W9-AOG-818

The Education of a Gentleman

The Education
of a
Gentleman

Theories of Gentlemanly Education
In England, 1660-1775

by

GEORGE C. BRAUER, JR.

COLLEGE & UNIVERSITY PRESS · *Publishers*

NEW HAVEN, CONN.

THIS COLLEGE AND UNIVERSITY PRESS *edition*
is published by Special Arrangement
with BOOKMAN ASSOCIATES

© *1959, by George C. Brauer, Jr.*

Library of Congress Catalog Card Number: 59-8395

LC
4945
G7
B7
1959

MANUFACTURED IN THE UNITED STATES OF AMERICA BY
UNITED PRINTING SERVICES, INC.
NEW HAVEN, CONN.

To

PROFESSOR LOUIS A. LANDA OF PRINCETON

A teacher and scholar in the finest sense of the term

Preface

The term "gentleman" as used in this book denotes anyone, from a duke to a country squire, who could claim an honorable family name and who was identified mainly with the landed interest rather than the trading interest, even though he perhaps augmented his fortune by marrying the daughter of a prosperous merchant. In the Restoration and eighteenth century, as in the Tudor and early Stuart periods, the gentleman's education in its broadest sense and in its every aspect was the subject of considerable discussion by courtesy writers and other theorizers on gentility or on pedagogy. Since the purpose of his education was to fashion him into a model man of quality, an examination of opinions regarding his upbringing must in large degree be a study in an ideal. Such an examination must take into account the attributes which theorists believed the gentleman should possess and their criticisms of him for not living up to the ideal, as well as their notions as to how his training should be conducted and what it should consist of in order that the ideal might be realized.

Those who wrote on the gentleman represented many walks of life. Some of them, such as Ramesey, Sir Matthew Hale, Sir George Mackenzie, Ramsay, and Chesterfield, were gentlemen themselves. A few, such as Panton and Forrester, were military officers. Many—for example, Penton, Grenville, Burnet, Brown, and Hurd—were clergymen, who may or may not have occupied elevated stations in the church. Others, notably Gailhard and Locke, were tutors, or like Law and Dalton, tutors and clergymen at the same time. The schoolmaster's profession contributed Clarke, Chapman, and several lesser theorists; Beattie, Bentham, Fordyce, and others taught at the universities. The educators, like a number of the divines, were not of genteel origin. Neither were the majority of men of letters who had significant comments to make on the gentleman, and who included Steele, Defoe, Swift, Coventry, Johnson, and Brooke.

Despite the variety of classes and vocations to which the theorists belonged, there was remarkable agreement among them as to what the gentleman should be and how the ideal could best be attained through education; commentators repeated the sentiments of their contemporaries and immediate predecessors, and sometimes the views of Renaissance authors. Shifts of opinion did occur from age to age, however, and on some points the theorists of a single age were in violent discord. The important differences are noted in their appropriate places, as are also the disparities between the gentleman's own conception of the gentleman and that subscribed to by the theorists. To a large extent I have let the commentators speak for themselves, quoting liberally from them and confining my own remarks to explication and interpretation.

The choice of a date *a quo*, 1660, was not entirely arbitrary. The concept of the gentleman in the Renaissance and early seventeenth century has already been treated admirably by such scholars as Miss Ruth Kelso and Professor W. L. Ustick. An investigation of the ideal of the gentleman in the eighteenth century, furthermore, must take into account the Restoration ideal, to which eighteenth-century theories were closely related. The choice of a terminal date was not entirely arbitrary either; after the publication of Chesterfield's letters to his son in 1774 and Croft's *General Observations* in 1775, little of importance appeared in the field of courtesy literature. When the occasion warranted it, however, I have gone a few years beyond 1775, just as I have for certain purposes considered works written prior to 1660. Although the majority of my sources belong within the realms of courtesy literature or treatises on education, I have at times attempted to show how the dramas, novels, and periodical essays of the eighteenth century reflected the age's ideas regarding the gentleman.

Acknowledgments

The author wishes to acknowledge his indebtedness to:

G. Bell & Sons, Ltd., for permission to quote from Jonathan Swift's *Prose Works,* ed. Temple Scott

The Cambridge University Press, for permission to quote from J. W. Adamson's "Education," chap. xv in the *Cambridge History of English Literature,* IX, and John Locke's *Some Thoughts Concerning Education,* in *The Educational Writings of John Locke,* ed. J. W. Adamson

The Clarendon Press, for permission to quote from Bernard Mandeville's *Fable of the Bees,* ed. F. B. Kaye

P. F. Collier & Son Corp., for permission to quote from William Penn's *More Fruits of Solitude,* ed. Charles W. Eliot, in The Harvard Classics, I.

E. P. Dutton & Co., for permission to quote from William Law's *Serious Call to a Devout and Holy Life,* and Oliver Goldsmith's *Citizen of the World,* ed. Austin Dobson

Gerald Duckworth & Co., Ltd., for permision to quote from the *Tatler,* ed. George A. Aitken

Routledge and Kegan Paul, Ltd., for permission to quote from the *Spectator,* ed. George A. Aitken

The University of Illinois Press, for permission to quote from Ruth Kelso's *Doctrine of the English Gentleman in the Sixteenth Century*

The Yale University Press, for permission to quote from Henry Fielding's *Covent-Garden Journal,* ed. Gerard Edward Jensen

TABLE OF CONTENTS

CHAPTER ONE

Virtue as an Aim in the Gentleman's Education

Courtesy writers in the late seventeenth and early eighteenth centuries frequently raised the question of whether birth or virtue constituted the greater claim to gentility. It could not be denied that a man was in actual fact a gentleman if he possessed an ancient and honorable name. Critics insisted, however, that on an ideal plane his ancestry was much less important than his virtue—that without virtue he was at best a most imperfect gentleman. One author, for example, called a gentleman's virtue as superior to his blood as the soul was to the body.[1] The ecclesiastic Denis Grenville, himself a gentleman, declared: "So far is Christian Vertue from being Incompatible with true Gentility, that to speak properly, and strictly, a Man cannot be a compleat Gentleman who is utterly void thereof."[2] According to Defoe, "if the vertue descends not with the titles, the man is but the shaddow of a gentleman, without the substance."[3] Indeed, no serious commentator would have questioned the proposition that virtue was the most essential qualification of true gentility. The present chapter will attempt to indicate its significance in the concept of the gentleman, its place in the scheme of his education, and prominent theories regarding its inculcation.

During the Restoration, writers went so far as to term virtue the very source of nobility and gentility. They inherited this view from the Middle Ages and Renaissance, and ultimately from antiquity.[4] All men were equal in the sight of God, seventeenth-century authors maintained, but some had been elevated above their fellows because of their outstanding moral qualities and exemplary conduct. " 'Tis virtue and merit," the

tutor Jean Gailhard affirmed, "which first of all did put a
difference between men: by this means his [i.e., a gentleman's]
Ancestors were raised to honor."[5] In discussing the aspects of
virtue responsible for advancement in rank, some commentators
placed considerable stress on heroic qualities: "*Tamberlaine,*
by most is reported to be the sonne of a Shepherd . . . admit
that his Virtues were not Christian, yet they were at least Moral,
and Heroick, raising him to a glorious Throne."[6] Among the
heroic virtues, signal patriotism was often mentioned; thus
Philip Ayres named as the founts of nobility and gentility
"noble and generous Enterprises and Designs" not only "for
the honour of God, defence of his true Religion," but also for
"the support and honour of the Prince, Gods Vicegerent, and
the publick Weal, for the general good."[7] The tracing of gentility to virtuous actions, particularly those performed in the
service of the nation, grew much less frequent in the eighteenth
century, but it still occurred occasionally. Defoe, for example,
said of the Venetian nobility: "True merit, fidellity to, and
services done for, their country, exalted the first patriots of the
State, and establish'd themselves as the rule for those noble
persons to act by in taking subsequent nobillity afterwards as
the reward of virtue."[8]

The gentleman's virtue, however, was to consist of much more
than heroic qualities and public service. It is sometimes said
that in the Renaissance the particular virtues required of the
gentleman were in large degree classical, influenced by Aristo-
telian ethics and embodying such attributes as valor and mag-
nanimity, but that in the seventeenth century the classical ideal
was replaced by an eminently Christian one emphasizing piety,
godliness, and an almost Puritanical morality.[9] This view should
be modified slightly. The distinction between classical and
Christian virtues is not always clear, Renaissance courtesy
literature was by no means devoid of Christian principles, and,
as has just been remarked, an admiration for the heroic virtues
was not dead in the Restoration, though it was certainly mori-
bund. Furthermore, many seventeenth-century works on the
gentleman, especially in the early Stuart period, were not pious
in any sense of the word; books of worldly advice, some of them

practical treatises on policy and expediency, formed a tradition possibly as important as the tradition of pietistic books.[10] Nevertheless, a change in the tone of much courtesy literature after 1600 is undeniable. It may be noted in such treatises as Nicholas Breton's *Mothers Blessing* (1602), James Cleland's *Institution of a Young Noble Man* (1607), and the *Basilikon Doron* of James I (published in an edition of seven copies in 1599, but actually brought before the public in 1603). The pietistic ideal received full expression in Richard Brathwait's important book *The English Gentleman* (1630), which made godliness an indispensable qualification of gentility. A Puritan influence on several such works is detectable, although many of them were not written by Dissenters; Brathwait himself was an opponent of Puritanism. In many respects, the alteration in the ideal must be attributed to the increasing articulateness of bourgeois society, which adopted a moralistic mood indeed when it viewed its superiors in rank.

This early seventeenth-century approach to gentility was transmitted to the Restoration and carried through into the eighteenth century, when scant attention was paid to the classical ideal and when the tracing of gentility to the heroic virtues almost vanished from courtesy literature. The Restoration attitude is represented by the publication in 1660 of *The Gentleman's Calling,* attributed to Richard Allestree, and Clement Ellis's *Gentile* [i.e., "Genteel"] *Sinner,* both embodying an extremely religious viewpoint. Among numerous early eighteenth-century works in the same vein, *The Gentleman Instructed* (1704), attributed to William Darrell, and Thomas Foxton's *Serino* (1721) may be singled out as egregiously pious. While such treatments of the gentleman were characterized by a very moralistic and at times even Puritanical tone, most of them were not written by Puritans; Darrell, in fact, was a Jesuit, and Allestree was a staunch royalist divine.

In insistent language and with many moral examples and Biblical references, these books exhorted the gentleman to regulate his life according to conventional Christian principles. Honesty was stressed and lying condemned, not so much because the gentleman's code of honor forbade lying as because Christian teaching forbade it. Avarice and covetousness were named as vices which the aristocrat should flee. The gentleman was strongly warned against the sin of pride and, especially during the Restoration, urged not to boast of his forbears, as "his Ancestors were raised to honor; not that he should brag of, but imitate them."[11] He was told to "hate and despise all human glory, for it is nothing else but human folly," and to "love humility in all its instances; practise it in all its parts, for it is the noblest state of the soul of man."[12] Critics of the gentleman demanded that he refrain from sexual misconduct, drunkenness, and gaming, and their lengthy remarks on these vices no doubt contributed to the Puritanical tone of their works. On Christian grounds, the genteel tradition of dueling was denounced.[13]

Moral and religious counsel went hand in hand; the gentleman was required to have a profound awareness of and reverence for God and Christian principles: "Your Endeavour and Hope is to know GOD and Goodness, in which alone there is true Enjoyment and good."[14] Any attitude disrespectful toward religion or suggestive of what the age termed "atheism" was, of course, reprehensible in the extreme. The gentleman who neglected his Christian duties was thought to be more censurable than less fortunately circumstanced men; he owed a special debt of thankfulness and service to God in return for the wealth and station which God had given him: "Consider, that your Estate and Honour are so far from excusing you, that they lay the greatest obligations on you to serve God . . . in point of Gratitude, that you, considering these *mercies of God, may present your soul and body as a living holy sacrifice,* most acceptable to him."[15] The demands that the gentleman be trained early and thoroughly in religion and that he lead a life of exemplary devotion to his Creator were probably the most noteworthy feature of discussions of his virtue.

Together with the requirement that the gentleman be virtuous came a severe condemnation of him for his alleged viciousness. The man of rank was almost never praised for moral qualities. One author announced that the Great Rebellion was due punishment for English gentlemen, who had brought their calamities

upon their own heads by their wickedness.[16] Criticism of the
gentleman for his lack of virtue had, of course, long been a
literary tradition, but it received an added impetus in the
Restoration, when commentators looked with moral indignation at the court of Charles II and remembered with nearly
as much indignation the court of Charles I. Ellis's *Gentile
Sinner,* a savage attack upon the gentleman for his impious
attitude and evil ways, set the tone of succeeding works. The
assault upon the genteel order for its godlessness was conducted by all serious critics, those who ranked as gentlemen as
well as those who did not. The well-born William Ramesey,
for example, exclaimed in horror that "he that will not
Blaspheme his maker, nay, and deny there is any such thing
as a Deity, and declare himself a down-right Atheist, is accounted no Gentleman."[17] Clergymen were especially vehement.
In his *Counsel and Directions* Denis Grenville accused fashionable youths of thinking that "the Practice of Religion, and
Devotion is inconsistent with a Gentleman" and of giving themselves "wholly up to their full swinge of Vice, and Leudness."
The Heathens, he asserted, had believed "that Virtue is the
truest Nobility" and that it was not right for even "the Ras-
cality to be sottishly vitious, when among us Christians, (to
our everlasting shame) it is many times become the distinguishing Character of Gentility" (pages 58, 60).

The same kind of indictment continued into the eighteenth
century. One author affirmed that not even the fear of God
could "awake our young Gallants, (like so many bewitched
Sampsons) they sleep in the Bosom of fascinating Pleasures.
. . . Their Study is to learn Sins; their Employment to commit
'em, and grand Diversion to applaud their Impieties."[18] Instead of fulfilling their obligation to be especially virtuous in
return for the favors bestowed on them by Providence, many
of them, as a clergyman said, practiced "the vile *Ingratitude* of
living only to dishonour their great Benefactor."[19]

In the mid-eighteenth century, when attacks on persons of
quality seem to have broken out with renewed violence, some
critics mentioned as a piece of common knowledge that the
genteel order was more prone to vice than the middle and

lower classes, and expressed fear that the examples of impiety
and immorality set by gentlemen would be followed by their
social inferiors or that the tendency toward sinfulness would
be inherited by future generations till all England suffered a
moral decline.[20] The moral fervor of the earlier period was
sometimes replaced in the mid-century periodicals by a more
delicate satire,[21] but the basic attitude remained unchanged.
There were, besides, many commentators who voiced their out-
rage as bluntly and furiously as had those of the Restoration.
Among these was the Reverend Dr. John Brown, who said of
the man of rank: "Should you propose to him the Renewal
of that *Family Devotion,* which concluded the guiltless Evening
Entertainments of his Ancestry? You would become an Object
of his Pity, rather than Contempt. The sublime Truths, the
pure and simple Morals of the Gospel, are despised and trod
under foot." English gentlemen were worse than atheists, Brown
added, as they did not even have sufficient interest in religious
questions to wonder whether they should be atheists or not.[22]
Drunkenness, gaming, and sexual misconduct were so often
ascribed to men of quality that they came to be termed the
genteel vices. Although an unknown author wrote a reply to
Brown's *Estimate* in which he disagreed with most of Brown's
opinions, he apparently did not find the churchman's judgment of men of fashion unwarranted, exclaiming in particular
against the prevalence of sexual misconduct: "The Commerce
of the Sexes never was so barefaced among the great. . . .
Modesty is trod under Foot; Rank, and the Ties of Matrimony
are forgot; the Guilty Passion is become a Subject of Vanity."[23]
Thomas Sheridan, father of the dramatist, threw up his hands
in dismay at what he considered the sinfulness of his well-born
contemporaries. They were so thoroughly indoctrinated in vice,
he thought, that all attempts to change them would be fruit-
less. The only hope lay in the young sons of gentlemen, who
might yet be led to virtue by right education.[24]

All this censure of the British gentleman for viciousness, no
matter how exaggerated or unreasonable it may have been on
occasion, is indicative of the very grave concern throughout

the Restoration and eighteenth century over the moral character and religious attitude of the man of quality. The consensus
of opinion was that the British gentleman should be a great
deal more virtuous than he actually was. And most commentators believed, with Thomas Sheridan, that he could be made
virtuous only through his education. According to many of
them, the young gentleman's studies, or at any rate certain
of his studies, could be of help in fashioning him into a good
man. "Nothing avails more that Learning and Institution,"
one author declared, "to turn our Hearts, excite our Wills,
and conform our Passions to Virtue."[25] Defoe called a lack of
learning "an enemy to temperance, to frugallity, to honesty,
and to the practise of all morall vertues."[26] Readings in the
Bible, often a part of early education, could be of considerable
help in giving the young gentleman a religious sense and in
teaching him Christian conduct; and history, from which in-
numerable moral examples could be drawn, furnished many
incentives to lead a good life.

Studies, however, were only one aspect of training in virtue.
Most writers, in calling education the source of virtue, were
thinking not merely of instruction in the arts and sciences but
of the whole upbringing of the well-born youth. They had
in mind the moral discipline and religious direction which,
they said, should commence almost at the moment of his birth
and be carried on without slackening, by parents, governors,
tutors, and schoolmasters, until he reached maturity.

The inculcation of virtue was regarded as the most important
aim of the gentleman's education thus broadly conceived, much
more necessary than lessons in the branches of learning. "The
first end in view," as Sheridan remarked in his *Plan of Education*, "is to make good men, and good Christians" (page 53).
Except in so far as a gentleman's studies were used to this end,
they were a very secondary consideration; knowledge for the
sake of knowledge was generally deprecated. "No Knowledge
. . . no Accomplishments of any kind," an anonymous eighteenth-century author declared, "can compensate for the want
of Virtue,"[27] and no one would have challenged this pronouncement. In Chapter XVIII of his *Serious Call*, Law intro-

duced a character named Paternus as a spokesman for his views on the gentleman's education. Paternus informed his son that he was teaching him Latin and Greek not for their own sake, but for the goodness and piety that resulted from a study of ancient literature. The classics, when they were studied as ends in themselves or as a means of making oneself a great critic, poet, or orator, were to be despised, "for the desire of these accomplishments is a vanity of the mind" (page 243).

Those writers who enumerated the objects of gentlemanly education consistently placed virtue at the head of the list; and sometimes, especially in the Restoration, they put the arts and sciences at the very bottom, occasionally even questioning their moral value. Bishop Gilbert Burnet spoke of "the ordering their [i.e., children's] morals, which I account the chieffe part of education," and said of learning: "I judge learning the meanest piece of education, and were it not that study preserves youths from idleness and worse exercises, I sould [sic] not very earnestly recommend it to the breeding of all youth: for indeed the right framing of their minds, and forming their manners, is most to be thought upon."[28] Locke ranked learning last among the aims of education, whereas he ranked "Virtue as the first and most necessary of those endowments that belong to a man or a gentleman." "Reading, and writing, and learning," he observed, "I allow to be necessary, but yet not the chief business."

> I say this [he added, addressing a genteel parent], that, when you consider of the breeding of your son, you would not have . . . Latin and logic only in your thoughts. . . . Seek out somebody that may know how discreetly to frame his manners; place him in hands where you may, as much as possible, secure his innocence, cherish and nurse up the good, and gently correct and weed out any bad inclinations, and settle in him good habits. This is the main point; and this being provided for, learning may be had into the bargain.

Unlike those theorists who had considerable faith in the moral efficacy of studies, Locke believed that although learning was "a great help" toward producing both virtue and wisdom "in well-disposed minds," nevertheless, "in others not so disposed, it helps them only to be the more foolish or worse men."[29]

This distrust of learning as an aid to virtue did not disappear entirely in the eighteenth century. Peter Shaw, for example, devoted much consideration to the question "Why learning has not farther advanced Morality." The instruction of youths, according to him, "should have two Views; the first to form them Men [i.e., men who act morally], and the second to form them Christians." Thus the only necessary branches of learning, in his opinion, were ones which taught morality and religion, and he did not include among these such studies as mathematics and the natural sciences. As for the abstract philosophical speculations of the universities, they were definitely harmful, not serving at all to further piety or morality.[30]

The majority of eighteenth-century theorists, as mentioned before, held that most studies at any rate did help to promote virtue. Like more severe critics of learning, however, they often suspected that abstract speculations and the minute erudition of the scholar were of little or no aid in the inculcation of virtue, and they deplored this type of learning on those grounds. "All that we call Improvement of our Minds, in dry and empty Speculation," one theorist observed; "all Learning or whatever else, either in *Theology* or other Science, which has not a direct Tendency to render us *honester, milder, juster,* and *better,* is far from being justly so call'd."[31] Other commentators criticized the public schools for emphasizing studies which did little to inspire the boys with worthy sentiments and for neglecting studies more valuable from the standpoint of virtue. Eustace Budgell, in the *Spectator* No. 337 (March 27, 1712), animadverted against the schools' practice of having boys compose Latin themes and verses on prescribed subjects; he felt that the children's time could more profitably be employed in finding moral lessons and examples in their Latin reading and in writing out their thoughts on these. Thomas Sheridan reproached the schools because, in his opinion, their purpose was "to make good Latin and Greek scholars" rather than to turn the students into moral Christian gentlemen.[32] A number of authors advocated the careful selection of reading material, so that only works which instilled virtuous principles would be put into the hands of young gentlemen. "All the [Latin] passages selected for translating, and declaiming," Sheridan announced, "should be such as are most likely to inculcate principles of Religion and morality."[33]

The precedence of virtue over learning as an aim of the gentleman's education was thus firmly established throughout the period under consideration, and it was generally recognized that even if studies afforded strong persuasions to goodness, other aspects of his upbringing were perhaps of more influence in molding a well-born youth into a virtuous gentleman. If he was indoctrinated early and thoroughly in moral ideas and pious beliefs through careful rearing as well as through studies, he would become the ideal gentleman which his critics so ardently wished him to be. Various pedagogical techniques for the inculcation of virtue were therefore discussed at great length, as in Locke's *Some Thoughts Concerning Education* (1693). A boy was to be taught virtue by precept and example, rewards bestowed with caution, severe punishments administered only as a last resort, the cultivation of a sense of honor through manifestations of approval, and the cultivation of a sense of shame through manifestations of disapproval. If a young gentleman showed undue possessiveness or selfish tendencies in games with other children, these faults must be checked; if he practiced cruelty towards animals and birds, he must be given lessons in kindness; if he lied or cheated, even in the smallest matters, his elders must evince great dismay and enlarge on the advantages of veracity. His playmates must be carefully chosen, as wickedly inclined children would have a bad influence on his character. He was not to consort familiarly with the servants, since they might teach him meanness. Tutors, governors, and schoolmasters were required to be virtuous beyond all else and to have the ability of transmitting their virtue to their pupils.

The actions and attitudes of a youth's father were of especial importance. "When God hath given a Man Children," Gailhard affirmed, "he ought to see them brought up and instructed in the fear of God." Fathers, he continued, "must withall take care to . . . teach them true morality."[34] Ideally, a parent was to be a paragon of piety and moral excellence and was to devote his efforts unstintingly toward leading his son in the path of goodness, overseeing the boy's religious training, curbing his sinful proclivities, patiently explaining the difference between right and wrong conduct, restraining his wilful passions, and inspiring him with a love of virtue by his own example. The fashionable father, however, was subjected to considerable criticism for doing exactly the opposite of all this. "Most Gentlemen," Ellis wrote sarcastically, "seem to make it a speciall piece of their *fatherly* care to stave off their *Children* as long as they can from *Vertue* and *Religion;* lest therein resembling *better men* than their *Fathers,* some might take occasion to think them *Spurious."*

> It is indeed most lamentable [he went on] to consider how very few of those we call *Gentlemen* endeavour to make their *Children* either *Honest* men or *Good Christians:* as if it were their onely *businesse* to *beget* them, and when they are come into the world, to *teach* them by their own *example,* how they may most *unprofitably* spend the short *leavings* of their own *Luxury.*[35]

The same type of criticism was rather frequent in the eighteenth century. In the *Connoisseur* No. 22 (June 27, 1754), the Earl of Cork afforded an illustration of a fashionable father, a "Colonel, who had served only in the peaceful campaigns of Covent-Garden," who by his own example influenced his son to lead an immoral life. "He enumerated . . . his midnight skirmishes with constables, his storming of bagnios, his imprisonment in round-houses, and his honourable wounds in the service of prostitutes." The son "could not fail of improving under so excellent a tutor, and soon became as eminent as his father."

When Chesterfield's letters to his son were printed in 1774, they must have impressed contemporaries as a further instance of a gentleman's inculcation of vice in his son. Despite the moral injunctions in some of the early letters, it was obvious

to readers that on the whole they did not express extremely
virtuous ideas. Chesterfield, perhaps assuming that young Philip's
morally irreproachable governor Mr. Harte would give him
sufficient instruction in virtue, paid comparatively little attention to this aspect of education himself; he strongly urged
the youth to have *liaisons* with women of quality on the Continent; when he did advocate virtuous conduct, he usually did
so not from an appreciation of its intrinsic value but from
the fear that vicious conduct would hurt the boy's reputation,
thereby rendering it difficult for him to shine in the world;
and he seemed to feel that the appearance of religion and
morality was more important and desirable than the actuality.
Although Chesterfield's letters to his son, which, of course,
were not intended for publication, ran contrary to the many
pious letters of advice to young gentlemen which were published throughout the seventeenth and eighteenth centuries, they
were in the tradition of the books of worldly advice and prudential counsel which constituted a significant part of courtesy
literature in the seventeenth century but which disappeared
during the eighteenth. In their treatment of virtue, therefore,
they were perhaps somewhat anachronistic. At any rate, they
alarmed Chesterfield's contemporaries, who, as is well known,
pointed to them as attempts on the part of a cynical and
vicious aristocrat to ruin the moral character of a young English
gentleman. Thus the author of a satirical skit made a well-
born youth recite, as a preliminary to baptism into what he
termed Lord Chesterfield's Creed: "I believe that . . . forni-
cation, and adultery, are within the lines of morality; that a
woman may be honourable when she has lost her honour, and
virtuous when she has lost her virtue, etc."[36] And thus Cowper,
in *The Progress of Error,* called Chesterfield the "Grey-beard
corrupter of our list'ning youth" (1. 342).

Many of the particular directions for making a young gentleman virtuous have already been mentioned and need not detain
us further. There were two, however, which, because of the
urgency with which they were uttered, deserve more detailed
consideration. Both were applicable to the moral education

of children in general, but their frequent occurrence in discussions of the upbringing of gentlemen's sons makes them
especially important in that regard.

The first of these directions was that the passions should be
kept under rigid control. Restoration commentators subscribed
to the notion, traceable ultimately to Plato, that "the inferiour
and more brutish part of the man" must be guided by his
rational faculty, that "a bridle" must be put "in the mouths
of these head-strong passions," until they were rendered "not
only captivated slaves, but good Subjects, obedient to the laws
of Reason."[37] "When in man passions are exalted above reason,"
one seventeenth-century courtesy writer explained, "nothing
follows but disorders, mischiefs, and unavoidable ruine both
within and without."[38] Locke was thoroughly convinced of this.
"It seems plain to me," he averred, "that the principle of all
virtue and excellency lies in a power of denying ourselves the
satisfaction of our own desires, where reason does not authorize
them." Teaching a young gentleman to govern his passions
was therefore one of the most important points in Locke's
educational scheme. The most infantile desires of the small
child, he said, should be opposed, for "if the child must have
grapes, or sugar-plums, when he has a mind to them, rather
than make the poor baby cry, or be out of humour, why, when
he is grown up, must he not be satisfied too, if his desires
carry him to wine or women?" Coddling children and gratify-
ing their whims and wishes was the greatest mistake that could
be made in early education, according to Locke; they "should
be used to submit their desires, and go without their longings,
even from their very cradles." Only in this way, he thought,
could the passions be made "subject to the rules and restraints
of reason."[39]

A belief in the necessity for training a young gentleman to
curb his passions by means of his reason was as characteristic
of the eighteenth century as of the seventeenth. The Reverend
John Dalton's *Epistle to a Young Nobleman,* a set of instructions in virtue written in 1736 by a gentleman's preceptor,
included the following exhortations:

'Tis now the time young passion to command,
While yet the pliant stem obeys the hand;
Guide now the courser with a steddy rein,
E're yet he bounds o'er pleasure's flow'ry plain:
In passion's strife, no medium you can have;
You rule a master, or submit a slave.[40]

Although Burgh did not, like Locke, require that training in control of the passions begin in the cradle, he did stipulate that "regulating the passions and appetites" should be taught "from the time a child can speak, throughout the whole course of education."[41] John Brown announced that the first three of his *Sermons on Various Subjects* "will be altogether confined to the primary and effectual Regulation of the Passions." With Locke, he believed that "if this general End be thoroughly obtained in Infancy, the secondary and succeeding Principles of Education . . . will naturally flow from these first Principles, as from their common Fountain." In the second sermon, where he treated this essential aspect of education most fully, he listed various evil qualities, such as envy, vindictiveness, and pride, which must be suppressed early in order to make room for good qualities, such as benevolence and humility. The average parent, he thought, paid too little regard to this early suppression in rearing his child, and the consequences were disastrous: "For . . . the same Want of Power to curb his Passions, which led him in his Infancy to gratify every childish Humour, will gain Strength in Youth and Manhood, and tend to lead him by Degrees to the highest Excess of every Sensual Gratification."[42]

The influence of Locke on passages such as those cited above is probable but not ascertainable. It can be conclusively assigned, however, to other eighteenth-century remarks on subjugation of the passions. Bishop Richard Hurd's *Dialogues on the Uses of Foreign Travel* was cast in the form of discussions between Locke and Shaftesbury, in the course of which Hurd appropriately gave to Locke the following statement concerning the gentleman's upbringing: "I require . . . That he be trained, by a strict discipline, to the command of his temper and passions; in one word, that he be inured to habits of self-government."[43]

The schoolmaster Chapman, who admired Locke for his "many ingenious observations . . . and many useful directions," also stipulated that the child "should not allow his lower appetites, or selfish passions, to usurp that place in his breast which is due to the nobler and more refined. . . . Are reason and conscience placed within us to check the impetuosity of our passions, and shall we despise their heavenly admonitions?"[44]

The second idea frequently propounded in Restoration and eighteenth-century discussions of training in virtue was that such training must begin extremely early. We have already noted in Locke and Brown the belief that the control of the passions was not taught soon enough. They felt that the same was true of other aspects of the inculcation of virtue; thus Locke gave many directions for curing children of their infantile vices and laid down a plan for instructing them in the principles of religion from the time when they were first able to comprehend any principles at all.[45] Some authors, deeply aware of the natural depravity of man, feared that unless a child's sinful proclivities were nipped in the bud, he was forever lost to virtue. "The inward principle being naturally corrupt," Gailhard said in his *Compleat Gentleman,* and "the will and affections deprav'd and prone to evil, if these natural dispositions be strengthened with evil practise, and become habitual, all that will not only be setled and confirmed, but also it will become inveterate and past remedy, without God's special grace" (First Treatise, pages 9-10). Other theorists, although they perhaps did not take quite so pessimistic a view of human nature, argued that attempts to inculcate virtue were most successful when a child was still young enough to be receptive of moral teaching and when evil tendencies had not yet become firmly rooted in him. "Children," it was thought, "should be moulded while their Tempers are yet pliant and ductile; for it is infinitely easier to prevent ill Habits, than to Master them . . . It should be consider'd too that we have the Seeds of Virtue in us, as well as of Vice; and whenever we take a wrong Bias, 'tis not out of a moral Incapacity to do better, but for want of careful Manage and Discipline to set us right at first."[46]

Related to this theory was, of course, the conception of a child's mind as a *tabula rasa*. It is hardly necessary to point out that this conception was at the basis of Locke's demand that education to virtue should start in the cradle itself. Boyer showed himself to be under the influence of this notion when he included in his *English Theophrastus* the following passage: "To speak all in a few words, *Children* are but *Blank Paper,* ready indifferently for any Impression, good or bad . . . and it is much in the power of the first comer to write *Saint* or *Devil* upon't, which of the two he pleases" (page 164). Oswald Dykes used another familiar image to express the same idea: "'Tis certain, that as Seals and Signets can easily make any Impression upon soft Wax, so wise Instructors may soon cast upon the pliant Minds of Youth, as in a Mould, the fairest Images and Ideas of Virtue, Piety, and Prudence." Dykes therefore asserted that "the surest Foundations of Virtue . . . may be said to be laid in our Cradles, and rais'd up in the Arms of our very Nurses."[47] Still another image to the same purpose was employed by Burgh: "The human mind resembles a piece of ground, which will by no means lie wholly bare; but will either bring forth weeds or fruits, according as it is cultivated or neglected. And according as the habits of vice and irreligion, or the contrary, get the first possession of the mind, such is the future man like to be."[48] Brown drew a parallel between learning virtue and learning speech. As an infant acquired the English language, he said, the organs of speech developed certain conformations which remained with him throughout his life. Similarly, as an infant acquired habits of virtue his mind developed certain conformations just as hostile to change.[49]

The exact age at which training in virtue should begin varied somewhat with various writers; not all of them, like Locke and Dykes, pushed it back quite so far as the cradle. The unknown author of the treatise *Of Education* thought that it "ought to exert itself, as soon as a Child shews any Power of Reason" (page 24) but did not specify when reason first manifested itself. Brown assumed that "the very *first Dawn* of *Reason*" occurred "before a Child is one Year old"[50] and advised commencing education to virtue at that date. Burgh, on the other hand, offered a list of moral and religious lessons which, in his opinion, were suitable for the child of three or four.[51] Although theorists may have differed slightly as to the precise age, however, they were in complete agreement that the inculcation of virtue should begin as early as was practicable.

According to Brown, the enemy of this important principle was Rousseau. Two translations of *Emile* (1762) were printed at London in 1763. The next year Brown, in his *Sermons on Various Subjects*, summarized Rousseau's position, justly or unjustly, in the following manner:

It were to be wished, that he had been more precise and determinate in delivering his Opinions: but so far as I understand him, his Principles are these.—1. "That no Kind of Habits ought to be impressed on Children; because they will inevitably check the natural Liberty of the Mind.—2. That you ought never to teach them Obedience as a Duty, because it will render their Minds tyrannical and capricious.—3. That if you leave them to the natural Consequences of their own Actions, these will sufficiently rectify the Mistakes they commit in Infancy.—4. That when Reason comes to exert itself in a maturer State, the Passions will naturally rectify themselves according to this Standard, if they are not corrupted beforehand by an improper Education." (Pages 14-15)

It may easily be seen how antithetical these ideas were to a belief in the necessity for careful early training in virtue, and, incidentally, training in the control of the passions. Brown set himself firmly against them. In opposition to Rousseau's first principle, he maintained that in a civilized life the freedom of the mind had to be checked for the good of society and that a small child must be taught to place his duties toward society above his personal freedom. In reply to the second, he affirmed that unless a parent imposed his authority on a child and exacted duties from him, the child's virtue could not be hoped for. He attacked the third principle by pointing out that since even an adult often did not learn by the consequences of his mistakes, surely a child never would, and that therefore the parents must exert their influence over infants and show them the error of their ways. He disposed of the fourth principle by repeating the traditional argument that if a human being was not brought up to virtue during his infancy and early childhood he would never acquire it, and all subsequent efforts to inculcate it would come too late to be effectual.[52]

Notes to Chapter I

1. See Capt. Edward Panton, *Speculum Juventutis* (London, 1671), pp. 3-4.

2. *Counsel and Directions Divine and Moral* (London, 1685), pp. 112-113.

3. *The Compleat English Gentleman,* ed. Karl D. Bülbring (London, 1890), p. 24. This is the 1st ed. of the work, apparently written 1728-29, and retains Defoe's somewhat eccentric orthography.

4. See Lewis Einstein, *The Italian Renaissance in England* (New York and London, 1902), pp. 66-68, and *Tudor Ideals* (New York, 1921), p. 157; John E. Mason, *Gentlefolk in the Making: Studies in the History of English Courtesy Literature and Related Topics from 1531 to 1774* (Philadelphia, 1935), pp. 6-8; and George McGill Vogt, "Gleanings for the History of a Sentiment: Generositas Virtus, Non Sanguis," *JEGP,* XXIV (1925), 102-124.

5. *The Compleat Gentleman* (London, 1678), 2nd Treatise, p. 109.

6. Panton, *op. cit.,* p. 26.

7. *Vox Clamantis* (London, 1684), p. 65.

8. *Compleat English Gentleman,* p. 24.

9. See Ruth Kelso, *The Doctrine of the English Gentleman in the Sixteenth Century,* Univ, of Ill. Stud. in Lang. and Lit., XIV (Feb.—May, 1929), 71-106, and W. L. Ustick, "Changing Ideals of Aristocratic Character and Conduct in Seventeenth-Century England," *MP,* XXX (1932), 147-166. Miss Kelso affirms that the Renaissance concept of the gentleman was characterized by an "over-emphasis on pagan virtues to the neglect of Christian," whereas "during the seventeenth century the bal-

ance was completely shifted; a distinctly religious point of view colored the handbook for the gentleman, and finally usurped the whole field, turning the complete gentleman into a Christian gentleman, and hardly a gentleman at all from the point of view of the sixteenth century" (pp. 72, 107).

10. See Mason, *Gentlefolk in the Making*, ch. vii, "Seventeenth-Century Treatises on Policy," and W. L. Ustick, "Advice to a Son: A Type of Seventeenth-Century Conduct Book," *SP*, XXIX (1932), 409-441.

11. Gailhard, *Compleat Gentleman*, 2nd Treatise, p. 109.

12. William Law, *A Serious Call to a Devout and Holy Life* (London and New York, 1906), p. 244. These exhortations were directed toward young gentlemen.

13. See Richard Allestree, attrib., *The Gentleman's Calling* (London, 1677), pp. 132-145; Panton, *Speculum Juventutis*, p. 335, remainder of Book VI, and Book VII; William Ramesey, *The Gentlemans Companion* (London, 1672), pp. 79-83; Gailhard, *op. cit.*, 2nd Treatise, p. 130; and William Darrell, *The Gentleman Instructed*, 6th ed. (London, 1716), pp. 23-24. Richardson's condemnation of dueling through the attitude of the hero in *Sir Charles Grandison* had a religious basis and was typical of the position of eighteenth-century commentators; typical also were the remarks of Addison in *Spectator* Nos. 9 and 99 and of Steele in *Spectator* No. 97.

14. Anthony Ashley Cooper, 3rd Earl of Shaftesbury, attrib., *Several Letters Written by a Noble Lord to a Young Man at the University* (London, 1716), p. 28.

15. Francis Brokesby, *A Letter of Advice to a Young Gentleman at the University* (London, 1751, repr. from 1st ed., 1701), p. 2.

16. See Allestree, attrib., *Gentleman's Calling*, "To the Bookseller."

17. *Gentlemans Companion*, p. 17.

18. Darrell, attrib., *Gentleman Instructed*, p. 34.

19. Bishop Thomas Wilson, *The True Christian Method of Educating Children*, 5th ed. (London, 1787), p. 23. This was a sermon preached on May 28, 1724.

20. See, for example, Mrs. Elizabeth Carter in *Rambler* No. 100 (March 2, 1751); the Earl of Cork in *Connoisseur* No. 22 (June 27, 1754); Henry Brooke, *The Fool of Quality*, with Biog. Pref. by Charles Kingsley and Life by E. A. Baker (Lon-

don and New York, 1860), p. 138; and even Chesterfield, who adopted the prevalent attitude of the age in *World* No. 189 (August 12, 1756).

21. See, in addition to the essayists cited in n. 20, George Colman the Elder and Bonnel Thornton in *Connoisseur* Nos. 74 (June 26, 1755) and 122 (May 27, 1756).

22. *An Estimate of the Manners and Principles of the Times,* 2nd ed. (London, 1757), pp. 54, 55-58.

23. "C. L. St.," *The Real Character of the Age* (London, 1757), p. 21.

24. See his *Plan of Education for the Young Nobility and Gentry of Great Britain* (London, 1769), pp. xiii, xv-xvii, 10-11, 52.

25. Oswald Dykes, *The Royal Marriage* (London, 1722), p. 16.

26. *Compleat English Gentleman,* p. 177. See also *Gentleman's Calling,* p. 22; Panton, *Speculum Juventutis,* p. 83; Ramesey, *Gentlemans Companion,* p. 14; Gailhard, *Compleat Gentleman,* 1st Treatise, pp. 23-24. 27-28; Edward Moore in *World* No. 20 (May 17, 1753); James Burgh, *The Dignity of Human Nature* (Hartford, Conn., 1802), pp. 109-110; and George Chapman, *A Treatise on Education, with A Sketch of the Author's Method,* 3rd ed., enl. (London, 1784), pp. 223-224. The cited ed. of *The Dignity of Human Nature* is a reprint of the 1st ed., London, 1754; Chapman's *Treatise* first appeared in 1773.

27. *Of Education* (London, 1734), p. 24.

28. *Thoughts on Education,* ed. John Clarke (Aberdeen, 1914), pp. 22, 30-31. This work, first published in 1761, was apparently written in 1668.

29. *Some Thoughts Concerning Education,* in *The Educational Writings of John Locke,* ed. John William Adamson (Cambridge, 1922), pp. 104-105, 115.

30. See *The Reflector* (London, 1750), pp. 35, 41-42, 52-57.

31. Shaftesbury, attrib., *Several Letters,* p. 21.

32. See his *Plan of Education,* pp. 41-42.

33. *Ibid.,* p. 61; see also pp. 99-100. For other instances of this tendency to select and bowdlerize, see Gailhard, *Compleat Gentleman,* 1st Treatise, pp. 69-71; *The Gentleman's Library, Containing Rules for Conduct in All Parts of Life* (London, 1715), p. 35; Shaftesbury, attrib., *Several Letters,* pp. 27-28, 34-35; James Beattie, *Remarks on the Utility of Classical Learn-*

ing, in *Essays* (Edinburgh, 1778), pp. 542-545; and Chapman, *Treatise on Education,* p. 171.

34. *Two Discourses* (London, 1682), pp. 11-12.

35. *The Gentile Sinner, Or, England's Brave Gentleman* (Oxford, 1660), pp. 24-25.

36. *Gentleman's Magazine,* XLV (1775), 131.

37. Allestree, attrib., *Gentleman's Calling,* pp. 32-33.

38. Gailhard, *Compleat Gentleman,* 1st Treatise, p. 30.

39. *Some Thoughts Concerning Education,* pp. 30-31.

40. *Two Epistles* (London, 1745), p. 3.

41. *Dignity of Human Nature,* p. 114.

42. *Sermons on Various Subjects* (London, 1764), pp. 6-7, 44-45. See pp. 35-51 in general.

43. *Dialogues on the Uses of Foreign Travel; Considered as a Part of An English Gentleman's Education* (London, 1764), p. 77.

44. *Treatise on Education,* pp. 40, 31-34.

45. See *Some Thoughts Concerning Education, passim.,* esp. pp. 105-109.

46. Abel Boyer, *The English Theophrastus* (London, 1702), pp. 164-165. Boyer drew and adapted from many sources and was more the compiler than the author of this work.

47. *Royal Marriage,* pp. 17, 15.

48. *Dignity of Human Nature,* p. 115.

49. See *Sermons on Various Subjects,* pp. 9-10.

50. *Ibid.,* pp. 28-29.

51. See *Dignity of Human Nature,* p. 116.

52. See pp. 15-27.

CHAPTER TWO

Public Spirit as an Aim in the Gentleman's Education

As a member of the leading class in his nation and as a man of wealth and leisure, the gentleman of the Renaissance had a duty toward society; it was his obligation to act in the service of king and country. Those virtues which resulted in the benefit of the nation were, in the sixteenth century, the main justification for conferring titles of nobility. During the Middle Ages the gentleman had been useful to the state principally in a military capacity; but in the Renaissance, although his military duties were still highly regarded, the emphasis shifted from the gentleman as warrior to the gentleman as statesman, fulfilling his function in the court and in Parliament, participating in affairs of government, giving counsel to the king, or representing his nation on diplomatic missions. Books on policy, instructing the aristocrat in conduct at court and in political expediency, were frequent in the later sixteenth century and most of the seventeenth. Preparing the gentleman for the execution of his national duties was an important aim of his education.[1]

During the Restoration, we recall, patriotic virtues and public service were sometimes named as the hypothetical origins of rank. But many Restoration commentators went further than this, adopting from the Renaissance and the earlier seventeenth century the view that the contemporary gentleman should represent those same qualities for which his ancestors were presumably raised to eminence. One author, for example, affirmed that he "hath those Qualifications, which render him useful, and he must give himself those Exercises, whereby he may become the most eminently so. If by just authority he be assigned

to any publick charge," this author went on, he should welcome
it as "a sphere wherein he may move the most vigorously in
the service of God and his Country."[2] The second of Gailhard's *Two Discourses* was entitled "Concerning the Statesman, Or Him who is in Publick Employments," and treated
the gentleman in that capacity. By Sir George Mackenzie,
public spirit was reckoned the greatest virtue of the gentleman.[3] Obadiah Walker, like many other Restoration commentators, listed various ways in which men of quality might
fulfill their obligations to king and country:

> As the *most considerable Members of a Common-Wealth,*
> they are ingaged in more peculiar Duties towards the Prince,
> and his subordinate Magistrates; *to* know and obey the
> Laws, and assist toward the observation of them by others.
> Besides this, to fit themselves for such imployments as they
> may probably be call'd unto. Whether to be
> *Courtiers,* and domestick Servants to the Prince.
> *Magistrates* in Peace. *Commanders* in War.
> *Counsellors* of, or *Officers* under, the Prince.
> Employed in forregin [*sic*] Parts, as *Agents, Ambassa-*
> *dors, &c.*
> Or in the Church as *Clergy-Men,* Secular or Religious,
> active or contemplative.[4]

Despite such statements as these, however, national service
was perhaps a somewhat less important component of the
gentlemanly ideal in the Restoration than it had been in the
Renaissance. Gailhard, recognizing without surprise or disap-
probation that many men of birth would not enter public life,
devoted the first of his *Two Discourses* to the gentleman who
intended simply to "live upon his own Estate, and according
to his quality, and to have no share in the Government, nor
hand in the management of Public Affairs" (page 5). Service
of one's country seems to have become even less prominent
in the gentlemanly ideal of the eighteenth century. As was
noted in Chapter I, the heroic virtues, especially virtues resulting in the public benefit, were now seldom mentioned as
the sources of nobility or gentility. The fact that treatises on

policy, most characteristic of the earlier seventeenth century, faded out of courtesy literature in the eighteenth,[5] suggests a waning interest in the gentleman as courtier and statesman. Critics such as Defoe and Swift complained that in contrast to his ancestors the contemporary gentleman neglected his national duties, which his ignorance rendered him incapable of performing.[6] To a degree, the prosperous and influential merchant class had taken over positions of national importance formerly held by noblemen, and members of the gentry and nobility were sometimes not rich enough to devote themselves to diplomatic careers, which did not always promise fortunes.

Yet notwithstanding the decrease in emphasis, service of the state still held a place in the gentlemanly ideal. Younger sons, who had to adopt professions in order to gain a livelihood, frequently obtained high commands in the Army or Navy. Many gentlemen entered Parliament, even if, as Defoe believed, they were too ignorant to be of much use there. Significant political offices were, as before, open to gentlemen as members of a privileged class and as the presumed leaders of the nation, and their rank qualified them for diplomatic missions abroad. Some of them, like their ancestors, engaged actively in politics at court. It was therefore maintained throughout the eighteenth century, though not quite so vehemently as in the Renaissance or even in the Restoration, that national service devolved upon the gentleman in consequence of his birth and that he deserved censure if he neglected this charge.

Government and legislation were thus mentioned by John Clarke as activities suitable for men of quality: "The proper Business of *Gentlemen* as such, is, I presume, to serve their Country, in the Making or Execution of the Laws; as likewise in preventing the Breach and Violation of them."[7] John Dalton was alluding mainly to service in the House of Lords when he somewhat extravagantly described the British nobleman as

> Born to redress an injur'd orphan's cause,
> To smooth th' unequal frown of rigid laws;
> To stand an isthmus of our well-mix'd state,
> Where rival pow'rs with restless billows beat,

And from each side alike the fury fling,
Of madd'ning commons, or incroaching king.
How mean, who scorns his country's sacred voice!
By birth a patriot, but a slave by choice.
How great, who answers this illustrious end,
Whom prince and people call their equal friend!
(*Epistle to a Young Nobleman*, in *Two Epistles*, p. 6.)

Some writers were less explicit as to the kind of service they expected of the gentleman; James Puckle simply remarked that a gentleman's youth was "to be employed in qualifying for the service of the commonwealth,"[8] and Burgh in his *Dignity of Human Nature* said only: "The proper and peculiar study of a person of high rank is the knowledge of the interest of his country" (page 161). Chesterfield, on the other hand, has left us a clear idea of the sphere of activity he envisioned for his son. Having been ambassador to the Hague, active member of Parliament, Lord Lieutenant of Ireland, and Secretary of State, he fondly dreamed of an equally distinguished political career for young Philip. "Your business," he told the boy, "is negotiation abroad, and oratory in the House of Commons at home." The office of Secretary of State was also one "for which," as he observed, "I have always intended you."[9] Young Harry Clinton, Henry Brooke's portrait of the ideal gentleman, was equally aware of the patriotic duties of a man of rank. He was destined, in partial fulfilment of the ideal, to "be a member of the legislature of Great Britain." He was, furthermore, invited by William III to serve him at court, a distinction "to which I aspire, answered Harry, as soon as I am capable of so high a duty."[10]

In addition to the services which the gentleman was to perform in a public capacity, there were others, no less a sign of his public spirit, which could be performed in a private capacity. These included founding or donating funds to charitable institutions, exercising liberality toward the poor, caring for his servants and tenants, and executing any number of other acts of generosity not related to his career as a soldier or statesman. Renaissance courtesy writers viewed liberality as an important qualification of the ideal gentleman,[11] and this view, together with the medieval idea that the rich man was the steward or trustee of his wealth, obliged by Christian duty to use it for the relief of the distressed, was still current in the Restoration and eighteenth century. Gailhard explained the concept of the stewardship of wealth for the benefit of his well-born readers who did not plan to participate actively in public affairs: "There is no man rich but by Gods Grace, disposition, or at least permission, which being supposed to be received from Gods hand, let him who enjoys it consider himself as a Tenant and a Steward, and therefore [to] make a good and right use of it, he ought to bestow it upon works of Piety, Charity and Necessity" (*Two Discourses,* page 68).

The same idea was emphasized by Gailhard's Restoration contemporaries. It was urged that God had given the poor "Bills of Assignment upon the plenty of the Rich, a right to be supplied by them."[12] "Persons of quality," Walker affirmed, had an obligation "to make all the advantage they can for bettering . . . others by their riches. They are Gods *Stewards* . . . not for *luxury, delicious* fare, or fatter; nor for *accumulating wealth,* the rust whereof will corrode their consciences as fire would their flesh."[13] "In this also consists your Gentility," Ayres admonished gentlemen, "that you abound in Charity towards the Poor, they are eminently yours, your Lot and Portion."[14] William Penn too stressed munificence as a debt owed by "our Great Men" to God, who gave them the advantages of rank and fortune for the express purpose of "playing the good Stewards, to the Honor of our great Benefactor, and the Good of our Fellow-Creatures."[15] Stephen Penton in 1688 was sarcastic toward men of fortune for not playing the good steward. "It is an ill-natur'd sort of Doctrine to preach, and will not hold at *Westminster*," he said, "that the *Poor* have a good *Title* to some of the rich man's Money: But it would be an unlucky *Disappointment* hereafter, if in stead of asking how many Lordships you left your Heir . . . God should demand, How many poor Widows have you sav'd from *starving*? . . . how many *decay'd* Families you have reliev'd; what did you give to a *Brief* for a Fire, Church, or Hospital, &c."[16]

Oswald Dykes's portrayal of a bountiful gentleman will illustrate the continuance of the idea of the stewardship of wealth into the early eighteenth century: "This liberal Hero looks upon it as a selfish Life, not to study the Benefit and Advantage of his Neighbour, as well as his own Grandeur. He believes Gentlemen of the greatest Estates, either real or personal, to be no more by right Reason, than God Almighty's Trustees; for the Relief of needy People with their superfluous Substance."[17] The stewardship of wealth was mentioned less frequently in the later eighteenth century, but it still occurred occasionally in discussions of the gentleman's duty of liberality; in *The Fool of Quality,* for example, the nobly born young Harry Clinton was informed by his uncle that "we are but the stewards of the bounty of our God" (page 250).

Even if the concept of the gentleman as a divinely appointed trustee received progressively less attention in the course of the eighteenth century, the demand that he be generous with his fortune remained constant throughout the period. The ideal of charity was, of course, widespread in the eighteenth century and was not confined to the gentleman, but it no doubt influenced the views of critics toward him. He was, in fact, severely censured when he did not show generosity. In the *Spectator* No. 372 (May 7, 1712), Steele blamed persons of rank for being less disposed to charity than Powell, the marionette man popular in fashionable circles, who intended to give the proceeds from his next performance to the poor children of the parish. " 'Our people of quality, who are not to be interrupted in their pleasure to think of the practice of any moral duty,' " should learn from Powell's example, Steele implied; they should " 'at least fine for their sins, and give something to these poor children; a litle out of their luxury and superfluity would atone, in some measure, for the wanton use of the rest of their fortunes.' " On the other hand, portraits of the ideal gentleman as the bountiful man were frequent. Among these portraits were the sketch of the munificent Manilius in the *Spectator* No. 467 (August 26, 1712), probably by Hughes, and Thomas Foxton's Serino. This latter individual, whose beneficence, according to Foxton, all gentlemen should imitate, was "the real Friend and powerful Patron of the Orphan and Defenceless at his Gates."

He daily supplied "with a free and promiscuous Bounty" the indigent who came to him for aid, even though some of them might be cheats and impostors. He had founded and supported a large charity school, and he contributed to the maintenance of several others. His stewards were employed in seeking out the neediest families in the neighborhood, to which he then gave money from his own purse, and his chaplain was required to look for those who had been reduced from comfortable circumstances to poverty, so that they also might be relieved in their distress.[18] Young Harry Clinton's uncle "Mr. Fenton" was intended by Brooke as a similar illustration of the gentlemanly virtue of charity. It was his practice to invite the poor of the neighborhood to his hall for dinner every Sunday and have money placed under their plates so that they could pay their debts and establish themselves in lucrative employments. This public-spirited uncle soon had as many as fifty impoverished guests per week.[19]

Caring for servants and tenants with all the solicitude of a father was closely related to the duty of charity. These people were the gentleman's special responsibility. Ayres thus directed the English gentry and nobility to "endeavour to promote the welfare of all under you, and the welfare of your poor Tenants, and that they may not only subsist but thrive under you; take heed of oppressing them."[20] Sir Roger de Coverley was an ideal gentleman in this respect. Steele remarked in the *Spectator* No. 107 (July 3, 1711): "I never saw, but in Sir Roger's family, and one or two more, good servants treated as they ought to be. Sir Roger's kindness extends to their children's children, and this very morning he sent his coachman's grandson to 'prentice." Perhaps Sir Roger had inherited his kindly disposition from his ancestor Sir Humphrey, who, he said, had been " 'as generous as a gentleman.' "[21] The opposite of the ideal was the selfish and malevolent Squire Bluster depicted by Johnson in the *Rambler* No. 142 (July 27, 1751): " 'It is his rule to suffer his tenants to owe him rent, because, by this indulgence, he secures to himself the power of seizure whenever he has an inclination to amuse himself with calamity, and feast his ears with entreaties and lamentations.' "

Just as education was believed to establish a moral and religious sense in the gentleman, so was it thought to establish
public spirit in him and to equip him for serving society both
as a politician and as a private citizen. Some aspects of public
spirit, such as charity and an unselfish concern for one's fellow
creatures, were, after all, among the Christian principles in
which a youth was to be indoctrinated early; others, such as
patriotism, loyalty to the king, and a desire to promote the
national welfare, had been named since the Renaissance as
virtues to be bred into the young man of quality. When a
young nobleman had been well trained he was, in the words of
one eighteenth-century theorist, "justly qualify'd . . . and capable of all imaginable Service to his King and Country . . .
sensible of his Duty to . . . his Sovereign, his Equals and Inferiors, through the vast Advantages of Education."[22] Joseph
Priestley even asserted that since the education of gentlemen of
lesser rank was generally superior to that of nobles, these men
of less eminent family were better suited for statesmanship,
even though the great nobles were by their birth the logical
occupants of important political offices.[23] Chesterfield's enormous faith in education as preparation for public affairs is
well known; perhaps the primary object of his scheme of training was to equip his son for his intended political career.

Seventeenth-century treatises on policy and prudential conduct were directed toward mature gentlemen and thus do not
come properly under the province of education; the second of
Gailhard's *Two Discourses,* for example, was designed to instruct incipient and practising statesmen whose education was
already completed. During the Renaissance and seventeenth
century, and to a lesser extent in the eighteenth century, a
knowledge of the world was named as very useful for the man
engaged in public life; in so far as a knowledge of the world
was a part of education, it is treated in Chapter IV. Two additional aspects of education related to a political career, namely
the grand tour and the public schools, are also reserved for
treatment later. Our immediate concern is with still other
factors in the young gentleman's training which were considered
as contributive to making him into a man of public spirit.

One of these was the process of instilling into a well-born youth a vivid awareness of his responsibilities toward society. Without such an awareness, he would not be eager either to devote himself to the welfare of his nation in a political capacity or to perform acts of charity in a private capacity. For this reason Bishop Hurd said of the young English gentleman: "I require . . . That his ambition be awakened, or rather directed, to it's right object, the *public good;* and, to that end, that his soul be fired with the love of excellence and true honour."[24] Of similarly high-minded sentiments was David Fordyce, for whom the inculcation of a fervent public spirit became an essential principle in all good instruction of youth. Fordyce appears to have had in mind mainly duties toward the nation, but he probably included under these the exercise of charity. He emphasized the fact that selfishness, the opposite of public spirit, must be destroyed through right education if a young gentleman was to be of benefit to society. "In the education of youth," he declared, ". . . nothing seems to me to deserve more care and pains, than to possess them strongly with a sense of the connection they have with the public, and the meanness of all selfish and narrow views." Euphranor, the headmaster of the ideal academy which Fordyce envisioned, endeavored to inspire the students "with the highest notions and strongest feelings of a steady regard for the public, and of our connexion with society." On entering the academy, a student was required to participate in a formal initiation ceremony during which Euphranor informed him that "all its [i.e., the academy's] orders and institutions" were calculated to make him a good citizen and patriot, that "the whole circle of arts and sciences, are only valuable and honourable, as they are subservient to this grand purpose," that he was henceforth to consider himself "as a part of the public, and made for the good of others," and that he was to view his education "as a course of instruction and discipline necessary to qualify him for serving the public."[25]

In his education of his nephew Harry, "Mr. Fenton" tried, by means of exhortation and example, to fill him with public spirit and generous impulses. He gave the youth clothes for distribution among the needy and informed him that he must furnish beggars with money for food—but not wearing apparel, as beggars preferred their own rags, which were more likely to excite pity. He adjured Harry that when he spied any poor travelers on the road he should take them in, clothe them, and feed them; and "Mr. Fenton's" methods were so successful that the young nobleman was soon "watching to intercept poor travellers, as eagerly as a fowler watches for the rising of his game." By the time Harry attained manhood he had already spent fifty thousand pounds of his uncle's fortune. His less bountiful father, the Earl of Moreland, inquired in astonishment where he could possibly have disposed of so large a sum. "In hospitals and in prisons, my father, answered Harry. In streets and highways, among the wretched and indigent, supplying eyes to the blind, and limbs to the lame, and cheerfulness to the sorrowful and broken of heart; for such were my uncle's orders."[26] Harry had learned his lessons well.

A young gentleman's studies were thought to be an important prerequisite to the performance of his duties both as a statesman and as a private individual. "Our Studies," Ramesey remarked in his *Gentlemans Companion,* "tend to . . . the welfare of our Country, and the advantage of Man, or Neighbour" (pages 15-16). Francis Brokesby told the well-born young recipient of his *Letter of Advice* that "Knowledge of worthy and excellent things will . . . fit you to do good both in a private and publick capacity" and therefore enjoined the youth to "pursue learning" (page 5). It was obvious to theorists that unless a man had an adequate degree of learning, he was ill constituted for filling a public office intelligently and capably. Book knowledge, according to Gailhard's *Compleat Gentleman,* qualified the man of rank for a seat in Parliament or the King's council (First Treatise, page 33). Defoe and Swift, we recall, attributed the failure of contemporary gentlemen to distinguish themselves in statesmanship largely to their lack of intellectual acquirements; indeed, Defoe demanded, with regard to the untaught gentleman: "Can he go thro' the office of a Secretary of State or a Secretary of War, a paymaster of the Navy or Army, a Commissioner of Trade and Plantacions, or the like;

or to come lower, to a Commissioner of the Navy, the Excise, or the Customes? All these must be men of letters and men of figures. They must be men of learning and languages; or what are they fit for?"[27]

Among particular studies, history and law, as will be demonstrated in Chapter III, were highly esteemed as preparation for service of the state, since they furnished the young gentleman with much information useful in a political career. Rhetoric and oratory were especially necessary for the member of Parliament; an elegant written style, for anyone called upon to compose letters and official documents. A familiarity with geography and chronology, the so-called handmaids of history, also helped the gentleman execute his political functions competently. As a branch of history, the study of politics was considered especially valuable. In order to equip his nephew for the public duties to which he would soon be called, "Mr. Fenton" educated him at great length in the necessity and nature of government, the idea of British liberty, and the origin and principles of the British constitution.[28] Chesterfield's insistence that his son be well acquainted with the political histories of the European nations was to the same purpose.

Like Ramesey and Brokesby, many commentators did not explain their view that studies could also aid a gentleman in the performance of his duties in a private capacity. Certain of his studies, however—especially history and readings in the Bible or in moral works suitable for children—provided examples illustrating the virtue of charity. A comprehension of law, furthermore, enabled the gentleman in retirement on his estate to serve as a justice of the peace (one of his charitable rather than political obligations) and to promote the welfare of his tenants and neighbors by extricating them from legal difficulties.

Since an ardent and unswerving patriotism was a corollary of service of the nation, many theorists recommended that the gentleman's training be given a patriotic turn—that it produce in him a strong devotion to his native land and an attachment to its government, laws, and political principles. Thus Burnet

affirmed in 1668 that the gentleman's governor "must . . . in-
fuse in him a love to his countrey, and duty to his prince."[29]
Four decades later Burnet complained that education, most
notoriously at the universities, seldom fulfilled this function
and that "our gentry are not betimes possessed . . . with a love
to their country, a hatred of tyranny, and a zeal for liberty."[30]
Hurd demanded that education furnish the young gentleman
with "a reverence for the legal constitution of his country, and
a fervent affection for the great community, to which he belongs."[31] At the ideal academy described by Fordyce, the stimu-
lation of a "love of one's country" was assured by showing
the youths public buildings and other symbols of the national
community calculated to excite devotion toward it.[32] Joseph
Priestley laid great stress on history, politics, commerce, and
law, in the belief that these studies would inspire well-born
youths with an ardent patriotism. He expatiated on the value
of this patriotic training for future national service:

> It is a circumstance of particular consequence, that this
> enthusiastic love for our country would . . . be imbibed
> by persons of fortune, rank, and influence in whom it might
> be effectual to the most important purposes, who might have
> it in their power, not only to wish well to their country,
> but to render it the greatest real services. Such men would
> not only . . . be able to employ the force of a single arm
> only in its defence, but might animate the hearts, and en-
> gage the hands of thousands in its cause. Of what unspeak-
> able advantage might be one minister of state, one military
> commander, or even a single member of parliament, who
> throughly [sic] understood the interests of his country, who
> postponed every other interest and consideration to it.[33]

The inculcation of British patriotism after 1715 was complicated by Jacobitism. When the eleventh Earl of Mar, leader
of the Scottish rebels in 1715, counseled his son to be of service
"to your country . . . and consequently to your king,"[34] he
was advocating loyalty to Scotland rather than to Great Britain
and to the Pretender rather than to George II. Advice such as
this was, of course, very disturbing to Hanoverians. Objections
against instilling seditious principles into the minds of young

gentlemen were directed less toward Jacobite noblemen, however, than toward Oxford, which, during the years following
each of the rebellions, made itself especially liable to such
criticism.

There is no doubt that the charges of Jacobitism leveled against
Oxford were, in some degree, founded on fact. At the accession
of George I, the Chancellor of the University was that Stuart
champion the Duke of Ormond; and when he was impeached,
Oxford promptly selected his equally disaffected brother Lord
Arran to fill his place. In 1715 Jacobite riots occurred at the
university, and the authorities, with questionable justice, sol-
emnly held the Whiggish Constitution Club responsible for
them. More disturbances followed, till in October the government was obliged to send a regiment of dragoons to Oxford
and to place both university and town under martial law.
In 1716 a student named Meadowcourt, Hanoverian and member of the Constitution Club, invited (or perhaps forced) a
Proctor to drink a toast to King George, and, apparently for
no greater crime than this, his name was entered in the Black
Book (which listed flagrant offenders against academic law)
and he was sentenced to be kept from his Master's degree for
two years; when the two years had elapsed he encountered
more opposition from the university authorities before he finally
succeeded in obtaining his degree. Evidently this case, which
attained some notoriety, was not the only instance in which
the authorities rendered it difficult for Hanoverian sympathizers
to be granted degrees. Stuart sentiment at Oxford waned during
the 1720's and 1730's, but with the rebellion of 1745 it ex-
perienced something of a resurgence. In February, 1748, the
loyal-principled Reverend Richard Blacow, Canon of Windsor,
found a group of Oxonians holding an enthusiastic Jacobite
demonstration and brought the three ringleaders before the
Vice-Chancellor for punishment; feeling that the sentences imposed on them were too light, he eventually had the three youths
tried at the King's Bench.[35] The next year, the staunch Jacobite
Dr. William King, Principal of St. Mary Hall, delivered at the
dedication of the Radcliffe Library an oration of a strongly
Jacobite flavor; the implication of its closing paragraphs, all

beginning with the word "Redeat" ("Restore"), was unmistakable. This address naturally provoked rebukes from loyal pamphleteers.[36] King defended himself with an acid pen,[37] and again Oxford was brought before the public as a center of Jacobitism. Disaffection gradually died out at Oxford, but the events which had occurred there as a result of the two rebellions did considerable damage to the university's reputation for loyalty.[38]

It is, of course, not always easy to distinguish between Jacobitism and Toryism, and Oxford's Whig critics, in the excess of party spirit, may sometimes have leveled charges at the university which were exaggerated or unfounded. Deserved or not, however, the opinion that Oxford possessed marked seditious tendencies was apparently quite widespread between 1715 and 1755, helped along, no doubt, by the number of political pamphlets arising out of Jacobite incidents at the university. Nicholas Amhurst, one of the most violent of the pamphleteers, after describing the early incidents, exclaimed sarcastically: "Are not all these very plain and undeniable marks of the stedfast *loyalty* and affection which our *learned old mother* preserves to crown'd heads, and the *anointed of the Lord?*"[39] Thomas Gordon, another Whig journalist, portrayed a squire who refused to drink to King George, apparently as a consequence of having received his education at Oxford.[40] Edward Bentham, a fellow of Oriel College, was gravely concerned in the late 1740's over "how liberally the Charge of general Disaffection to his Majesty's Person and Government hath of late been thrown upon the University of Oxford." "The Nation," he said, "hath taken the Alarm."[41]

The suspicion under which Oxford lay induced some Whig parents not to send their sons to the university, lest the youths' thoughts be tainted with seditious principles by rebellious fellow students and a disloyal faculty. If parents felt this way, Amhurst implied, they had good reason to do so. He described the situation in the following terms:

Either we must keep our youth at home, by our chimney-corners, and put them into possession of our estates, in-

structed no better than our grooms, without one qualification, from the knowledge of mankind, to make a figure in
the world worthy their birth and fortune; or, by sending
them to the pretended seminaries of virtue and learning
[i.e., Oxford specifically], prostitute them to the base designs of those [faculty members] whose business we see it
has been, and is, to ensnare them into all the traps that
giddy boys can be caught in; and make them, at any rate,
the tools of *their* ambition and craft.[42]

After the second rebellion Bentham, in his *Letter to a Fellow
of a College,* expressed the fear that as long as Oxford remained
under the stigma of Jacobitism, parents would send their sons
abroad to be educated. Nor were they to be blamed for this
course, if, as they believed, the university, instead of qualifying
a young gentleman for serving his nation, engrained into him
the most unpatriotic and disloyal sentiments:

> What Parent, that hath a true Concern for the publick
> Welfare, or for the Success of his Child, will care to hazard
> the first Formation of his Mind among such Companions,
> or under such Governors? Will the Fears be at all un-
> natural, that He may possibly be led into immediate Danger
> of his Life and Fortunes by Rebellion;—that His Attention,
> and Study will be diverted from procuring such Qualifica-
> tions as may be useful to himself and his Country;—that
> His Temper will be sour'd against his Superiors;—that He
> will be influenced to a Way of thinking and behaving,
> contrary to the publick Good . . .? (Pages 50-51.)

But Bentham tried to convince parents that they did not need
to be so afraid of an Oxford education. Much fonder of the
university than Amhurst was, he wished to exonerate it from
the charge of teaching Jacobitism. In an admonition addressed
to a Jacobite student, he reproved the youth for joining with
other rebels in "the several Stages of their treasonable Frol-
icks,"[43] when his training at the university should have shown
him how wrong such conduct was. He announced that his
Letter to a Fellow of a College was written "in order to show
that, agreeably to Our public Professions, We [i.e., the Oxford

faculty] do regard the training up of Persons to be good Subjects as a principal Object in the Business of Education."
Oxford's reputation for Jacobitism, he maintained in this
pamphlet, was exaggerated and was based on the treasonable
activities of a small minority. He admitted that the university
authorities were doing nothing to prevent students from hanging
portraits of the Pretender and his sons in their chambers or
from drinking the health of the Chevalier of St. George, but,
he said in extenuation, this was perhaps only because the faculty
had "higher Notions of the Authority of Academical Discipline,
than the Licentiousness of the Age will well permit to be
exercised." Such leniency, he affirmed, must cease; whenever
the faculty did evince Jacobite sentiments, they should be strongly discouraged; the covert teaching of Jacobite principles should
be stifled, for "the secret Efforts of Disloyalty are the more
dangerous, and make deeper Impressions on the Minds of
young People."[44] Genteel parents would then resume sending
their sons to Oxford, and the inculcation of patriotism and
preparation for service of the nation would again be, as they
should, important aims of education at the university.

Notes to Chapter II

1. For the views in this paragraph, see Einstein, *Italian
Renaissance in England,* pp. 89-91, and *Tudor Ideals,* pp. 53-55,
164-167; Kelso, *Doctrine,* pp. 14-15, 27, 39-40, and "Sixteenth
Century Definitions of the Gentleman in England," *JEGP,*
XXIV (1925), 378, 380-381; Mason, *Gentlefolk in the Making,*
pp. 48, 51-52, 124, 130, 143, and chap. viii, "Seventeenth-Century
Treatises on Policy"; and William H. Woodward, *Studies in
Education During the Age of the Renaissance 1400-1600* (Cam-
bridge Univ. Press, 1906), pp. 295-296.

2. Allestree, attrib., *Gentleman's Calling,* p. 26.

3. See his *Moral Gallantry* (Edinburgh, repr. at London,
1669), pp. 97-103.

4. *Of Education, Especially of Young Gentlemen,* p. 33.

5. See Mason, pp. 220, 252.

6. See *Compleat English Gentleman,* pp. 175-181, 239-240,
and Swift's *Essay on Modern Education,* in *Prose Works,* ed.
Temple Scott (London, 1897-1908), XI, 47-57.

7. *An Essay upon Study*, 2nd ed. (London, 1737), p. 215. 1st ed. was 1731.

8. *The Club* (London, 1817), p. 75. 1st ed. was 1711.

9. *Letters,* ed. Bonamy Dobrée (London, 1932), IV, 1443, and III, 831.

10. *Fool of Quality*, pp. 258, 303.

11. See Kelso, *Doctrine,* pp. 88-89.

12. Allestree, attrib., *Gentleman's Calling,* p. 55.

13. *Of Education, Especially of Young Gentlemen,* p. 32.

14. *Vox Clamantis,* p. 33.

15. *More Fruits of Solitude,* in Harvard Classics, ed. Charles W. Eliot, I (1909), 412-413.

16. *The Guardian's Instruction, Or, The Gentleman's Romance,* with introd. by Herbert H. Sturmer (London, 1897), pp. 14-15.

17. *Royal Marriage,* p. 71. Louis A. Landa in "Jonathan Swift and Charity," *JEGP,* XLIV (1945), 337-350, discusses the concept of the stewardship of wealth with regard to Swift and his clerical contemporaries.

18. See *Serino: Or, The Character of a Fine Gentleman,* 2nd ed. (London, 1723), pp. 39-41. 1st ed. was 1721.

19. See *Fool of Quality,* p. 55.

20. *Vox Clamantis,* pp. 32-33.

21. *Spectator* No. 109 (July 5, 1711).

22. John Littleton Costeker, *The Fine Gentleman: Or, The Compleat Education of a Young Nobleman* (London, 1732), pp. 51-52.

23. See his *Essay on the First Principles of Government,* 2nd ed., corr. and enl. (London, 1771), pp. 16-17. 1st ed. was 1768.

24. *Uses of Foreign Travel,* p. 77.

25. *Dialogues Concerning Education* (Glasgow, 1768, repr. from London, 1745), I, 32-34, 296-297.

26. See *Fool of Quality,* pp. 54-56, 346.

27. *Compleat English Gentleman,* p. 178.

28. See *Fool of Quality,* pp. 258-284.

29. *Thoughts on Education,* p. 67.

30. *History of His Own Time* (Oxford, Clarendon Press, 1823), VI, 197-198.

31. *Uses of Foreign Travel,* p. 77.

32. See his *Dialogues Concerning Education,* I, 298-299.

33. *An Essay on a Course of Liberal Education for Civil and*

Active Life (London, 1765), pp. 33-34.

34. *My Legacie to My Dear Son Thomas, Lord Erskine,* ed. the Hon. Stuart Erskine, in *Scottish History Soc.,* 1 Ser., XXVI (Edinburgh, 1896), 178-179. Dated March, 1726.

35. Blacow described this affair in *A Letter to William King . . . Concerning a Particular Account of a Treasonable Riot at Oxford, February 1747* [i.e., 1748] (London, 1755).

36. See *Remarks on Dr. King's Speech at the Dedication of Dr. R———'s Library* (1749) by John Burton (pseud. Phileleutherus Londinensis); *Oxford Honesty or A Case of Conscience* (1749); and *A Satire upon Physicians* (1755). The oration itself was printed in 1749 and 1750 as *Oratio in Theatro Sheldoniano habita. Die Dedicationis Bibliothecae Radclivianae.*

37. See his *Elogium Famae Inserviens Jacci Etonensis* (1750), a satire against his Whig opponent John Burton; *The Last Blow* (1755); and *Dr. King's Apology* (1755), an attack on Blacow's *Letter.* This last pamphlet was itself attacked anonymously in *A Letter to Dr. King Occasioned by His Late Apology* (1755) and *The Principles of the University of Oxford, as far as Relates to Affection to the Government, Stated* (1755).

38. For further discussion of the material in this paragraph, see A. D. Godley, *Oxford in the Eighteenth Century* (New York and London, 1908), pp. 237-241, 244-259, and (Sir) Charles Edward Mallet, *A History of the University of Oxford* (London, 1924-27), III, 38-43, 45, 50-54.

39. *Terrae-Filius: Or, The Secret History of the University of Oxford,* 2nd ed. (London, 1726), I, 32. The *Terrae-Filius* essays were originally published periodically; the above citation is from No. 6 (Feb. 1, 1721).

40. See *The Humourist,* II (London, 1725), 73-74.

41. *A Letter to a Fellow of a College* (London, 1749), pp. 5, 51. This work was ridiculed by William King in *Some Remarks on the Letter to a Fellow of a College* (1749).

42. *Terrae-Filius,* I, 49-50. From No. 9 (Feb. 15, 1721).

43. *A Letter to a Young Gentleman of Oxford* (Oxford, 1748), p. 9. This work was ridiculed by the indefatigable William King in *A Proposal for Publishing a Poetical Translation . . . of . . . Bentham's Letter to a Young Gentleman of Oxford* (1748) and his *Poetical Abridgement . . . of . . . Bentham's Letter to A Young Gentleman of Oxford* (1749).

44. See *Letter to a Fellow of a College,* pp. 51-55, 61, 71.

CHAPTER THREE

Intellectual Acquirements as an Aim in the Gentleman's Education

No definite position can be assigned to learning among the qualifications of the ideal gentleman in the Restoration and eighteenth century. Opinions on the place of intellectual acquirements among the gentlemanly attributes, unlike opinions on the place of virtue, were inconsistent except for the fact that nobody ranked these acquirements first. Educational theorists also differed as to the degree of learning necessary for men of birth and as to the desirability of certain studies. Perhaps the majority of gentlemen, furthermore, held views on learning quite divergent from those held by the theorists, many of whom were tutors, schoolmasters, or clergymen. It is sometimes assumed that after the Elizabethan period learning declined in importance as a component of the gentlemanly ideal in England,[1] but the extent of the decline, if there was an appreciable decline at all, is a debatable matter.

The complex question of the relationship of learning to gentlemen might be first approached through a consideration of the state of learning among men of quality as seen by their critics. If we are to credit the complaints of these critics, the average Englishman of rank, in both the Restoration and the eighteenth century, was abysmally ignorant, knowing very little about history, mathematics, Latin grammar and literature, and the other studies traditionally required of him. Certainly some well-born youths attended private schools, and others attended public schools despite the fact that many people of fashion evidently looked upon public education with disfavor. Others, again, received instruction at home from tutors, who in many instances were very well qualified. A few spent some time at academies or universities abroad, and some went to Oxford or Cambridge. Notwithstanding their opportunities for improving their minds, however, English gentlemen were so frequently accused of a lack of learning that we must assume some basis in fact behind the complaints.

Three types in particular were thus accused. These were the country gentleman, who lived mainly on his ancestral estate in the provinces; the so-called fine gentleman, who passed most of his life in the fashionable circles of London; and the well-born student at Oxford or Cambridge.

The country gentleman was characterized as a thick-headed individual who, rather than engage in any intellectual pursuits, spent his existence in hunting foxes or partridges and in drinking ale. Squire Western in *Tom Jones,* for whom hunting was the main concern of life, was a more sympathetic picture of the unlearned country gentleman than many produced in the period. Elsewhere Fielding satirized squires' sons who returned ignorant from schools to their fathers' country seats and stayed there for the remainder of their lives, doing nothing toward the improvement of their minds, earning the appellation of clowns by simply wasting their time on the estates, "where Racing, Cock fighting, and Party become their Pursuit, and form the whole Business and Amusement of their future Lives."[2] The conversation of such a man, one writer affirmed, was "wholly taken up by his Horses, Dogs, and Hawks, and the more senseless Animals that tend 'em."[3] According to another author, had a squire of his acquaintance "hunted less, and read more . . . he might have been Company for Men," but instead, he was "a Child and a Coxcomb at Threescore."[4] Descriptions like these are reminiscent of the lines of verse by Tickell which Steele included in the *Spectator* No. 532 (November 10, 1712), as a portrait of country gentlemen:

> At length despised, each to his fields retires,
> First with the dogs, and king amidst the squires;
> From pert to stupid sinks supinely down,
> In youth a coxcomb, and in age a clown.

Sometimes, it appears, the squire scarcely even knew how to write English,[5] and we recall that in Act IV of *She Stoops to Conquer* Tony Lumpkin was revealed as unable to read. Defoe, perhaps the most outspoken critic of the ignorant country gentleman, depicted him in *The Compleat English Gentleman* as one who "enjoys his espous'd brutallity, hunts, hawkes, shootes, and follows his game . . . drinks with his huntsman, and is excellent company for two or three drunken elder brothers in his neighbourhood; and as here is his felicity, so here is the uttmost of his acomplishments." If he should inherit the estate, "'tis not the same onely but worse; for, his pride encreasing without his sence, he comes at last to the perfeccion of a fool, namely to be proud of his ignorance" (pages 39-40). Cultivated and intelligent aristocrats, such as Chesterfield, deplored the lack of learning displayed by squires on their estates; Chesterfield called them "our English bumpkin country gentlemen" and counseled his godson not to follow their "rustic illiberal sports."[6] Apparently, however, Chesterfield's attitude did not prevail among men of quality in the provinces.

According to his critics, the fine gentleman who spent most of his life in London was often as ignorant as his country cousin. His waking hours were taken up with the ritual of dressing in careful conformity to the current mode, attending balls and ridottos, carrying on amours, and gaming at the clubs. His preoccupation with these elegant but frivolous pastimes left him little opportunity to cultivate his intellect. Thinking that "the chief end of Man is to *Dress well*," he had, as one writer observed, "more Learning in his *Heels* than his Head."[7] His paucity of sound knowledge was frequently illustrated from the superficiality of his conversation, which, instead of including intelligent ideas on significant subjects, was said to consist of "sweet Chit-chat, and tender Prittle-Prattle, Shreds of Sentiments, and *Cuttings* of Sentences," revolving around such topics as "Furniture, Equipage, Dress, the Tiring Room, and the Toyshop."[8] There had been a time, some authors thought, when the man of fashion was qualified to discourse on deep and weighty matters; but that time was dead, and, as Thomas Gordon remarked ironically, custom had now "happily made an Excess of Knowledge unnecessary to *modish Conversation;* for otherwise, the finest Assemblies in the Nation would not be much different from silent Meetings."[9] Steele's portrait of Will Honeycomb in the *Spectator* No. 2 (March 2, 1711) was in part intended as a satire on the empty-headed Londoner of fashion. Will's knowledge and conversation did not extend beyond modes, scandals, and intrigues.

The reading habits of the fine gentleman were, according to some authors, another indication of his lack of interest in learning. If he read at all, these authors implied, he chose books on horse racing, treatises on card playing, and French romances, which supplied him with as much knowledge as he needed in order to cut a figure in his own circle of fashionable fools.[10] The unknown author of the *World* No. 64 (March 21, 1754) satirically described a visit to the library of a "Lord Finical," whose collection of books, of which the nobleman was inordinately proud, seemed magnificent indeed, including works of the best authors, with all the volumes elegantly bound. When the visitor took down several of the books, he discovered that their pages were uncut. Lord Finical freely admitted that he never read any of the volumes; his interest was in the splendor of their bindings only. Mid-century commentators were appalled at the apathetic attitude of people of quality toward serious literary works, and some of them, such as John Brown in his *Estimate,* averred that this state of affairs, like the superficiality of modish conversation, was peculiar to their own age: "A Knowledge of Books, a Taste in Arts, a Proficiency in Science, was formerly regarded as a proper Qualification, in a Man of Fashion. The Annals of our Country have transmitted to us the Name and Memory of Men, as eminent in Learning and Taste, as in Rank and Fortune. It will not, I presume, be regarded as any kind of Satire on the present Age, to say, that among the higher Ranks, this literary Spirit is generally vanished" (pages 41-42).

The country gentleman and the fine gentleman had both completed their formal education, and attacks leveled at them for their ignorance were attacks on the finished product. But the well-born university student, who was still in the process

of being educated, was also the object of frequent satire. Young
men of rank entered Oxford or Cambridge as gentleman-com-
moners or fellow-commoners, and their status entitled them to
certain privileges with regard to observance of discipline, attendance at lectures, and exercises. Their abundance of free
time and spending money made them liable to more temptations from study than were youths of lower station, so that they
often conducted themselves in such a manner "as to render a
College Life quite ineffectual, sometimes living, as if they were
sent there only for their Recreation, and Divertisement, or to
. . . swagger in a Tavern, or . . . Tipple in a Chamber."[11]
In addition, they were likely to have entered college with a
determination not to profit by it intellectually.

Opinions varied as to whether their own anti-intellectual
attitude or their university was more at fault for their lack of
learning. Being ill-disposed toward Oxford for many reasons,
Nicholas Amhurst, as might be expected, put the blame on
the nature of the university rather than on the well-born
student's distaste for intellectual pursuits, declaring: "The
education of a person of distinction at OXFORD, instead of being
. . . the most strictly taken care of, is of all the most neglected;
a nobleman may bring any thing from college but learning. . . .
A gentleman-commoner, if he be a man of fortune, is soon told,
that it is not expected from one of his form to mind exercises."[12]
Most writers, however, seem to have believed that the genteel
undergraduate's ignorance was largely voluntary. One, for example, described him as passing "his whole Winter's Morning
in dividing and subdividing his Cinders" or as lying idle until
dinner time.[13] James Miller included in his comedy about
Oxford a certain Ape-all, the dramatic portrait of the well-
born undergraduate whose ignorance was entirely self-chosen.
Ape-all was described in the cast of characters as "a trifling
ridiculous Fop, affecting Dress and Lewdness, and a Contemner
of Learning." He avoided study so successfully that when some-
one mentioned Plutarch's *Morals,* he said in an aside: "That
must be some Bawdy Book that I have not seen."[14] In the
Connoisseur No. 41 (November 7, 1754), Colman and Thornton
ironically suggested that Newmarket be made a supplement to

Cambridge, so that fellow-commoners, whose "rank exempts them from the common drudgery of lectures and exercises," might study the horse races and thus derive at least some profit from their years at the university; for "though they never will be scholars," they might perhaps "turn out excellent jockeys."

No doubt the critics, as satirists, often indulged in exaggeration; moreover, portraits of the unlearned country squire and the superficial Londoner of fashion had almost reached the status of literary conventions, which must be viewed with some reservations as factual evidence. Such conventions, however, would not have arisen without cause, and the frequency and violence of complaints about the ignorance of gentlemen are irrefutable indications of a very real condition. A considerable number of eighteenth-century gentlemen were undeniably quite uninformed. With many of them, furthermore, their ignorance may in large part be attributed to the notion that learning was incompatible with gentility. Defoe was perhaps not speaking in unduly extravagant terms when he exclaimed in his *Compleat English Gentleman*:

That our gentlemen are illiterate and untaught is true; but 'tis as true that where there is one gentleman who complains of it and thinks himself the worse for it, there are 20 that boast of it, value themselves upon it, think their ignorance sits well upon their quality, and that contemn the men of letters and books as below them and not worth their regard; who think learning unfashionable, and, at best, useless to them, and that to write their names is enough for men of fortunes, that they have nothing to do but sit still and enjoy the world and roll in the abundance of it, that the rest is all bussiness and bustle, that 'tis below them and not worth their notice. (Page 237).

The same persuasion that learning and gentility were incompatible was characteristic of much of the genteel order in the Restoration. Clement Ellis referred to it in 1660, when he affirmed that "care is taken for the good [university] *Tutor*, that if his *Schollar* chance to return home (as too seldome he does) with . . . Schollarship . . . he shall then have the *Credit* or

Discredit (call it what you will) of *making* the *Schollar,* or *spoiling* the *Gentleman.*"[15] A similar attitude toward learning obtained in the seventeenth-century Scottish aristocracy, prompting Archibald Campbell, eighth Earl and first Marquis of Argyle, to tell his son that history and mathematics were the only studies fit for gentlemen, the others being suitable for scholars and those who had to live by their learning.[16]

Such statements, however, do not constitute reliable evidence that learning declined in importance as a component of the gentlemanly ideal during the seventeenth century. A contempt for learning was, in fact, an old genteel tradition, originating in the Middle Ages, when the proper province for a knight or nobleman was believed to be the active life, particularly that of a warrior, as opposed to the contemplative life of a scholar.[17] It is true that during the Renaissance learning came to be treated as indispensable to the ideal gentleman by authors of courtesy books and other theorizers on gentility. Yet to a considerable extent the Tudor aristocracy and gentry retained an anti-intellectual outlook despite the opinions of their critics.[18] Some Renaissance gentlemen, such as Sir Philip Sidney, Sir Henry Wotton, and Sir Walter Raleigh, combined the active life of a soldier, statesman, or courtier with intellectual acquirements, just as some gentlemen did in the seventeenth and eighteenth centuries; but an antipathy toward learning on the part of many men of rank throughout the Tudor period is not to be denied. It was less strong than it had been in the Middle Ages, partly because the Elizabethan respect and enthusiasm for learning had some effect on the aristocratic order and partly because, with the Tudor shift in emphasis from the gentleman as warrior to the gentleman as statesman, a degree of learning became requisite to the performance of public duties; but it remained a powerful current in the gentleman's own conception of the ideal. Elyot complained about an aristocratic scorn for learning in 1531, and James Cleland uttered a similar complaint in 1607: "False and fantastical opinion preuaileth so against reason now a daies, that ignorance is thought an essential marke of a Noble man by many."[19]

The fondness of seventeenth-century English aristocrats for the French academies, which made little pretense of cultivating the intellect, is therefore not surprising, although it perhaps does not indicate, as one authority believes, that learning for gentlemen fell into disesteem *after* the Renaissance.[20] It illustrates a genteel attitude far older than the seventeenth century. Furthermore, the alleged ignorance of men of quality in eighteenth-century England does not offer substantial ground for supposing that their views toward learning were a great deal less sympathetic than those of their Renaissance ancestors, even if the critics did occasionally look back to a vague former period when men of birth and title had been learned. The more probable conclusion is that anti-intellectual gentlemen of the eighteenth century were simply following a long-established and deep-rooted tradition of their class. The extent of their ignorance cannot, of course, be precisely determined, nor can their antagonism toward learning be accurately compared with that of Elizabethan gentlemen, since many of the most prejudiced were, in both ages, inarticulate. The most one can say with certitude, on the basis of the evidence discussed so far, is that their distaste for intellectual acquirements was by no means new.

There were, however, two factors not yet touched upon which, in the Restoration and eighteenth century, probably combined with and bolstered the fashionable antipathy toward learning. These were the relationship between learning and pedantry, and the relationship between learning and "the world."

The disgust with which the Restoration and eighteenth century regarded pedantry, or the pursuit and ostentatious display of obscure erudition, needs little comment. Gentlemen and critics alike agreed with Locke's pronouncement that pedantry was a quality "than which there is nothing less becoming a gentleman."[21] Even aristocrats who had a high respect for learning were wary of the acquisition of pedantry; thus Chesterfield, who had subjected his son to a more rigorous course of study than that which many well-born youths received, warned the boy: "Great learning . . . if not accompanied with sound judgment, frequently carries us into error, pride, and pedantry." "Wear your learning, like your watch, in a private pocket: and do not merely pull it out and strike it merely to show you have one."[22]

Youths who had attended a university were held to be especially liable to pedantry. One Restoration writer cautioned a young gentleman who had recently graduated from a university: "When you come into Company, be not forward to show your *Proficiency*, nor impose your *Academical Discourses*, nor glitter affectedly in *Terms of Art*."[23] In the *Guardian* No. 24 (April 8, 1713), Steele illustrated this university-inspired parade of erudition by means of Jack Lizard, who had just returned home after a year and a half at Oxford, and in whose conversation a "vein of pedantry" had consequently become prominent. "He told us, upon the appearance of a dish of wild fowl, that, according to the opinion of some natural philosophers, they might be lately come from the moon." He offended his sister "with several questions, relating to the bigness and distance of the moon and stars; and after every interrogatory, would be winking upon me, and smiling at his sister's ignorance."

During the eighteenth century the opprobrious term "pedant" was used so indiscriminately and irresponsibly that it came to be applied, by those who knew no better, to almost anyone who exhibited signs of learning. "With many People," the *Gentleman's Library* declared, "*Learning* and *Pedantry* are Synonimous" (page 39). Johnson, in the *Rambler* No. 173 (November 12, 1751), maintained that every educated man was in peril of being called a pedant and that from a fear of bringing this stigma upon themselves, some well-informed persons tried to hide their very knowledge. Loveybond made a similar assertion in the *World* No. 13 (October 10, 1754).

This extensive and gratuitous application of the term "pedant," combined with the inherited fashionable aversion toward intellectual pursuits, induced some gentlemen actively to avoid learning. From bias or conviction, they appear to have identified even a nominal amount of it with pedantry. As early as 1671, Panton described genteel parents who were "of Opinion, that to breed Gentlemen at Schools, and in Learning, is the way to make them meer Scholists and Pedants." As a critic of aristocratic ignorance, Panton himself held that while "Gentlemen ought not to be so long ty'd to their Studies, as should render them pedantique,"[24] they should at least be given an adequate training in the fields of specific knowledge. The exaggerated fear of pedantry which he mentioned, however, grew more characteristic of people of fashion in the eighteenth century. One reason why the country gentleman rejected learning, according to a satiric portrait, was that "he has such a fear of Pedantry always before his Eyes, that he accounts it a Scandal to his Gentility to talk Sense, and write true *English*."[25] In Nicholas Amhurst's belief, the well-born university student neglected his studies partly because "*pedantry* to him all learning seems."[26] Colman and Thornton, in the *Connoisseur* No. 24 (July 11, 1754), explained the disinclination of fashionable people to read informative works by suggesting that they did not wish pedantry to be imputed to them. An ignorant gentleman sketched by Defoe would have nothing to do with learning because "as to books and reading, 'tis a good, dull, poreing work for the parsons and pedants" (page 65). A number of gentlemen, such as Chesterfield, could see that the danger of pedantry arose only when a man's information became extraordinarily deep and was misused, but the unreasonable fear of incurring the obnoxious title of pedant certainly contributed to make many members of the nobility and gentry men of little learning.

From the Middle Ages through the eighteenth century, the proper field of activity for a gentleman was always "the world" in one form or another. For the medieval knight or nobleman, as we have seen, the world usually meant a military life, whereas in the Renaissance it more often meant a political life. Although Renaissance theorists believed that learning helped a gentleman to play a wise and successful part in government and legislation, even they declared that an excessive erudition, specialized and remote and hardly practical, would not assist a man in performing the duties of an active political or military life but, in fact, would probably hinder him.[27] We have noted that while the gentleman's role as politician was still important in the eighteenth century, it received less attention than it had earlier. For the eighteenth-century gentleman, the world seemed

to imply mainly polite society, conversation, and social intercourse in general. Since the old antithesis between the world
and the study persisted, however, people came to fear that
learning would disable a gentleman from taking part in social
activities. This fear contributed materially to the theory that
the scholar was incompatible with the gentleman, and it no
doubt reinforced the traditional genteel dislike for learning.
If the erudite man was not indulging in pedantic ostentation
in company, he was, people assumed, acting awkward and ill
at ease; he had no grace, poise, or polish, but only an unpleas-
antly bookish air. Such an individual was obviously the opposite
of what the gentleman wanted to be, as the gentleman's own
ideal was the Chesterfieldian one of unstudied elegance, charm,
and affability.

Ludicrous portraits of the scholar in society became as much
a literary convention in the eighteenth century as portraits of
the unlearned country squire or empty-headed town gentleman.
Steele, it may be recalled, wrote for the *Spectator* No. 362 (April
25, 1712) a letter supposedly contributed by a person who had
spent most of his life with books, so that " 'by conversing
generally with the dead,' " he " 'grew almost unfit for the
society of the living.' " Realizing that he had " 'contracted an
ungainly aversion to conversation' " and talked with " 'little
entertainment to others,' " he resolved to force himself into
company, in the hope that a change could still be effected.
But his efforts failed miserably until he fell in love with a
socially competent woman; by imitating her, he finally developed some ability to comport himself with ease in the world.
A similar picture of the learned man in company was drawn
by Fordyce, who had a well-born student say that most scholars
seemed "to be afraid of company," could not "bear to have the
eyes of others fixed upon them," and were "utterly at a loss
what to do with their hands, or how to dispose of their limbs!"
The genteel youth observed in conclusion: "What a reproach
does it cast on learning, to see its friends wearing so mean and
ridiculous a garb?"[28]

Among literary descriptions of the awkward figure which the
scholar cut in society, those which Johnson included in the

Rambler deserve mention. For No. 157 (September 17, 1751) he wrote a letter supposedly penned by a certain Verecundulus ("The Bashful One"), who, having entered society from the seclusion of a university, found himself " 'blasted with a sudden imbecility.' " Since the subjects of conversation were not erudite, he was unable to utter anything except " 'negative monosyllables, or professions of ignorance.' " To crown his embarrassment, he dropped his teacup, scalding a lapdog and staining a lady's petticoat. In No. 159 Johnson assured the desperate Verecundulus that although deep learning disabled a man initially from engaging in social intercourse, his "imbecility" was curable. Yet in No. 179 (December 3, 1751) he depicted another learned man, a mathematician named Gelasimus ("The Frozen One"), whose social ineptitude was not curable. Gelasimus tried to charm others by facetiousness and hilarity; but since his years of solitary study had not taught him how to be amusing, he succeeded only in acquiring a reputation as a buffoon.

Just as some gentlemen exaggerated the danger of becoming pedantic through learning, some exaggerated the danger of becoming unfit for social intercourse through learning. Their inherited contempt for erudition probably predisposed them to make this exaggeration. Swift suggested that the genteel distrust of learning originated during the War of the Spanish Succession, when officers returned from the Continent to regale their admiring audiences with such sentiments as "D——n me, a scholar when he comes into good company, what is he but an ass?"[29] In answer to the well-born student's scornful description of scholars, Fordyce asserted in his *Dialogues Concerning Education*: "People presume, without examining, because some men, reputed learned, have been mere simpletons in the common affairs of life, that therefor [*sic*] *all* men of learning must be so." He observed with disapproval that "one kind of knowledge has been thought necessary to furnish a *learned head,* and quite another [i.e., knowledge of the world] to form a *gentleman*" (I, 90-91).

The fashionable tendency to emphasize the world at the expense of book learning was satirized by Johnson in the

Rambler. In No. 109 (April 2, 1751), he portrayed a youth whose genteel mother seriously considered dismissing his tutor so that the boy would not be in peril of acquiring this man's awkward manner, and determined that her son should immediately be introduced to the world as a corrective to his studies. Notwithstanding his awareness that a Verecundulus or Gelasimus was the possible product of an excess of learning, Johnson thought the mother's apprehensions unreasonable, as he showed in No. 132 (June 22, 1751), where he expressed his own opinions through a letter supposedly from the tutor:

> "I remonstrated against too early an acquaintance with cards and company; but . . . she said that he had been already confined too long to solitary study, and it was now time to show him the world; nothing was more a brand of meanness than bashful timidity; gay freedom and elegant assurance were only to be gained by mixed conversation, a frequent intercourse with strangers, and a timely introduction to splendid assemblies; and she had more than once observed, that his forwardness and complaisance began to desert him; that he was silent when he had not something of consequence to say; blushed whenever he happened to find himself mistaken; and hung down his head in the presence of the ladies, without the readiness of reply and activity of officiousness remarkable in young gentlemen that are bred in London."

The mother, of course, erred in interpreting her son's actions as signs that he was losing the social graces; but she had her way, and he showed " 'a speedy acquisition or recovery of her darling qualities.' " More than that, he soon developed his fashionable parent's scorn for learning. " 'He begins already to look down on me with superiority,' " the tutor affirmed, " 'and submits to one short lesson in a week, as an act of condescension rather than obedience.' " In time, this youth would probably turn into one of those fine gentlemen of London conspicuous for their ignorance—and all because his mother had an unwarranted fear of learning as prejudicial to participation in the world.

One further cause of a lack of learning among eighteenth-century English gentlemen ought to be noted briefly. This was the theory, endorsed, apparently, by many fashionable parents, that although learning was desirable for younger sons because they might have to make their own way in the world by entering careers or professions, it was superfluous for the eldest son, who, being assured of a handsome fortune, did not need to be equipped for acquiring one. Swift affirmed that this attitude prevailed in "all families, where there is wealth enough to afford, that their sons (at least the eldest) may be good for nothing. Why should my son be a scholar, when it is not intended that he should live by his learning?"[30] Mrs. Hardcastle, in Act I of *She Stoops to Conquer,* remarked as an excuse for her son's ignorance: "No matter, Tony Lumpkin has a good fortune. My son is not to live by his learning." If we are to credit Defoe, this kind of reasoning, perhaps more than any other single factor, accounted for what he considered the deplorable stupidity of eldest sons:

> The bright and the dull, the blind and the clear, the man of sence and learning and the blockhead, is as often to be disscern'd as the heir and the cadet are seen together, where one is untaught and good for nothing because he is to have the estate, and the other is polish'd and educated because he is to make his fortune; the last is to be prepar'd to liv by his witts, and the other is to have no wits or, at best, no learning, because he can liv without them.

In Defoe's opinion, eldest sons usually agreed with their parents that learning was not necessary for them. He invented a conversation in which an elder brother told a younger: " 'The heir you kno' has no need of the wit, if he has but the estate.' " The younger brother observed: " ' Most eldest sons are of your mind, and that makes us see so many heirs that can't write their own names.' " But the elder replied: " ' No matter, if they can but read their own names in the deeds of their inheritance.' "[31]

The foregoing discussion of genteel ignorance and the genteel attitude toward learning is not intended to imply that there were not many gentlemen in the Restoration and eighteenth

century who entertained a great respect for learning and acquired considerable erudition, and many others who were certainly cultivated and well-informed. We must remember that
a very significant minority of Restoration and eighteenth-century men of quality—figures such as Evelyn, Sir William Temple,
the first and second Earls of Clarendon, the first Marquis and
first Earl of Halifax, Shaftesbury, Chesterfield, and Horace
Walpole—were distinguished for intellectual pursuits and that
some of them engaged in scholarly activities, though perhaps
with an assumed air of effortlessness, casualness, and aristocratic nonchalance which differentiated them from pedants
and professional scholars. It is, however, the majority rather
than the minority that we are concerned with here—the thou-
sands of gentlemen who had little learning and preferred not
to have any more. The fear of becoming pedants and the
fear of acquiring bookish manners may possibly have made them
even less sympathetic toward learning than their Renaissance
forbears; and if this is so, then learning *had* declined somewhat
as a requirement in the gentleman's own ideal of the gentleman.
The question is, however, a debatable one.

In any case, the views held by gentlemen are not indicative
of the views held by theorists and commentators on gentility,
many of whom, as mentioned before, were not members of
fashionable society. If we turn to their opinions and recommendations, we may determine how they felt on the matter of
learning as a qualification for gentlemen and to what extent
their attitude differed from that of anti-intellectual aristocrats.

It should already be obvious from the storm of complaints
about the ignorance of men of quality that commentators required the gentleman to have more learning than many gentlemen themselves thought necessary. Theorists deprecated and
satirized the illogical identification of moderate learning with
pedantry, the exaggerated fear that book knowledge would
disqualify a man from participation in polite society, and the
persuasion that an eldest son should be intellectually impoverished because he was not to live by his learning.

On the other hand, most theorists agreed with gentlemen that the man of birth should not have so much learning as to become pedantic or awkward. Their ideal was not an antiquarian, such as Gray, but an enlightened, well-informed man— a person whose store of knowledge was broad and liberal but did not embrace obscure, useless details or result in bookish, ungraceful manners. Even Defoe, who in his *Compleat English Gentleman* so strongly insisted that the man of rank acquire learning, did not wish him to be what was commonly regarded as a scholar. "I distinguish between a learned man and a man of learning," he said, "as I distinguish between a schollar and a gentleman." The former was "a meer book-case . . . a creature buryed aliv in heaps of antients and moderns, full of tongues but no language." The latter, "a man of polite learning," was "a gentleman and what a gentleman should be" (page 203).

It is true that an occasional writer contested the fashionable theory that the scholar and the gentleman were irreconcilable opposites, "he that is a Scholar having one principal part, if not the best part of a Gentleman,"[32] as Ayres maintained. An anonymous author early in the eighteenth century regretted that learning was under the gentleman's "disgrace and contempt" and ascribed this condition to the fact that many scholars were poor and shabby. His own unusual and undemocratic solution was to prevent indigent youths from attending schools and universities; this course, in his opinion, would rid the term "scholar" of its ungenteel connotations and thereby "Reconcile the Gentleman with the Scholar."[33] Such attempts at reconciliation, however, were rare. We may take as more representative of the opinion of theorists, in the eighteenth century as in the Restoration, Walker's statement that the well-born youth should attain only "a sufficient perfection" in his studies, "not so much as is required for a *Professor,* but so much, as is necessary or requisite for *a* Gentleman."[34] In other words, the man of rank was generally required to be well-informed but not egregiously erudite.

The attitudes of theorists regarding the importance of learning for gentlemen demand closer investigation, however, as there were shades of difference and sometimes marked discrepancies. In Chapter I, mention was made of Restoration commentators who placed learning last among the aims of gentlemanly education; and many authors, we recall from Chapter I, asserted that studies were useless unless they were conducive to virtue. The opinions of these writers are possibly indicative of a decreased emphasis on learning by theorists after the Renaissance. The distrust which some seventeenth-century commentators manifested toward speculative or abstruse learning as vain, profitless, and impractical, and which continued into the eighteenth century, is perhaps significant of the same trend. But a large number of authors did not share the distrust, and in any case it did not disqualify a great deal of learning, being particularly irrelevant to such studies as history, arithmetic, law, and the modern languages. More illuminating are views as to the relative rank of book knowledge and a knowledge of the world among the gentlemanly attributes.

Quite a few critics seemed to think that a knowledge of the world (or, in other words, of human nature) was fully as valuable for the gentleman as book knowledge, if not more so, and that no gentleman could be complete if he neglected the study of man in favor of the arts and sciences. Writers in the Restoration sometimes expressed the belief, already current in the Renaissance,[35] that a gentleman's learning should never be so great as to lead him to forsake the active life for which he was destined or interfere with the performance of his public functions. Thus one Restoration theorist informed a young gentleman that well-born youths should not embrace a life of study after graduating from a university, since "there is a Husk and Shell that grows up with the Learning they acquired, which they must throw away, caused, perchance, by the Childishness of their State, or Formalities of the Place, or the Ruggedness of Retirement, the not considering of which hath made many a great Scholar unserviceable to the World."[36] In his *Humane Prudence* (1680), one of the books of advice on prudential conduct so popular in the seventeenth century, William de Britaine rated worldly knowledge superior to book knowledge.[37] Locke in *Some Thoughts Concerning Education* was firmly persuaded that "to judge right of men, and manage his affairs wisely with them," was of far greater benefit to the gentleman than "to speak Greek and Latin" or even "to be well versed in the Greek and Roman writers." He consequently called the young gentleman's studies "but as it were, the exercises of his faculties, and employment of his time, to keep him from sauntering and idleness, to teach him application, and accustom him to take pains, and to give him some little taste of what his own industry must perfect," whereas "of . . . knowledge of the world . . . he cannot have too much" (pages 74, 76).

A similar tendency to rank a knowledge of the world above book knowledge was manifest in subsequent years. Thus Boyer's *English Theophrastus* contained the following observation: "*Study* makes a greater difference between a *Scholar* and an *Ignorant* Man, than there is between an *Ignorant* Man and a *Brute*. But the *Air* of the World, yet makes a greater distinction between a *Polite* and a *Learned* Person. *Knowledge* begins the *Gentleman;* and the Commerce of the World compleats him" (page 255). Eighteenth-century educational theorists of gentle blood were also inclined to consider an acquaintance with the world more desirable than an acquaintance with books, even though they, unlike their less enlightened compeers, had no particular bias against learning. Typical of their view was Chesterfield's attitude in the education of his son. He stressed book learning more than did many fashionable fathers, especially during young Philip's childhood, but he called a knowledge of the world "still more necessary than that of books." Therefore, although he dwelled heavily on the importance of learning in the early letters, he looked forward to a time when worldly experience would be substituted for it: "I neither require nor expect from you great application to books after you are once thrown out into the great world." When Philip, as a young traveler on the Continent in 1748, did begin to participate in the world, his father strongly recommended such participation, urging him, for example, to enter fully into the splendors and diversions of the court of Berlin and to devote only the mornings to study. As Philip grew older, the world was to usurp more and more of his time, until the period arrived when the perusal of books should yield to it almost *in toto*. Thus Chesterfield told Philip in 1751: "The world is now the only book you want, and almost the only one you ought to read." "Let every other book . . . give way," he said, "to this great and necessary book, the World."[38]

It would be wrong to assume that even those writers who placed a knowledge of the world so high deprecated book learning. They simply feared that the gentleman might become inappropriately erudite for his calling. Furthermore, there was a definite counter trend to the emphasis on worldly experience. In the Restoration, for example, Panton, while not denying that "experience is much to be esteem'd in the affairs of the World," considered it inseparable from learning (or "science," as he termed it) and flatly declared that "Science is to be preferr'd in our search before Experience." He supported his preference by many arguments—that it was easier to gain a given amount of knowledge from books than from worldly experience; that the teachings of books were more general and at the same time more certain than the teachings of experience; that books distinguished clearly between cause and effect, which often appeared confused in the world; that books delved more deeply into things than experience did; that experience was often deceptive and misleading; and that since all the wisdom in books presupposed experience, the latter was necessary only as a means to an end.[39]

By the middle of the eighteenth century the tendency to regard book learning as more valuable than a knowledge of the world was perceptibly stronger than it had been during the Restoration, and was perhaps even the prevailing attitude among theorists. The unknown author of *An Essay on Modern Education* (1747) believed that the world would be "a Means . . . of getting Understanding, more agreeable, and even more profitable by far than Books, provided a Man could, with equal Ease, blend himself into the Society of living Companions, as instructive and learned as those in his Study." But since one's companions rarely answered these qualifications, the "airy" (or empty) gentlemen who rejected their studies for worldly experience were to be condemned (page 7). In the *Mirror* No. 15 (March 16, 1779), J. A. Home stood diametrically opposed to

Locke's view that a knowledge of the world was more necessary than learning, especially a solid training in the classics. "There can be little doubt," he affirmed, "to which the preference belongs"—it belonged to a classical education. Home tried to excuse Locke by saying that "from a prejudice, to which even great minds are liable," Locke mistakenly extended his justifiable dislike for pedantry to all learning.

The recognition that a knowledge of the world sometimes meant little more than a knowledge of the world's vices, a matter to be discussed in Chapter IV, contributed to influence many commentators against it. Perhaps the cumulative effect of years of criticism directed against ignorant gentlemen was also partly responsible for the stress on learning in the mid-eighteenth century. People felt that fashionable society emphasized a knowledge of the world unduly. "We of this generation," Colman and Thorton wrote ironically in the *Connoisseur* No. 24 (July 11, 1754), "are wiser than to suffer our youth of quality to lose their precious time in studying the *belles lettres,* while our only care is to introduce them into the *beau monde."* Pope's dictum, "Men may be read, as well as books, too much," was quoted by them in the *Connoisseur* No. 136 (September 2, 1756). Another writer complained that "an early acquaintance with the World is now deemed of such consequence, that both the intellectual and moral accomplishments lose their weight."[40]

Some commentators thus placed learning high among the requirements for gentlemen, even though nobody considered it more important than virtue. Many arguments were advanced in favor of learning. The first of these, discussed in Chapter I, was that various studies could be of aid in the attainment of virtue. Some authors, besides, praised learning as an ornament of the gentleman, or even likened it to a spiritual ennobling.[41] The obvious point that a training in the arts and sciences developed and brought to fruition the natural capacities of the gentleman's mind was frequently mentioned; without such training these potentialities "may be interr'd in the Bosom of the Part that possesses them, and entirely lost to the World."[42]

The notion that a considerable degree of learning was necessary to the able execution of the gentleman's public functions has been mentioned in the preceding chapter. This conviction gave rise to much criticism and satire of the ignorant gentleman who tried to take a hand in statesmanship. The ill-educated country squire occupying a seat in Parliament was described as one who "shews his *Wisdom* best by his Silence, and serves his Country *most* in his *Absence*."[43] It was Swift's aim in his *Essay on Modern Education* "to prove that some proportion of human knowledge appears requisite to those, who by their birth or fortune are called to the making of laws, and, in a subordinate way, to the execution of them."[44] In *The Modern Fine Gentleman* (1746), Soame Jenyns drew a scathing portrait of the uninformed young gentleman in Parliament:

> There safe in self-sufficient impudence,
> Without experience, honesty, or sense,
> Unknowing in her int'rest, trade, or laws,
> He vainly undertakes his country's cause:
> Forth from his lips, prepar'd at all to rail,
> Torrents of nonsense burst like bottled ale.[45]

Defoe furnished several reasons why the gentleman of little learning who entered Parliament did injury to the nation or, at the very least, was of no help whatever. Too uninformed to think for himself, such a man simply voted as cleverer and perhaps unscrupulous individuals told him. He was the unwitting tool of corrupt courtiers and politicians, and the liberties of Britain were consequently endangered. Since his ignorance often made him incompetent to manage his estate economically, he was sometimes in want of funds and was therefore susceptible to the bribes of factions and crafty politicians who wanted only to enslave their country. Many times the ignorant gentleman sat idle at home, doing nothing in the service of his nation, and this was just as harmful as participation in government, since when gentlemen did not occupy the offices which should naturally devolve upon them, those offices were filled instead by "knaves and polititians" and "mercenaryes." Defoe regarded with longing a former period of English history, when, according to him, the gentry and nobility had intelligence enough to protect their nation against fraud, oppression, and the mismanagement of public affairs.[46]

Learning was also of practical advantage to some gentlemen, especially younger sons, because, as has been mentioned previously, it equipped them for entering the professions and thereby attaining fortunes. The material advantages of learning were sometimes not highly praised by commentators on the gentleman; Brokesby, for example, warned his well-born correspondent at a university not to look upon the achievement of riches as the main end of learning, and Fordyce stipulated that the instruction of youth should be aimed principally at nobler goals than that of amassing a fortune.[47] A number of writers, nevertheless, were very much aware of the material benefits of learning; in fact, as will be demonstrated toward the end of the present chapter, some of them strenuously advocated more specific training for a career or profession than the young gentleman usually received.

Thus in the eyes of courtesy writers and other educational theorists, learning remained an important qualification of the ideal gentleman in the Restoration and eighteenth century, even if it was somewhat less important than it had been during the Renaissance. The opinion of commentators that a gentleman should not possess a scholar's erudition was not new with the period and in no way disqualified a large degree of learning as a gentlemanly attribute. While writers recognized the dangers inherent in excessive erudition, they also enumerated the many advantages of learning. On the whole, a regard for learning probably reached its low point in the Restoration, when some writers ranked it last among the components of the aristocratic ideal or at any rate thought it inferior to a knowledge of the world, and when vain speculation was so actively distrusted. In the eighteenth century, learning seems to have assumed a somewhat more prominent position among the requisites of the complete gentleman. Criticism of the ignorant portion of the gentry and nobility became perhaps more pronounced than ever before, and many commentators reacted against an emphasis on worldly knowledge at the expense of book knowledge. In any case, writers on the gentleman during both ages subscribed to an ideal which gave a higher place to learning than did the ideal held by those many men of quality who were under the influence of the traditional genteel prejudice against intellectual pursuits.

Despite the prejudice, a large number of gentlemen obviously acquired more learning than did the illiterate ones sketched by Defoe and other critics. Few were in the position of Tony Lumpkin, who never got an education at all. The training of well-born youths in the arts and sciences may have been conducted inefficiently at times; their parents may have minimized its importance; and they themselves may perhaps have avoided it as much as possible, regarded it with marked antipathy, profited little by it, forgotten most of it the moment their education was at an end, and determined not to follow intellectual pursuits during the remainder of their lives; but most of them were at least exposed to some course of studies, whether they were educated under tutors, at fashionable private schools, at public schools, at the universities, or abroad. The range of subjects recognized as being valid or proper for young gentlemen therefore affords some intimation of the intellectual training which they received. To conduct an exhaustive examination of this range of subjects in all its particulars is unnecessary. The approved course of study may be summed up in a few words. With some variations in emphasis, it held true no matter whether a youth was brought up under a good tutor or at a public school. The following outline is to be understood, however, as the ideal curriculum, of which the real was only an approximation, sometimes very close and sometimes quite defective. As a reduction from many sources, it necessarily presents a general picture which was by no means always followed in all its details.

At the earliest period of his education, the gentleman's son was taught to read English, using, perhaps, Aesop's *Fables* and select passages from the Scriptures, and to write a good hand.[48] At a slightly later date he was instructed in the rudiments of Latin grammar and assigned as reading matter the easiest Latin prose authors.[49] He acquired a speaking knowledge of French and perhaps also of Italian.[50] An introduction to arithmetic was essential to the beginning student, and his mathematical knowledge was afterwards expanded to include geometry and algebra.[51] He learned geography and chronology as the hand-maids of history.[52] The study of history itself was commenced at an early stage in his training and broadened in later years until he knew history both sacred and profane, ancient and modern, domestic as well as foreign.[53] He advanced in Latin to an acquaintance with the Roman historians, dramatists, orators, and poets.[54] Greek possibly became a part of his cur-riculum also,[55] and rhetoric and oratory assumed a significant place in his education; an oratorical ability was considered very desirable in view of the likelihood that he would become a statesman or a divine.[56] An ability to write English correctly and elegantly and an appreciation for English literature were apparently sometimes neglected in the midst of these other pursuits; but he was not infrequently required to polish his English style, since in his future capacity as public servant he might have to draw up many letters, speeches, and documents,[57] and some theorists urged that his taste be cultivated by a read-ing of the most admired British poets and prose-writers.[58] He was also perhaps made familiar with logic, ethics, and meta-physics.[59] Finally, he might be taught the fundamentals of the natural sciences and obtain an understanding of theology and law as well.[60]

Simultaneously with his training in these traditional branches of learning, he took lessons in the polite accomplishments of drawing, music, and dancing, which will be discussed later in this chapter. Furthermore, he engaged in physical exercises adapted to his physical development at various periods of his childhood and adolescence, such as running, swimming, wrest-ling, and riding.[61] Fencing, as might be expected, held a promi-nent place among these exercises.[62]

It should be borne in mind not only that the education of many gentlemen did not cover nearly all the subjects mentioned above but also that certain fields of study were sometimes just briefly touched on, while others were stressed unduly. If a gentleman was educated under a tutor, for example, he often received a very thorough training in French and perhaps in the other modern languages, whereas if he was brought up in a public school Latin was sure to be emphasized. He might be given little or no instruction in any of the natural sciences except possibly botany and animal husbandry, which would be of use in the management of his estate. On the other hand, his curriculum on occasion included studies which have not so far been mentioned, such as astronomy and Hebrew.[63] Stress on certain subjects also varied somewhat from age to age. The young gentleman of the Restoration would more probably be required to study theology, Greek, logic, and meta-physics than would the well-born youth of the mid-eighteenth century, and the physical exercises of the former almost in-evitably embraced lessons in riding the great horse; the reading of British authors, however, was more often a part of eighteenth-century than of seventeenth-century education of children. The course of studies outlined above does not represent an average, as there was no average. When the young gentleman's educa-tion was carried out with care and thoroughness, however, it usually comprehended the subjects which I have named, and its pattern was at least roughly approximate to that suggested here. The above program, is, then, to be regarded in the light of a common denominator.

Several points about this program need to be examined in more detail. The first of these is the importance of history, which was viewed by the theorists as "the properest study for a Gentleman."[64] A knowledge of history enabled a gentleman to profit by the experience and example of others who had gone before him so that, without personal risk, he could acquire wisdom of action, learning what mistakes to avoid and what course to pursue; he could "enjoy the fruit of other mens labors, be wise at their own costs, and receive benefit from every thing they have done, whether bad or good, avoiding them in one, and imitating them in the other."[65] It was this belief that prompted Chesterfield to tell his son that through his-torical studies "un jeune homme peut, en quelque façon, ac-quérir l'expérience de la vieillesse; en lisant ce qui a été fait, il apprend ce qu'il a à faire."[66]

Among the most valuable lessons taught by history were lessons in virtue. The conviction that history was rich in moral examples and could be of great influence in guiding young gentlemen along the paths of righteousness was inherited from the Renaissance,[67] and it remained very common in both the Restoration and eighteenth century. Burnet thus advised the gentleman's governor to use historical examples in order to teach morality, and Gailhard attested to the value of history in demonstrating moral ideas and illustrating the virtues and vices of mankind.[68] Similarly, in *The Royal Marriage* Dykes counseled educators to teach children virtue "by setting before their Eyes the good and bad *Examples,* of Virtue and Vice, in reading true *Histories,* that they may learn how to follow the *Former,* and forsake the *Latter*" (page 330). According to Burgh, "There is not indeed a lesson in the whole compass of morals, that is not, in the most advantageous and pleasing way, to be learned in history and biography, taking in ancient and modern, sacred and profane."[69] J. A. Home's defense of classical studies in the *Mirror* No. 15 (March 16, 1779) rested partly on the claim that the ancient historians impressed their readers with a love of virtue. Even Chesterfield, who paid comparatively little regard to morality in his letters to his son, told the boy that "the utility of history consists principally in the examples it gives us of the virtue and vices of those who have gone before us" (II, 396-397).

In the Renaissance, history was deemed especially suitable for inculcating morality because it was a demonstration of God's providence, showing how God rewarded the good with glory and the evil with punishment, how he set his mercy and justice at work in the world. Although a providential view of history was mentioned less often in the eighteenth century, it persisted in some force. Joseph Priestley, for instance, declared: "History tends to strengthen the sentiments of virtue by the variety of views in which it exhibits the conduct of Divine providence, showing important events brought about by inconsiderable means, or contrary to the intention of those persons who were the principal agents in them. A regard to Divine providence heightens our satisfaction in reading history, and tends to throw an agreeable light upon the most gloomy and disgusting parts of it."[70]

History was probably considered the most valuable study for enabling a gentleman to serve his nation in a political capacity. The political usefulness of historical knowledge was stressed during the Renaissance.[71] It was perhaps less often emphasized in the eighteenth century than in the earlier period, but it received frequent mention even so, and was sometimes given extraordinary attention. In order to occupy an important public office intelligently, a gentleman had to have a considerable knowledge of political principles and events of the past, and to be able to determine a course of policy on the basis of past policies which had failed or succeeded. From a study of history, Burgh observed in his *Dignity of Human Nature,* a man would "learn every honest art of government" (page 139). An acquaintance with English history was particularly desirable for the well-born Englishman embarking on a political career. Clarke, for example, declared: "As for *History,* I think a Gentleman can scarce be too minutely acquainted with that of his own Country; especially if he has, or aspires to a Seat in Parliament: the frequent Occasion for that Kind of Knowledge in the Business transacted there, makes it absolutely necessary for a Gentleman, that proposes to be of any great Use to his Country, or to cut a reputable Figure in such a Station."[72] But ancient history too had its political value, partly because it impressed a young gentleman with right ideas of government. He must be taught Greek and Roman history, Burnet said, "that the difference between a just and a vicious government may be well apprehended." The decline of the Roman Empire would show him the unfortunate consequences of absolutism. In fact, the main aim of all a young gentleman's historical studies, in Burnet's opinion, should be "to possess a young mind with noble principles of justice, liberty, and virtue, as the true basis of government; and with an aversion to violence and arbitrary power, servile flattery, faction and luxury, from which the corruption and ruin of all governments have arisen."[73]

Among the warmest advocates of history as preparation for a political career were Sheridan, Chesterfield, and Priestley.

Sheridan proposed a school at which the well-born pupils were to be divided into various groups according to the careers or professions for which they were destined, each group to have its own curriculum, dictated by the special requirements of its members. History was a subject proper for all young gentlemen in the school, but it was particularly necessary for those who intended to be, as Sheridan termed them, legislators.[74] Many of Chesterfield's early letters to his son and godson were nothing but lessons in history, for, as he informed the godson, "a perfect knowledge of history is absolutely necessary for a . . . minister of state, which you intend to be." When his son had advanced beyond the stage of simplified lessons in this branch of learning, Chesterfield counseled him to read nothing *but* history and to begin specializing his study of it, with the object of obtaining an exhaustive knowledge of certain significant historical periods and political events, information which would be of enormous help toward becoming an influential figure in public affairs. An understanding of comparatively recent occurrences was of incalculable benefit; even earlier he had urged his son: "Modern history, by which I mean particularly the history of the last three centuries, should be the object of your greatest and constant attention, especially those parts of it which relate more immediately to the great Powers of Europe."[75]

Since "all improvement in the science of government," according to Priestley, was "derived from history," this subject should be the primary study of those gentlemen who "have . . . the greatest interest in the fate of their country, and who are within the influence of an honourable ambition to appear in the character of magistrates and legislators in the state, or of standing near the helm of affairs, and guiding the secret springs of government." Because Priestley included all right-thinking young gentlemen under this definition, his conception of a liberal education amounted to little else than the study of history and related fields, "such as the theory of laws, government, manufactures, commerce, naval force &c. with whatever may be demonstrated from history to have contributed to the flourishing state of nations, to rendering a people happy and populous at home, and formidable abroad."[76] He complained that history was neglected in the curriculum of schools and universities,[77] and, on the extremely broad scale which he envisioned, it no doubt was, although the subject was one in which many gentlemen were given some training even if they acquired little other learning. At the public schools they usually read the Roman and perhaps the Greek historians. At home or on the Continent under tutors, they received extensive instruction in history.

Law, like history, had been regarded as a very advantageous study for the gentleman since the Renaissance.[78] It was advocated for him no matter whether he had any intention of ever entering the legal profession. English law was particularly advisable. Thus all the sons of the gentry and nobility, one writer affirmed just prior to the Restoration, should spend some time at the Inns of Court after graduating from a university and before embarking on the grand tour.[79] "It would be strange," Locke observed in *Some Thoughts Concerning Education,* "to suppose an English gentleman should be ignorant of the law of his country" (page 152). Burnet was of a similar mind, affirming that without a knowledge of the laws of England a man was "but a poor nobleman or countrey man."[80]

If a gentleman lived principally on his estate, occupying no office except, perhaps, that of justice of the peace, his comprehension of English law could be of enormous benefit to his neighbors and tenants and thus could help him fulfill his duty of service in a private capacity.[81] After advising the well-born young addressee of his *Letter of Advice* to "do all the Good you can to others," Brokesby explained the helpfulness of law in this regard: "Being learned in the *Law,* will enable you to advise your Neighbours and Tenants in their concerns, and hereby to prevent many inconveniencies and streights, into which, through ignorance they frequently plunge themselves; and, to preserve peace among them, by determining their differences without Law-suits, to their own and others quiet" (page 10). This latter function, that of settling disagreements before they took the form of lawsuits, was no inconsiderable service, as a moment's reflection upon the legal snarls and tangles of Restoration and eighteenth-century England will make clear. Other

writers also were aware of its value; Clarke, for example, declared that a knowledge of law was "very useful and necessary
for a Gentleman . . . especially in preventing of Law-Suits, by
Arbitration of Differences amongst Neighbours; which is none
of the least important Branches of a Gentleman's Business as
such."[82] If a gentleman held a high political office, an acquaintance with law, like an acquaintance with history, was
indispensable to his performing the duties of that office capably.
For this reason Chesterfield had his son instructed in civil law
at Leipzig by a Professor Mascow, a celebrated authority on the
subject, at whose home young Philip lodged.[83] An extensive
acquaintance with law was certainly requisite for those individuals who, presumably, would some day be members of the
nation's law-making body; without legal knowledge, they could
not even be expected to vote intelligently, much less express
intelligent opinions on issues under debate. Brokesby told his
correspondent, who must "endeavour to be fitted to serve your
King and Country in Parliament," that to this end "the Laws
and Constitutions of this Kingdom . . . call for your perusal"
(page 14). Burnet also believed that "a competent skill" in
English law would make a gentleman "very useful to his country
. . . and, which ought to be the top of an English gentleman's
ambition, to be an able parliament man." Calling Parliament
"the fountain of law, and the fence of liberty," Burnet affirmed
that "no sort of instruction is so necessary for a gentleman, as
that which may qualify him to appear there with figure and
reputation."[84] Hurd, who termed the well-born youth "our
young Senator" in the assumption that he would be elected to
the House of Commons or be entitled by blood to a seat in the
House of Lords, required that he have a thorough comprehension of the constitution of his country in order to fill his
post adequately.[85]

As the object of Priestley's educational scheme was to prepare the gentleman for his destined life of action and service,
he considered the study of law an essential part of his education, devoting a large section of his *Essay on a Course of Liberal
Education* to a syllabus of lectures on the laws of England,
just as he had already done with history. The introductory

lecture contained perhaps the definitive statement on the necessity of legal knowledge for the gentleman as statesman. If such knowledge was important even for the average person, Priestley said, it was

> of much more importance . . . to those persons whose fortune, and whose station in life give them any degree of influence over their fellow subjects, and who may laudably indulge the ambition . . . of appearing in the character of magistrates, or legislators in the state; to have a voice in its councils, and to be concerned in enacting and repealing its laws, and in regulating its whole internal policy. It requires no words to show, how absolutely unqualified is the man of mere wealth and rank in life to fill these important stations, without a knowledge of those laws, and that constitution of his country of which he is appointed the guardian. It is evidently as preposterous, as for a Physician to undertake to prescribe medicines without knowing the structure of the human body, and the manner in which medicines operate upon it. (Pages 88-89.)

Whereas everyone was convinced of the desirability of history and law for gentlemen, there was little agreement with regard to classical studies. The young gentleman customarily received instruction in the Latin language and Latin literature if he was given a public education and usually if he was brought up privately, and Greek was perhaps also included in his curriculum. Even in the Renaissance, however, there were theorists who questioned the stress on Latin in education.[86] During the eighteenth century the reaction against the place of the learned languages in the curriculum attained greater proportions, partly, perhaps, because of the Ancients-Moderns controversy, which was tangential to it if nothing more. This reaction, of course, did not pertain solely to gentlemanly education, but it was particularly important in that connection. By the latter part of the eighteenth century, it had become so pronounced that champions of the traditional system of training, such as James Beattie (a professor at the University of Aberdeen), J. A. Home, and the schoolmaster Vicesimus Knox, felt obliged to defend classical studies against calumniators. The notion that "the study of the Classic Authors was a necessary part of polite education" was one which, as Beattie flatly declared, "has of late been not only questioned, but denied."[87]

Writers who minimized the importance of the ancient languages for gentlemen did not advocate the total exclusion of these languages from the curriculum, but they believed that too much time was spent on them and maintained that an understanding of them was not essential to a gentleman, though it was to a scholar. Thus Burnet thought that if a noble youth showed an antipathy toward Latin and was incapable of learning it, his education was "not for that to be despaired of," as many fields of learning could be mastered with only a knowledge of English and French and could "make a gentleman very knowing, though he has not a word of Latin."[88] The distinction between the learning necessary for the gentleman and that necessary for the scholar also influenced Locke's views regarding classical studies. While Locke called Latin "absolutely necessary to a gentleman," he did not believe it indispensable to younger sons destined for mercantile careers, nor did he think that speaking and writing Latin were nearly so important to the gentleman as speaking and writing English with elegance. Furthermore, he said that the gentleman, in contrast to the scholar, did not need to know Greek.[89] Hurd endorsed Locke's position as to Greek, and Sheridan advised this language only for those well-born youths who planned to enter the medical or clerical professions.[90]

Typical of the opposition to a traditional classical education was the attitude of Defoe, who, despite his vehement condemnation of the genteel order for a lack of learning, deprecated the great emphasis customarily accorded the ancient languages. "Is it worth any gentleman's while," he said, "to go seaven year to the Grammar Bridewell (the school) and there beat Greek and Latin, as whores beat hemp?"[91] Defoe did not believe that the ancient languages should be thrown entirely out of gentlemanly education, but, on the other hand, he did not regard them as essential to the cultivated man of quality and denied the common assumption that no individual could possess learning without knowing the learned languages. If a gentleman's studies had been neglected during his youth and he had been taught to read nothing but English, he could still, by following various intellectual pursuits, "be *a gentleman of learning.*"[92] Defoe described two men of rank who were well versed in such fields as mathematics, geography, astronomy, philosophy, and history, and who, in his opinion, merited the term "gentlemen of learning" notwithstanding their ignorance of Latin and Greek. Since the works of the ancients were obtainable in translations, he added, an inability to read them in the original was of little moment.[93]

According to many theorists, a young gentleman's course of studies should be useful to the extent of preparing him for the life he would lead as an adult. This persuasion, as has already been indicated, underlay the recommendations of history and law for gentlemen. Whereas the benefits of Latin were seldom entirely negated, a number of commentators, aware of the usefulness of other branches of learning, were opposed to the heavy concentration on Latin at the public schools to the neglect of these other subjects. Even Clarke, an author of Latin textbooks,[94] reprimanded the schools for insisting too strongly on Latin at the expense of such valuable studies as "History and Geography, both Ancient and Modern, with Chronology, and the most necessary and useful Things in Divinity, &c."[95] Although Burgh admitted in his *Dignity of Human Nature* that some acquaintance with Latin was desirable for the gentleman, he demanded "whether the most perfect knowledge of two dead languages is, to any person whatever . . . worth the expence of ten years study, to the exclusion of all other improvements?" Inclined to ally himself with the defenders of the Moderns as against the Ancients, he even asked "whether any knowledge of the learned languages, besides being qualified to understand the sense, and relish the beauties, of an ancient author, be of any use?" (pages 124-125). Sheridan deprecated the emphasis on Latin and Greek in the public schools because, while these languages had been indispensable in the Renaissance, they had lost their relevance to the affairs of an active life. The students, he said, were "employed wholly in studies which will produce little future benefit to them or advantage to the world; whilst such as would contribute most to public and private prosperity, that is to say, Religion, Morality, and the English language, are utterly neglected."[96] In 1758 an unknown author published an attack on Sheridan's lectures on the education of the young British gentry and nobility, the precursor of his *Plan of Education*. This author, however, raised no objection to Sheridan's relegation of Latin to a comparatively inferior position in the curriculum. In fact, he proposed that until boys were eleven or twelve they should "be taught the English language altogether, without any mixture of Latin." Those destined for a university could then be given an adequate grasp of the language; those destined for professions not requiring a university education might be "instructed . . . in some particular cases, in the easiest Latin prose Writers" and in other cases receive no training in Latin at all but be satisfied with "reading English translations of the most valuable of the Antients, such as might render their Literature and Manners familiar to them, without the drudgery of learning Languages to them useless."[97] Sheridan's anonymous opponent thus carried the reaction against classical studies to a further extreme than did most other educational theorists.

The reaction was probably applauded by a number of gentlemen, who associated the learned languages with pedantry and scholarly pursuits. In the *World* No. 137 (August 14, 1755), an unknown writer complained that whereas gentlemen in former ages could at least translate a Latin couplet, " 'nowadays the case is altered; it is pedantry to know any other language . . . but the fashionable modern ones.' " This author, however, was grossly exaggerating, since despite all the criticisms of the emphasis on Latin and Greek, a classical training remained in common practice even in private education and was, of course, characteristic of the public schools. Those who attacked it were iconoclasts. Many theorists, furthermore, still warmly advocated Latin for gentlemen.

The usual method of teaching Latin was to subject the student to detailed and painstaking lessons in grammar, including comprehensive analyses of syntax and the memorization and recitation of numerous rules. The conversational as opposed to the grammatical method, however, had been favorably regarded even by some Renai-sance theorists,[98] and it was not infrequently put into use as a preliminary or supplement to the other system. It was especially well liked by tutors, who, having perhaps just one boy under their care and at the most only three or four, could talk at length in Latin with their pupils. The great schools, where such lengthy colloquies were less feasible because of the large number of students under each master, had to employ the grammatical method almost exclusively. Some educational theorists were undecided as to which system of teaching Latin was better; Penton, for example, said in *The Guardian's Instruction* (1688) that "whether it be sooner learn'd by the *Rules* of Grammar as is done in Schools, or barely by Construing *Authours* and talking Latin with the Child always, by which sometimes Gentlemen are taught, I am not able to answer mine own Arguments for each" (page 67). Other writers, however, violently opposed the schools' emphasis on grammar. During the period under consideration, Locke raised the loudest outcry against the grammatical method, setting forth views on the subject which, directly or indirectly, were to influence later theorists.

Locke preferred the conversational to the grammatical method because the latter, he felt, was an unnatural way in which to learn a language; if an English child learned English and sometimes other modern languages through conversation, Latin could best be acquired in the same manner. Because the public schools relied on the grammatical technique, they were, for that reason among others, not fit for the education of well-born youths; a child should be taught Latin at home through conversations with his tutor. Furthermore, Locke said, the complexities of grammar were beyond the comprehension of children; if lessons in grammar were given at all, they should at least be delayed until a boy had advanced to a familiarity with Latin. Most significant from the standpoint of gentlemanly education was Locke's opinion that a knowledge of Latin or Greek grammar was neither needful nor advisable for gentlemen but only for scholars, the "sort of men who apply themselves to two or three foreign dead (and which amongst us are called the learned) languages." In order that they might "be critically exact" in an ancient tongue, scholars "ought carefully to study the grammar of it"; for men of quality, a reading knowledge was sufficient. Training in correct and polished English, on the other hand, was essential for children of quality, since it had great relevance to the business of their future lives.[99]

Later theorists, even if they may not in all cases have been influenced directly by Locke, disapproved of the grammatical method because they shared his wish to distinguish between a gentleman's learning and a scholar's learning and, like him, insisted on the usefulness of a gentleman's studies. Burnet, for example, called "it a great error, to waste young gentlemen's years so long in learning Latin, by so tedious a grammar," since a reading knowledge alone was requisite for them; no one but "those who are bred to the professions in literature must have the Latin correctly; and for that, the rules of grammar are necessary."[100] Burgh, similarly regarding the emphasis on grammar as a fault of the schools, demanded "whether the superfluous time, bestowed in learning grammar rules, would not be much better employed in writing, arithmetic, elements of mathematics, or other improvements of indispensable use in life?"[101]

There were theorists who opposed the grammatical method not because they viewed a comprehension of Latin grammar as inappropriate to gentlemen but because they believed that Latin could be more thoroughly mastered through conversation. The unknown author of *An Essay upon Education* (London, 1711) went so far as to suggest a boarding school at which children who were just learning to talk would be addressed solely in Latin so that they would forget any English they might have acquired beforehand; they would learn English in time anyway, and giving them an extraordinary facility in Latin was the greater object (see pages 4-5). This author's conception of the importance of Latin was, however, excessive for his age.

At the public schools and sometimes in private education, the grammatical method of teaching Latin was combined with the obligatory composition of Latin themes and verses on prescribed subjects. Milton had attacked this pedagogical technique in *Of Education,* and it was very harshly criticized by Locke. Requiring a well-born student to write Latin themes on such topics as *"Omnia vincit amor"* and *"Non licet in bello bis peccare"* was, according to Locke, a waste of time, seldom fulfilling its purpose of giving him an elegant style. Having little knowledge or experience on which to rely for these themes, a boy had to "set his invention on the rack, to say something where he knows nothing, which is a sort of Egyptian tyranny, to bid them make bricks who have not yet any of the materials." At a loss for what to say, a boy would "go to those of higher forms with this petition, 'Pray give me a little sense.'" Furthermore, writing themes in Latin, "a language . . . long since dead everywhere" and "far different from ours," would "very little improve the purity and facility of his English style," which was of more practical importance since in public life he might have to write speeches, letters, and documents. Much attention should therefore be paid to endowing him with elegance of expression in English. Composing Latin verses was, in Locke's opinion, perhaps even less necessary than composing Latin themes and could be actually dangerous if it induced a gentleman to follow the useless, unlucrative, and unfashionable profession of a poet.[102]

Commentators who assailed the composition of Latin themes and verses held Locke's view that these exercises were not characterized by the usefulness which should determine a gentleman's studies, whereas English composition could be extremely useful. In the *Spectator* No. 230 (November 23, 1711), Steele, under the guise of a person who wished to found an academy for genteel youths, suggested that " 'it would be requisite to exercise their style in writing any light pieces that ask more of fancy than of judgment; and that frequently in their native language, which every one methinks should be most concerned to cultivate, especially letters, in which a gentleman must have so frequent occasions to distinguish himself.' " Contriving Latin verses was looked on as particularly useless. "Tho' it be a pleasant and entertaining Amusement," said the unknown author of *An Essay upon Education,* "yet it contributes very little towards making us Useful in our Generation" (page 21). Clarke regarded it as dangerous and observed that even when it had no ill effects, "the best you can make of it is but a Diversion, a degree above Fidling."[103] Burgh also raised the question "whether the time spent in making *Latin* themes and verses is not wholly thrown away?"[104]

An indebtedness to Locke is especially noticeable in Clarke's *Education of Youth in Grammar-Schools* and Sheridan's *Plan of Education.* Clarke said of the enforced composition of Latin themes and verses: "It is not only an Egyptian Tyranny, as Mr. *Locke* properly calls it, but devours their [i.e., the students'] time to no purpose," time which could be spent much more advantageously "in the Reading of Authors, or other Exercises more suitable to their Years and Improvement" (page 60). Latin theme-writing, according to Sheridan's paraphrase of Locke, "cannot be better exposed, than by a representation of the behaviour of the poor boys upon this occasion (set like the Israelites to make bricks without straw)," who in their desperation appealed to the more advanced students "in this ridiculous phrase, '*Pray give me a little sense.*'" Poetical exercises, Sheridan exclaimed, were an "extravagant attempt to force all to be poets in spite of nature . . . and that in a dead language too." Such requirements were "so opposite to common sense, that it is a wonder how they could ever have obtained footing in a civilized country" (pages 44-45).

Objections to the making of Latin verses had become so prominent in the later eighteenth century that arguments against this device were repeated for purposes of refutation by its defenders. "Poetry may have its use," Beattie said in imitation of traducers of the practice; "but it will neither fill our warehouses, nor fertilise our soil, neither rig our fleet, nor regulate our finances. . . . No, no, Sir," he added, probably satirizing the genteel parents whose opinions of verses he strongly disapproved of; "a garret in Grubstreet, however honourable in your eyes, is not the station to which I intend to breed my son."[105] But Beattie did not need to be so worried; notwithstanding the virulence of the critics, changes in the traditional system were slow in coming about. Chesterfield's son was writing Latin poetry for his tutor at the age of eight.[106] In 1779 Vicesimus Knox, another champion of the long-established method of instruction, remarked in *Essays Moral and Literary* No. 141, with regard to the composition of Latin verses: "No part of classical education has been more generally censured and more firmly adhered to." Its opponents constituted a group of iconoclasts whose views were seldom put into execution, and then only in private education.

The polite accomplishments, or skills in music, drawing and painting, architecture, and dancing, were not properly studies but had been included in the gentleman's curriculum ever since the Renaissance.[107] Although some proficiency in them was often recommended by Restoration and eighteenth-century writers on the gentleman's education,[108] these writers, like those in the Renaissance, frequently accompanied their recommendations with reservations. An ability in musical performance, for example, might lead a gentleman to associate with vulgar and undesirable company, professional performers.[109] More important, if the well-born youth devoted too much attention to the polite accomplishments, which were of a frivolous and frothy nature, his weightier and more useful studies were likely to suffer.

Occasionally one of the polite arts could serve a useful purpose; thus a skill in drawing was of practical advantage if a gentleman wished to sketch buildings or machines seen on the Continental tour or if, as a military officer, he had to draw fortifications or plans of battles and sieges. But the accomplishments were in the main diversions on which a great deal of time should not be spent. Locke, while recognizing the usefulness of drawing or painting, stipulated: "I do not mean that I would have your son a perfect painter; to be that to any tolerable degree, will require more time than a young gentleman can spare from his other improvements of greater importance" (page 124). An early eighteenth-century author, after admitting the ornamental value of music and dancing to gentlemen, added the qualification that "those Embellishments are more *noble* and *rich* that lie in the Brain, than those that sink

into the Feet, or *perch* on the Finger's End."[110] Burgh similarly
counseled against any undue stress on dancing, music, drawing,
and other elegant acquirements, since it might result in an
ignorance of what he called "solid and useful knowledge.."[111]
Remarks such as these testify to the significance still attached
to learning by commentators on the gentleman in the eighteenth century, as well as to the conviction that the gentleman's
education should be primarily a useful one.

It was apprehended that if the well-born youth became too
much engrossed in the polite accomplishments, he would in-
dulge in them too frequently as an adult and thereby be dis-
tracted from his important duties and occupations, such as
serving his nation in a political capacity. "Many, especially men
of fortune," Burgh complained in his *Dignity of Human Nature,*
"do pursue the study of those elegances to lengths inconsistent
with . . . the awful and serious business" to which their lives
should be given over. Anyone who followed "what is merely
ornamental, to the neglect of the useful business of life," he
declared, ". . . does not understand, nor act up to, the true
dignity of his nature" (pages 150-151).

Gentlemen sometimes shared Burgh's fear that members of
their own class, enamored of the fashionable diversions, would
turn into idlers and useless dilettantes. Thus the Chevalier
Ramsay, after praising music, painting, and dancing, warned
against becoming too much interested in them. "Nothing," he
said, "is more dangerous, and nothing incapacitates a Man more
for Business. If these accessory Accomplishments be made the
End of Study, young Gentlemen become Men-triflers, lose their
Taste . . . for the great Duties of life."[112] Although the Earl
of Mar recommended music to his son as a pursuit "than w^ch
there cannot be a more agreeable, innocent amusement," he
cautioned him against indulging in it to excess, as such recreations "ought never to make us neglect our affairs or what we
may be more usefully emploied about, for the service of our
ffamily, generation or country, in respect of wch amusements or
what the Italians call virtu are but trifles." Mar reproached
himself for wasting too many hours in the diversion of architecture[113]—a reproach which seems undeservedly severe when

we recall that he found time to be Secretary for Scotland under Queen Anne, to lead the Scottish rebels in 1715, and later to serve the Old Pretender on the Continent. Chesterfield thought that a gentleman should be acquainted with painting and sculpture, yet only "to a certain degree," for "they must only be the amusements, and not the business of a man of parts." And a person of quality, he held, should not acquire an ability to play a musical instrument. Since his son was traveling through Italy, "a musical country," the Earl feared that Philip would come under the pernicious influence of this art. It was permissible for the youth to attend operas and concerts or to pay musicians to play for him, but, his father declared, "I insist upon your neither piping nor fiddling yourself." The indulgence of a skill in musical performance "takes up a great deal of time, which might be much better employed."[114]

As one of the polite accomplishments, dancing was usually the subject of cautions, but it occupied a unique position because it filled a special need for the gentleman. Desirable as a knowledge of the current dances obviously was for the man of rank and fashion, the impartation of this knowledge was only one aim of his dancing lessons. An equally important aim was to give him an habitual grace of carriage and gesture even when he was not dancing—"a comely posture of his body in his salutations of others," and in general "a good and gracefull motion of the body."[115] Largely because it performed this function, dancing was often considered more valuable than the other polite accomplishments, since the gentleman, as will be shown in Chapter V, had to possess a graceful manner as part of his good breeding.

Indeed, lessons in dancing were frequently accompanied by training in genteel posture and elegant carriage, which perhaps did more than the actual dance steps toward making the young gentleman graceful. Such training was highly regarded by many commentators, among them Gailhard, who observed in his *Compleat Gentleman*: "It is not enough to be able to Dance *a Branle, a Gavote, a Courante, a Boree,* &c. I will have a Master to teach a Gentleman how to keep his body in a good posture, when he stands, sitteth, or walketh; how to come in or go out of a

Chamber where is company; he must be taught how to carry his head, his hands, and his toes out, all in the best way, and with the handsomest presence: In a word, how to do things with a *Bonne grace,* and in the finest and most gentile manner that the person is capable of" (Second Treatise, pages 48-49). At Paris Chesterfield's son was put under the celebrated Marcel, who was not only to perfect him in the minuet but to give him instructions of the kind mentioned by Gailhard. In his letters, Chesterfield urged his son to make sure that he received such instructions: "Desire him to teach you every genteel attitude, that the human body can be put into; let him make you go in and out of his room frequently, and present yourself to him, as if he were by turns different persons; such as a minister, a lady, a superior, an equal, an inferior, etc. Learn to sit genteely in different companies; to loll genteely, and with good manners, in those companies where you are authorised to be free; and to sit up respectfully where the same freedom is not allowable" (IV, 1721).

When the dancing master provided such lessons as these, it is little wonder that even writers who considered dancing a very superficial acquirement, deserving no high place in the education of the gentleman, conceded that it had its use in bestowing upon him "a graceful Appearance in Company, that he may preserve as long as he lives."[116] Thus although Burgh was violently opposed to any emphasis on the accomplishment, he granted, perhaps somewhat grudgingly: "It is evidently an advantage, that a young gentleman be, from his infancy almost, put into the way of wielding his limbs decently, and coming into a room like a human creature."[117]

In addition to the polite accomplishments, there were other recreations which commentators considered suitable for gentlemen. These were sometimes recommended with great enthusiasm. They ranged from the manual arts and crafts to avocations of a scientific nature. Hale in his *Letter of Advice* advocated gardening and botanical study, mathematical observations, surveying, and "smithery, watch-making, carpentry, joinery works of all sorts" (page 128). In Penn's opinion, "a Garden, an Elaboratory, a Workhouse . . . and Breeding,"[118] or animal husbandry, were fit employments for leisure hours. Like the polite accomplishments, these recreations were not to be pursued to excess. They had an advantage over the polite accomplishments, however, because they generally served some useful purpose. Horticulture and animal husbandry were of obvious use in the management of estates, and even such avocations as watch-making and carpentry were of more practical value than playing a violin or dancing a minuet and were certainly to be preferred over the fashionable diversions of hunting and gaming, which were usually frowned upon.

Locke strongly advised such arts as "perfuming, varnishing, graving, and several sorts of working in iron, brass, and silver." For the country gentleman, "gardening and working in wood, as a carpenter, joiner, or turner" were particularly appropriate. On the other hand, the gentleman who spent most of his life in town "may learn to cut, polish, and set precious stones, or employ himself in grinding and polishing optical glasses." Perhaps rightly assuming that many of his genteel readers would regard these pursuits as beneath the notice of a man of quality, Locke, like other theorists, defended them on the grounds of their utility. They would not only "relax and refresh," he declared, but also "may produce what will afterwards be profitable."[119] Johnson, in the *Rambler* No. 85 (January 8, 1751), approved of Locke's suggestions; and Sheridan, though he considered diversions too distracting for young gentlemen who planned to enter a career, sanctioned Locke's list of avocations for the leisured country gentleman and town gentleman, affirming that instruction in them should be given to all students at his proposed school not destined for professions. He thought that, in addition to the pursuits mentioned by Locke, a prospective country gentleman "may also learn to make nets, and fishing tackle; he should be shewn the whole management of a gun, and all it's mechanism, so as to be able to keep it in order. The same as to clocks and watches." A boy intending to lead the life of a town gentleman might benefit by being taught "varnishing, graving, turning in wood or ivory."[120] Bentham wandered even farther afield, recommending weaving and masonry and stating that the young gentleman could turn his leisure time to advantage "by examining the many engines and mills for shortening of manual labour;—the process of various manufactures."[121] Almost any recreation, in fact, was acceptable to the theorists as long as it could be of some use or profit to the gentleman. The purely decorative or inutile was what they sought to avoid.

The emphasis on usefulness which underlay enthusiastic recommendations of history and law, attacks on a classical education and on methods of teaching Latin, cautions against the polite accomplishments, and advocacy of more practical diversions, also gave rise to a demand on the part of some theorists that the gentleman's studies should include specialized training for a profession or career.

Professions approved for gentlemen included law, medicine, divinity, the Army and the Navy. Trade was not yet entirely acceptable to the man of birth, although a number of theorists claimed that he could be brought up as a merchant with no loss of dignity.[122] Parliament, the offices of government, and the diplomatic service, unlike the professions, were often entered by gentlemen not obligated to earn a living. Suggestions that the gentleman choose his studies with a particular profession or career in view occurred occasionally in the Restoration and eighteenth century. Gailhard, for example, said that youths planning to be clergymen, physicians, lawyers, or military men should study what was appropriate to their callings and needed to know comparatively little of what appertained to other callings.[123] Burgh listed studies necessary for those who were to become lawyers, physicians, and divines, and Waterland prescribed the complete curriculum to be followed at a university by a young gentleman destined for the church.[124] The curriculum which Chesterfield laid down for his son, with its stress on history, oratory, government, politics, and the modern languages, was designed to prepare him for his intended career as a statesman and diplomat.

Despite scattered instances of an interest in specialized training, however, most theorists concerned with the gentleman did not deal with it at all, either being unaware of its significance or else tacitly assuming that all gentlemen, if they were to be instructed according to any ideal system, should be instructed alike. They realized the practical advantage of learning in equipping a gentleman for a future profession or career, but this realization seldom suggested the notion that youths destined for different occupations should be educated in different ways. The following remarks by the author of the pamphlet *Of Education* may be taken as typical of a very common attitude: "It is not the Business of Education to fit a Man for such a particular Employment or Character, but to render him capable of entering into any one, which his own Choice, or that of his Friends, or Opportunity, shall present to him. This makes it necessary for him to enter into parts of Learning, which perhaps will be but of little use to him in his future way of Life; but which, had he gone into some other Path, would have been absolutely necessary" (page 17).

Furthermore, the actual process of education, especially at the public schools, was not such as would prepare a young gentleman in any adequate fashion for a future employment. Thus the studies recommended by Burgh as proper for particular professions were not to be commenced until a gentleman had already reached maturity and his formal training was finished. At the public schools all the boys were submitted to one curriculum; it is significant in this regard that, except for a few years at Westminster, Chesterfield preferred to have his son brought up under tutors. At the universities, the ideal of professional training in our modern sense scarcely existed. During the Commonwealth the Puritans had tried to introduce into the universities vocational and utilitarian studies, especially applied science, but their attempts were futile and were popularly viewed as outrageous.[125] The universities were generally regarded as places for broad humanistic education, not as places where lawyers, physicians, etc., could be trained as in a modern college. Some provisions had been made for the specialized education of gentlemen, but these existed outside the universities. Lawyers trained at the Inns of Court; physicians sometimes attended the Royal College of Surgeons, although many went to Continental universities, notably Leyden. The

Royal Military Academy at Woolwich was established in 1741, but large numbers of military men still simply bought commissions.

Whereas most theorists did not deplore the lack of specialized education, there were a few who did. If a gentleman's training was to be primarily useful, they implied, it could certainly be made a great deal more useful with regard to future employment. Gentlemen engaged in the professions, Priestley affirmed in his *Course of Liberal Education,* would agree that most of the knowledge necessary for them was not acquired "till they had finished their studies at the University." In fact, said Priestley, "many gentlemen, who have had the most liberal education their country could afford, have looked upon the real advantage of such liberal education as very problematical" (pages 5-6). It was perhaps Sheridan's *Plan of Education,* however, that contained the loudest complaints about the absence of vocational instruction:

> In the present course [of education] there is not a single step taken towards qualifying a man to discharge the important office of a legislator. A divine, is one who has taken a batchelor's degree in arts. A lawyer, is one who has eaten commons at the Temple during a stated number of terms. A physician, is one, who being of a certain standing at either of the English universities, obtains a degree upon the observation of certain forms, and paying his fees. And an officer, is one who purchases a commission in the army, or obtains it by interest.
>
> The person who is to make laws for the good and preservation of the state, is never made acquainted with the constitution of the state. The divine, except his catechism at school, is never taught one tittle of his profession; nor is he ever instructed in the only art which can qualify him to discharge his function properly, or even with decency; I mean the art of speaking. The lawyer has no one to point out the way to him, thro' a most perplexed labyrinth. And the physician and soldier must seek for knowledge in their several professions, in other countries.
>
> Instead of preparing each for that sphere of life in which they are afterwards to move, they are all trained in one

and the same course, which fits them for no one employment upon earth. (Pages 15-16.)

Such criticisms, like criticisms of an excessive stress on Latin
and of the prevailing techniques in teaching Latin, constituted
not only a reaction against the traditional method of educating
gentlemen but also a plea for reform. Indeed, they were often
accompanied by constructive suggestions for reform. The unknown author of *Proposals For the Reformation of Schools &
Universities* (1704), after complaining that no adequate training
in medicine and law was offered by English educational institutions and that young gentlemen therefore had to prepare for
these professions on the Continent, asked Parliament to set
aside a certain amount of money in order to establish medical
and legal instruction in England on an equal footing with that
on the Continent (see pages 9-10). A much more elaborate
suggestion was put forth by Lewis Maidwell, who in 1705
affirmed that public schools should be founded in England
for the express purpose of teaching navigation to gentlemen's
sons interested in a naval career. On the floor of the House of
Commons, Maidwell offered up his own house in Westminster
as a site for such a school. The curriculum was to be of a
very specialized kind, including mechanics, castramentation,
perspective, trigonometry, the principles of calendars, and
military, civil, and naval architecture.[126] Priestley also "would
humbly propose some new articles of academical instruction,
such as have a nearer and more evident connection with the
business of active life" than those which usually occupied a
young gentleman's time at school. His plan, however, was
broader and less specialized than some. The "new articles"
consisted mainly of the extremely extensive training in law,
history, and related subjects previously referred to, subjects
which were, Priestley thought, "calculated to form the statesman, the military commander, the lawyer, the merchant, and
the accomplished country gentleman." Although Priestley thus
made no distinction between the studies necessary for one
career and those necessary for another, his proposal was still
a recognition of the need for vocational education, and he was

also aware that it was irrelevant to those youths wishing to enter the "learned professions," or medicine and divinity, who would have to receive a different kind of instruction.[127]

Far more extreme was the scheme devised by Sheridan. Only the boys in the lower school at his proposed institution were to be instructed alike; as soon as they reached the upper school, they would be placed in divisions according to their intended careers or professions, and each division would study subjects necessary to the intended vocation of its members. Religion, history, civil law, English literature, and oratory were the only studies proper for all the sections of the upper school, and boys planning to enter a Parliamentary career were to be given especially thorough training in them. Students choosing divinity as their profession should, in addition, read various religious works and should know some Greek, which would be a waste of time for pupils in the other divisions. Anatomy and botany were essential to the fledging physicians. The special studies of prospective lawyers included books on law as well as "some of the practical part belonging to the attorney's business, as the forms of drawing bills, pleadings, &c." Those looking forward to a military career needed little classical learning but should read biographies of eminent military figures and should be taught such fundamentals of their trade as gunnery, fortification, navigation, and perspective. For well-born youths who would become merchants, calligraphy, merchants' accounts, and mathematics were very important, and books on commerce should also have a prominent place in their curriculum. The useful recreations have been mentioned previously as appropriate to boys whose independent fortunes would enable them to pass leisurely lives as country gentlemen or town gentlemen, engaging in no lucrative occupation; town gentlemen should also know the keeping of accounts and the principles of the polite arts.[128] Such a system of education would ensure the adequate preparation of every student for his future life.

The anonymous author of *An Enquiry into the Plan and Pertensions of Mr. Sheridan* was particularly critical of Sheridan's ideas on specialized education. Boys were too immature, he affirmed, to know what course of life they would like to enter, and assigning them studies essential to their intended callings was therefore ridiculous. "When a Man," he said, "talks to us of parcelling out Boys, in a Grammar School, into Classes of Legislators, and Classes of Military Men, and Classes of Private Gentlemen in Town, and Classes of Private Gentlemen in the Country, &c. &c. &c. &c. I believe he hardly expects, that we should sit down with him to grave argument." The prospective divine might turn out to be a military commander, and the prospective general might end up as a lawyer. The unknown author derisively called Sheridan "our Classer of Geniuses" and furnished him with an assistant who could discover the peculiar genius of any individual by means of a "cephaloscope" which interpreted the lines on the membranes of people's heads (pages 33-35).

Notwithstanding his objections against commencing specialized training too early and giving it too much emphasis, however, Sheridan's antagonist agreed with him as to fundamental principles. He asked: "Is there not an impropriety in compelling the Boys of a School, who surely cannot be designed all for one Profession, and many of whom may be destined to Professions altogether opposite the one to the other, to ply all in one tract?" "Another method," he asserted, "is much wanted." Consequently, he had his own proposal to make. It was less revolutionary than that of Sheridan and did not include the division of a school into six classes with a particular curriculum for each, but it was a step in the direction of specialized instruction. He wished to give all boys an identical training untl they were twelve years old, at which time they would be separated into two groups, according to whether they planned to go on to a university or to adopt careers for which a university education was not necessary. Each of these groups was to have its own curriculum, and many studies desirable for one would be given scant attention, if any, in the other (see pages 36-38). This plan was a compromise between the very generalized training characteristic of British schools and the very specialized training advocated by Sheridan.

The length of the present chapter and the large number of

ideas discussed in it render a short summary advisable.

During the Restoration and eighteenth century the gentleman underwent severe censure for his ignorance. Country squires were characterized as boors and boobies. Fine gentlemen of the town were said to be fit only for frivolous conversation and to read nothing except books of very superficial nature. Well-born students at the universities were accused of a determination to idle away their college years and learn as little as possible. The apparent ignorance of much of the genteel class is traceable in part to the traditional aristocratic antipathy toward learning. This had existed since the Middle Ages; whether it became more pronounced in the period under consideration is a debatable matter. Throughout this period, however, it was accompanied by a fear on the part of gentlemen that even a minimal amount of learning would lead to pedantry or to awkwardness in social intercourse. The fear was often exaggerated and unwarranted, but the safer course, chosen by many gentlemen, was not to be learned. Still another cause of ignorance among people of quality was the attitude of some parents that learning had merely a practical value and was therefore desirable only for younger sons, who had to gain their own livelihood.

Educational theorists wished the gentleman to be more learned than he was, but they did not want him to be a scholar. The fashionable notion that the scholar and the gentleman were irreconcilable was in some degree shared by them. A number of them, especially in the Restoration, accorded fully as much importance to a knowledge of the world as to book knowledge among the requirements for the ideal gentleman; a few even ranked a knowledge of the world higher. Others, however, deprecated the aristocratic emphasis on "the world" at the cost of learning; such deprecation seems to have become especially prominent in the mid-eighteenth century. The question of whether learning declined as a component in the theorists' ideal of the gentleman after the Renaissance is not definitely answerable. Perhaps it declined somewhat, notably in the Restoration. On the other hand, learning was recognized as possessing many advantages. It was a powerful promoter of virtue, an ornament of the gentleman, and a spiritual ennobling; it served to develop his natural potentialities and was especially necessary if he was to benefit his nation in a political capacity. For younger sons, furthermore, learning could be helpful in attaining a fortune.

In so far as the gentleman did receive an adequate education, history was very important; it enabled him to profit by the experience of others, afforded him many moral lessons, and was indispensable to serving the state well in a political capacity. Legal training also prepared him for a public office; in addition, it enabled him to settle differences and preserve order in a private station, as a country squire and justice of the peace.

Latin traditionally bulked large in the gentleman's course of studies, but some educational reformers opposed the emphasis on it, affirming that such stress was unnecessary, that it detracted from studies of greater importance, and that a scholarly knowledge of Latin was inappropriate for gentlemen. The grammatical method of teaching Latin was also called inappropriate by some commentators, since an exhaustive acquaintance with the grammar of the language was necessary only for scholars. A gentleman's studies were supposed to be useful; training in grammar, according to the iconoclasts, did not satisfy this requirement. Neither did the composition of Latin themes and verses, in their opinion. All these criticisms were referent mainly to public schools, which were hostile to any alteration in their long-established system.

The polite accomplishments were considered more ornamental than useful, and the gentleman was consequently warned not to devote too much time to them; they might usurp the place of more serious studies or interfere with the main business of an active life. Dancing, however, held a unique position because of its value in giving the gentleman an habitual grace of carriage. Of more practical benefit than the accomplishments were other recreations, such as the manual arts and crafts and experiments in botany and animal husbandry.

As the schools and universities of the eighteenth century afforded little specialized training, some critics demanded that their curricula be revised so as to prepare the young gentleman in a more adequate fashion for his future profession or career. Such demands afford further evidence of a tendency to stress the usefulness of the gentleman's studies. Many educators, however, evidently believed that his studies were already useful enough; pleas and proposals for specialization, like objections to the emphasis on and modes of teaching Latin, were of an iconoclastic nature.

Notes to Chapter III

1. Clare Howard, for example, suggests that during the seventeenth century learning for gentlemen fell into disesteem in England and that the French ideal, which emphasized the martial at the expense of the erudite and which was embodied in the French academies, greatly influenced the English; see her *English Travellers of the Renaissance* (New York, 1913), pp. 104-108, 121-123, 128-130. Ricardo Quintana traces through the seventeenth century the reaction against the vain speculations of the universities and of many scholars and the effect of this somewhat anti-intellectual reaction on educational theory, including views on the education of gentlemen; see his "Notes on English Educational Opinion During the Seventeenth Century," *SP*, XXVII (1930), 265-292.

2. *Covent-Garden Journal,* ed. Gerard Edward Jensen (New Haven, London, and Oxford, 1915), II, 65-66. From No. 56 (July 25, 1752).

3. Boyer, *English Theophrastus*, p. 59. The sketch in which this passage occurs was adapted by Boyer from a sketch appended to *An Essay in Defence of the Female Sex* (London, 1696), attrib. to Judith Drake or Mary Astell.

4. Darrell, attrib., *Gentleman Instructed,* p. 15.

5. See Boyer, p. 58, and Defoe, *Compleat English Gentleman,* pp. 127-132. Steele's examples of a Yorkshire gentleman's faulty spelling in the *Spectator* No. 328 (March 17, 1712) were probably intended to ridicule the near-illiteracy of the provincial gentleman as well as the Yorkshire dialect.

6. *Letters,* VI, 2781; see also VI, 2828.

7. Boyer, p. 51. See above, n. 3.

8. *The Pretty Gentleman,* in *Fugitive Pieces, on Various*

Subjects (London, 1761), I, 206, 203. This essay, which is anonymous, was first published in 1747.

9. *The Humourist* (London, 1720), p. 101. This is Vol. I; Vol. II did not appear until 1725. See also Brown, *Estimate,* p. 38.

10. See, for example, Dr. Richard Bathurst in the *Adventurer* No. 35 (March 6, 1753) and Colman and Thornton in the *Connoisseur* No. 24 (July 11, 1754).

11. Grenville, *Counsel and Directions,* pp. 78-79.

12. *Terrae-Filius,* I, 47. From No. 9 (Feb. 15, 1721).

13. *An Essay on Modern Education* (London, 1747), pp. 24-25. This anonymous work should not be confused with Swift's essay of the same name.

14. *The Humours of Oxford* (London, 1730), "Dramatis Personae" and p. 8.

15. *Gentile Sinner,* p. 26.

16. See Mason, *Gentlefolk in the Making,* p. 74. This opinion occurred in Argyle's *Instructions to a Son,* written in 1661.

17. See Kelso, *Doctrine,* pp. 115-119, and Frederick J. Furnivall, "Education in Early England," *EETSOS,* XXXII (1868), xi-xiv.

18. See Einstein, *Tudor Ideals,* pp. 163-164; Kelso, *Doctrine,* pp. 111-114; Elbert N. S. Thompson, *Literary Bypaths of the Renaissance* (New Haven, 1924), p. 156; and Woodward, *Studies in Education,* pp. 293-294.

19. *The Institution of a Young Noble Man,* ed. Max Molyneux (New York, 1948), p. 134. See *The Boke Named the Gouvernour,* ed. H. H. S. Croft (London, 1880), I, 98-113.

20. See above, n. 1, s. v. Howard.

21. *Some Thoughts Concerning Education,* p. 142.

22. *Letters,* III, 1105-06, 1108.

23. Dr. Richard Lingard, attrib., *A Letter of Advice To a Young Gentleman Leaving the University,* ed. Frank C. Erb (New York, 1907), p. 9. 1st ed. was Dublin, 1670.

24. *Speculum Juventutis,* pp. 104-105.

25. Boyer, p. 58. See above, n. 3.

26. *Strephon's Revenge: A Satire on the Oxford Toasts,* 4th ed. (London, 1724), p. 6.

27. See Kelso, *Doctrine,* pp. 55-57, and Einstein, *Tudor Ideals,* pp. 54, 336-337.

28. *Dialogues Concerning Education,* I, 90.

29. *Essay on Modern Education,* in *Prose Works,* XI, 53.

30. *Ibid.,* 56.

31. *Compleat English Gentleman,* pp. 68, 54. See also pp. 118-119, 274.

32. *Vox Clamantis,* p. 73. See also *Gentleman's Library,* pp. 31-32.

33. *Proposals For the Reformation of Schools & Universities* (n. p., 1704), p. 5.

34. *Of Education, Especially of Young Gentlemen,* p. 112.

35. See Kelso, *Doctrine,* pp. 55-57, and G. C. Gordon, ed., *Peacham's Compleat Gentleman 1634* (Oxford, 1906), pp. xiv-xv.

36. Lingard, attrib., *Letter of Advice,* p. 3.

37. See Mason, *Gentlefolk in the Making,* p. 163.

38. *Letters,* III, 779, 1066, and IV, 1275-76, 1702, 1703.

39. See *Speculum Juventutis,* pp. 92-95.

40. G. Croft, *General Observations Concerning Education* (Hull, 1775), p. 17.

41. See, on the first point, Panton, pp. 76-77; Puckle, *The Club,* p. 77; and Budgell in *Spectator* No. 353 (April 15, 1712); and on the second point, Brokesby, *Letter of Advice,* p. 5; Defoe, *Compleat English Gentleman,* p. 89; and Burgh, *Dignity of Human Nature,* pp. 108-109.

42. *Gentleman's Library,* p. 15. See also Dykes, *Royal Marriage,* p. 15; Defoe, pp. 105, 163; and Fordyce, *Dialogues Concerning Education,* I, 107.

43. Boyer, p. 60. See above, n. 3.

44. *Prose Works,* XI, 56.

45. *Works,* ed. Charles Nason Cole, 2nd ed. (London, 1793), I, 66.

46. See pp. 175-181, 239-240.

47. See *Letter of Advice,* p. 5, and *Dialogues Concerning Education,* II, 74-75, 301-306.

48. See Burnet, *Thoughts on Education,* p. 18; Sir Matthew Hale, *A Letter to His Grandchildren* (Boston, 1817), p. 118; Locke, *Some Thoughts Concerning Education,* pp. 115-123; Costeker, *Fine Gentleman,* p. 17; Brooke, *Fool of Quality,* p. 55; Thomas Sheridan, *Plan of Education,* p. 88; and Chapman, *Treatise on Education,* pp. 65-66. Hale's *Letter,* first printed in the cited ed., was written ca. 1673. Although Burgh agreed that a young child should receive much instruction in reading English, he was unique in suggesting that a boy should not

be taught to write until the age of twelve; see *Dignity of Human Nature,* pp. 127-128.

49. See Burnet, *Thoughts on Education,* p. 38; Hale, pp. 118-119; Walker, *Of Education, Especially of Young Gentlemen,* p. 109; Gailhard, *Compleat Gentleman,* 1st Treatise, pp. 35-38; Locke, pp. 125-130, 133-146; the Chevalier Andrew Michael Ramsay, *A Plan of Education for a Young Prince . . . . To which is added, A Thought relating to Education, Offer'd to the Examination of such as have Noblemen and Gentlemen . . . under their Care* (London, 1732), pp. i-ii; Costeker, p. 18; *Of Education,* p. 6; Burgh, pp. 127-128; Priestley, *Course of Liberal Education,* p. 18; Brooke, p. 57; Sheridan, p. 88; and Chapman, p. 65.

50. See Burnet, *Thoughts on Education,* pp. 37-38, 54-55, and *History of His Own Time,* VI, 205; Locke, pp. 124-125; Costeker, pp. 18, 29; *Of Education,* pp. 10, 12; Priestley, *Course of Liberal Education,* p. 18; and Sheridan, p. 88. Chesterfield wrote several letters in French to his son and many to his godson while they were still children; by the time the son was seventeen or eighteen Chesterfield assumed that he had a good knowledge of Italian as well (see *Letters,* IV, 1565). It should be added, however, that instruction in the modern languages was not yet characteristic of the public school curriculum; the young gentleman usually learned French, and perhaps Italian, under a tutor at home. Some critics, among them Swift in his *Essay on Modern Education,* objected to the importance accorded to a French tutor in fashionable houses. Later a gentleman improved his facility in the modern languages on the grand tour.

51. See Panton, *Speculum Juventutis,* p. 288; Walker, pp. 112-113; Gailhard, *Compleat Gentleman,* 1st Treatise, pp. 69-70; Locke, pp. 146-149; Ramsay, p. ii; *Of Education,* pp. 10-11, 18; Burgh, pp. 128, 131; *An Enquiry into the Plan and Pretensions of Mr. Sheridan* (Dublin, 1758), p. 36; Priestley, *Course of Liberal Education,* p. 19; and Sheridan, p. 88. Burnet, however, did not advise mathematics until a youth was fifteen (see *Thoughts on Education,* p. 61), and Hale did not advise arithmetic until a youth was sixteen or seventeen (see p. 119).

52. See Burnet, *Thoughts on Education,* p. 45, and *History of His Own Time,* VI, 204; Panton, p. 288; Penton, *Guardian's Instruction,* p. 67; Locke, pp. 146-147, 149-150; *An Essay upon*

Education; Shewing How Latin, Greek, and Other Languages May Be Learn'd more easily, quickly, and perfectly, than they commonly are (London, 1711), p. 20; Steele in *Spectator* No. 230 (Nov. 23, 1711); Chesterfield, *Letters*, II, 374, 375; *Enquiry into the Plan and Pretensions*, p. 36; and Sheridan, p. 88. Burgh did not advise geography and chronology until a youth was fourteen or fifteen (see p. 131).

53. See Panton, p. 288; Gailhard, *Compleat Gentleman*, 1st Treatise, pp. 43-48; Locke, pp. 146, 151; *Essay upon Education*, etc., pp. 20-21; Steele in *Spectator* No. 230; Clarke, *Essay upon Study*, p. 127; Ramsay, p. 15; Costeker, p. 30; *Of Education*, p. 23; Chesterfield, II, 373-374, and IV, 1565; Daniel Waterland, *Advice to a Young Student*, 2nd ed. (Oxford, 1755), p. 14; and Chapman, pp. 158-159. The 1st ed. of Waterland's *Advice* also appeared in 1755, although the work had appeared in an incorrect and shorter form in *The Republick of Letters* for Dec., 1729.

54. See Hale, pp. 16-17; Gailhard, *Compleat Gentleman*, 1st Treatise, pp. 35-36; *Essay upon Education*, etc., p. 21; Steele in *Spectator* No. 230; Ramsay, pp. v-vi; Costeker, pp. 19, 29; *Of Education*, pp. 13-14; Chesterfield, II, 318, 362; Burgh, pp. 128-129; Sheridan, pp. 99-100; and Chapman, pp. 167-168, 195-196.

55. Among those who recommended Greek were Burnet, *Thoughts on Education*, pp. 51-52; Hale, p. 119; Gailhard, *Compleat Gentleman*, 1st Treatise, pp. 35-36; Penton, *Guardian's Instruction*, pp. 59, 67; Clarke, *Essay upon Study*, p. 127; Ramsay, pp. i-ii, v-vi; Costeker, pp. 19, 29; Chesterfield, II, 362, 400, 410, and IV, 1565; Burgh, p. 129; Brooke, pp. 168, 257; Chapman, pp. 167-168; and Croft, p. 11. Some of these authors, however, advised it with reservations. Locke did not deem Greek necessary for the gentleman (see pp. 163-164), and Sheridan advised it only for those well-born youths who planned to enter the medical or clerical professions (see pp. 104-106).

56. See Burnet, *Thoughts on Education*, pp. 37-38, 69; Walker, p. 109; Hale, p. 118; Ramesey, *Gentlemans Companion*, p. 15; Gailhard, *Compleat Gentleman*, 1st Treatise, p. 42; Clarke, *Essay upon Study*, pp. 218-219; Chesterfield, IV, 1454-56; Waterland, pp. 14, 27; and Sheridan, pp. 102-103, 122. The importance that Chesterfield attached to oratory in his son's

education need scarcely be pointed out. Sheridan's *British Education: Or, The Sources of the Disorders of Great Britain* (1756) was an attempt to show that training in oratory would cure Britain of her ills. An orator himself, Sheridan understandably exaggerated the case, but few would have denied the advantages of oratorical training for the gentleman.

57. See Locke, pp. 154-158; Steele in *Tatler* No. 234 (Oct. 7, 1710) and *Spectator* No. 230; Budgell in *Spectator* No. 353 (April 15, 1712); Defoe, pp. 115-116, 122; John Clarke, *An Essay upon the Education of Youth in Grammar-Schools* (London, 1730), pp. 116-117; *Of Education,* pp. 9, 15; Chesterfield, II, 332-333, 381, and V, 1799-1801; *Enquiry into the Plan and Pretensions,* p. 36; Sheridan, *Plan of Education,* pp. 56-58, 60-61; Chapman, pp. 192-194; and Croft, pp. 11-13. A shorter ed. of Clarke's *Education of Youth* appeared in 1720.

58. Among those theorists were Steele in *Spectator* No. 203; Chesterfield, II, 362-363, 410-413; Burgh, p. 128; the author of *An Enquiry into the Plan and Pretensions,* p. 36; Sheridan, *Plan of Education,* pp. 100-102; Chapman, pp. 197-198; and Croft, pp. 11-13. From the tone of many of these passages, one gathers that such instruction was often neglected in the education of gentlemen. It is, however, interesting to note that the *Spectator* was sometimes used as a schoolbook or advised for the perusal of university students; see George C. Brauer, Jr., "Recommendations of the 'Spectator' for Students During the Eighteenth Century," *N & Q,* CC (1955), 207-208.

59. See Panton, p. 288; Ramesey, p. 14; Hale, p. 120; Walker, p. 110; Gailhard, *Compleat Gentleman,* 1st Treatise, pp. 42-43; Locke, pp. 158-161; Costeker, pp. 20-24; Clarke, *Essay upon Study,* pp. 218-219; Waterland, p. 14; Chesterfield, IV, 1565; and Sheridan, *Plan of Education,* p. 95. Burnet, however, cautioned against teaching logic too early and considered it rather useless anyway (see *Thoughts on Education,* pp. 37-38, 63). Locke was opposed to teaching ethics too early and believed that the gentleman should have little training in logic (see pp. 151-154). Burgh (pp. 131-132) agreed with Locke's views on logic.

60. See Burnet, *Thoughts on Education,* pp. 60-61; Hale, pp. 20-21; Ramesey, p. 14; Walker, pp. 113-116; Gailhard, *Compleat Gentleman,* 1st Treatise, pp. 43, 48-49, 69-70; Locke, pp. 161-163 (Locke, however, stressed the limitations on scientific

knowledge); Costeker, pp. 19-20, 24-26, 29; *Of Education,* p. 23; Burgh, pp. 132, 143-145, 150; and Waterland, pp. 13-14, 26, 28-31. Dr. Richard Davies, in *The General State of Education in the Universities* (Bath, 1759), complained that the universities did not provide enough training in science (see esp. p. 40). But he was answered in the anon. *Observations on the Present State of the English Universities* (London, 1759), whose author maintained that scientific training was not neglected by them (see pp. 26-27). These authors were not, of course, speaking with particular reference to gentlemanly education. The place of law in the gentleman's education is treated later in this chapter.

61. See Burnet, *Thoughts on Education,* pp. 24, 64; Ramesey, pp. 133-134; Walker, pp. 68-71; Gailhard, *Compleat Gentleman,* 1st Treatise, pp. 79, 81-85, and 2nd Treatise, pp. 50-51; Locke, pp. 166-167; Dykes, *Royal Marriage,* p. 19; Costeker, p. 45; *Of Education,* p. 23; Fordyce, *Dialogues Concerning Education,* I, 30; Brooke, *Fool of Quality,* pp. 56, 127; Sheridan, *Plan of Education,* p. 115; Beattie, *Utility of Classical Learning,* in *Essays,* pp. 495-496; and Chapman, pp. 6-7, 133-136. Panton, however, maintained that a youth should have no violent exercise until the age of eighteen, although from then on he advised strenuous forms of exercise (see pp. 217-218).

62. See Gailhard, *Compleat Gentleman,* 2nd Treatise, p. 49; Locke, pp. 166-168; Costeker, pp. 44-45; Chesterfield, III, 1171, and IV, 1345, 1732; Brooke, p. 127; and Chapman, p. 136. Burnet, however, believed that a child should not be trained in arms too early (see *Thoughts on Education,* pp. 64-65), and Burgh, though he recognized that the gentleman was customarily taught to fence, spoke grudgingly of the practice (see p. 133).

63. See Burnet, *Thoughts on Education,* pp. 53, 62; Gailhard, *Compleat Gentleman,* 1st Treatise, p. 70; Locke, pp. 148-149; Steele in *Spectator* No. 230; Defoe, pp. 242-243; *Of Education,* p. 16; Chesterfield, IV, 1270-71; Waterland, p. 14; and *Enquiry into the Plan and Pretensions,* p. 36.

64. Brokesby, *Letter of Advice,* p. 7. See also Locke, p. 149; Clarke, *Essay upon Study,* p. 18; and Chesterfield, VI, 2587.

65. Gailhard, *Compleat Gentleman,* 1st Treatise, pp. 45-46.

66. II, 340. See also Burgh, p. 137, and Chapman, p. 215.

67. See Kelso, *Doctrine,* pp. 133-134; Foster Watson, *The Be-*

ginnings of the Teaching of Modern Subjects in England (London, 1909), p. 53; and Woodward, *Studies in Education,* pp. 287, 300-301.

68. See *Thoughts on Education,* pp. 45, 47, and *Compleat Gentleman,* 1st Treatise, pp. 44-45.

69. *Dignity of Human Nature,* p. 139. See also Priestley, *Course of Liberal Education,* pp. 40-41, and Chapman, *Treatise on Education,* pp. 215-217.

70. *Course of Liberal Education,* p. 41. See also Brokesby, *Letter of Advice,* pp. 7-8, and Burgh, p. 138.

71. See Kelso, *Doctrine,* p. 133; Mason, *Gentlefolk in the Making,* p. 236; Watson, *Beginnings,* pp. 54, 69-70; and Woodward, *Studies in Education* p. 287.

72. *Essay upon Study,* pp. 223-224. See also Sheridan, *Plan of Education,* pp. 97-99.

73. *History of His Own Time,* VI, 205.

74. See *Plan of Education,* pp. 95-97.

75. VI, 2587; V, 1887-92; and III, 1155-56.

76. *Course of Liberal Education,* pp. 40, 9-10.

77. See *ibid.,* pp. 5-7.

78. For recommendations of legal studies for gentlemen in the Renaissance, see Kelso, *Doctrine,* p. 137; Mason, pp. 126, 236; Ustick, *SP,* XXIX (1932), 415; and Woodward, p. 315.

79. See William Higford, *Institutions: Or, Advice to His Grandson* (London, 1658, repr. by W. Bulmer & Co., 1818), p. 63.

80. *Thoughts on Education,* p. 72.

81. See Hale, *Letter of Advice,* p. 125; Penton, *Guardian's Instruction,* p. 13; and Burnet, *History of His Own Time,* VI, 201.

82. *Essay upon Study,* p. 223.

83. See III, 972-973, 1076.

84. *History of His Own Time,* VI, 201.

85. *Uses of Foreign Travel,* pp. 78-79.

86. See J. W. Adamson, *Pioneers of Modern Education 1600-1700* (Cambridge, 1905), pp. 22-23, and James Oliphant, ed., *Educational Writings of Richard Mulcaster* (Glascow, 1903), pp. 227-229.

87. *Utility of Classical Learning,* in *Essays,* p. 489.

88. *History of His Own Time,* VI, 200-201. It may be recalled that this passage was quoted by Richardson in Letter VI of

Sir Charles Grandison, at the end of an argument over the importance of classical studies in education.

89. See *Some Thoughts Concerning Education,* pp. 125-126, 157-158, 163-164.

90. See *Uses of Foreign Travel,* p. 78, and *Plan of Education,* pp. 104-106.

91. *Compleat English Gentleman,* p. 217.

92. *Ibid.,* p. 203.

93. See *ibid.,* pp. 196-217, 223-225.

94. E. g., his *New Grammar of the Latin Tongue* (1733) and *Introduction to the Making of Latin* (1740), and his editions, for schoolchildren, of select colloquies of Corderius (1718) and Erasmus (1720).

95. *Education of Youth,* p. 9; see also pp. 7-8.

96. *Plan of Education,* pp. 41-42; see also pp. 16-17.

97. *Enquiry into the Plan and Pretensions,* pp. 36-38.

98. For example, although Elyot included grammar in his educational scheme, he advised commencing Latin by the conversational method, as did Erasmus also; and Mulcaster relegated grammar to a comparatively inferior position.

99. See *Some Thoughts Concerning Education,* pp. 126-127, 135-138, 154-158.

100. *History of His Own Time,* VI, 200. Quoted by Richardson in Letter VI of *Sir Charles Grandison.*

101. *Dignity of Human Nature,* p. 124. Although Clarke opposed Locke's pronouncement that grammar was not necessary, he agreed that training in it should be delayed until a youth was already familiar with Latin; see his *Education of Youth,* pp. 11-14, 104-105. The anon. author of *Of Education,* who like Clarke had read Locke, objected to the grammatical method; see p. 6.

102. See *Some Thoughts Concerning Education,* pp. 138-142, 154-158.

103. *Education of Youth,* p. 61.

104. *Dignity of Human Nature,* p. 124.

105. *Utility of Classical Learning,* in *Essays,* p. 517.

106. See *Letters,* II, 410.

107. See Kelso, *Doctrine,* pp. 140-141; Thompson, *Literary Bypaths,* pp. 142, 158; and Woodward, *Studies in Education,* pp. 277-278.

108. For recommendations and discussions of the polite ac-

complishments, see, in addition to the citations on the following pages, Higford, *Institutions,* pp. 84-88; Burnet, *Thoughts on Education,* p. 50; Gailhard, *Compleat Gentleman,* 2nd Treatise, p. 52; Steele in *Spectator* No. 230; Dykes, *Royal Marriage,* p. 19; Costeker, *Fine Gentleman,* pp. 48-49; Chesterfield, III, 1171, and IV, 1651, 1653; and Brooke, *Fool of Quality,* p. 127.

109. See Locke, *Some Thoughts Concerning Education,* p. 165; Chesterfield, IV, 1331; and Sheridan, *Plan of Education,* pp. 90-91.

110. Darrell, attrib., *Gentleman Instructed,* p. 20.

111. *Dignity of Human Nature,* pp. 133, 150. Ranking the "sciences" in the order of their importance, Burgh placed the polite arts last (see p. 157).

112. *Plan of Education for a Young Prince,* p. ix.

113. *Legacie to My Dear Son Thomas,* ed. cit., p. 186.

114. IV, 1420, 1330-31.

115. Higford, *Institutions,* p. 88, and Walker, *Of Education, Especially of Young Gentlemen,* p. 69, resp. See also Locke, pp. 47, 165; Steele in *Spectator* No. 334 (March 24, 1712); Costeker, *Fine Gentleman,* pp. 42-43; and Chapman, *Treatise on Education,* p. 136.

116. *Of Education,* p. 11.

117. *Dignity of Human Nature,* p. 133.

118. *Some Fruits,* ed. cit., pp. 344-345.

119. *Some Thoughts Concerning Education,* pp. 169-173.

120. *Plan of Education,* pp. 112-114.

121. *Advices to a Young Man of Fortune and Rank* (Oxford, n. d.), pp. 25-26.

122. Edward Waterhouse in his *Gentleman's Monitor* (1665) recommended trade for the younger sons of noblemen (see Mason, *Gentlefolk in the Making,* p. 151). Malachy Postlethwayt's *The Merchant's Public Counting-House* (1751), incorporating a plan for breeding youths to trade, included *"some remarks on the benefit of this instruction to the young nobility and gentry"* (title page). Sheridan, as will be shown shortly, provided for training young gentlemen as tradesmen, and Brooke, who conceived of Henry Clinton as an ideal gentleman, demonstrated that his gentility was in no way damaged by his connection with commerce. But the more common aristocratic attitude was represented by Clinton's brother the Earl of Moreland, who said of Henry: "I looked upon him as a branch cut off from

the family-tree" (*Fool of Quality*, p. 24). Most theorists did not even consider the question of trade for gentlemen. Johnson, however, suggested that a well-born youth brought up to trade lost the marks of his gentility; see *Rambler* Nos. 116 (April 27, 1751) and 123 (May 21, 1751).

123. See *Compleat Gentleman*, 1st Treatise, pp. 99-100.

124. See *Dignity of Human Nature*, pp. 157-159, and *Advice to a Young Student*, pp. 13-14 ff.

125. See R. F. Jones, "The Background of the Attack on Science in the Age of Pope," in *Pope and his Contemporaries: Essays presented to George Sherburn*, ed. James L. Clifford and Louis A. Landa (Oxford, 1949), pp. 100-104.

126. See *An Essay Upon the Necessity and Excellency of Education* (London, 1705), pp. 36, 44-45, 53 ff.

127. See *Course of Liberal Education*, pp. 1, 8-10, 13.

128. See *Plan of Education*, pp. 95-114.

CHAPTER FOUR

Worldly Experience as an Aim in the Gentleman's Education

"The world" has already been defined in its Restoration and eighteenth-century acceptation as mankind, and a participation in the world as a participation in society rather than an engrossing concern with books. For the gentleman the world was, of course, often restricted to genteel company; "the man of fashion," Colman and Thornton observed in the *Connoisseur* No. 136 (September 2, 1756), "seeks it no where but in the polite circle of the *beau-monde.*" Middle-class commentators sometimes objected to this limitation; Bentham, for example, admonished a young gentleman at Oxford that "if you mistake lowness of fortunes for meanness of manners, and so confine your acquaintance to persons of your rank in understanding because they are so in fortune, you certainly lose the most valuable benefit of a public education."[1] Whatever level of company gentlemen may have had in mind as constituting the world, however, it is certain that they deemed the world their special province and, as has been indicated in the preceding chapter, laid an extraordinary emphasis on it. A remark put into Shaftesbury's mouth by Hurd was expressive of the aristocratic attitude: "The proper business of men, especially those of rank and quality, lies among men. The first and last object of a Gentleman should be an intimate study and knowledge of his species."[2]

We have seen in Chapter III that although some theorists, particularly in the mid-eighteenth century, deprecated the fashionable stress on the world, others ranked a knowledge of the

world alongside or above learning. There were consequently
many commentators who were eager than the well-born youth
be introduced into company, which was the best tutor in worldly
knowledge, if not the only one. Thus Burnet said of the gentleman of eighteen or older that his "work sould be to know the
world; and therefore how retired soever I could wish a youth
were kept, before this age, now sould he be much abroad,
and in all company."[3] According to Gailhard, when boys em-
barked on the tour of the Continent it was time to acquaint
them with the world. "I will bring them out of their study,
and from amongst the dead," he announced, "to converse with
the living. We must now make them look abroad, raise them to
a higher form, and teach them how to know the world."[4] As
will appear in Chapter VI, a common argument in favor of
the grand tour was that it served as an introduction to a
knowledge of the world by providing a great deal of social
intercourse for the gentleman. Some theorists, mentioned in
Chapter VII, preferred public to private education because at
a public school, where a young gentleman mingled with many
other students, he learned more about the world than he did
in the seclusion of his own home. All this emphasis on the
desirability of social intercourse in gentlemanly upbringing was
justified by the several advantages which were said to accrue
from a participation in society, and which will be looked into
now.

One of those advantages was the acquisition of good breeding, treated in Chapter V. Another was that through conversation a gentleman gained much factual information, thereby
widening the scope of his practical knowledge. The well-born
youth on his travels, Gailhard stipulated in his *Compleat
Gentleman,* should "frequent persons of Quality, by whom
he may be well informed of affairs" (Second Treatise, page
74). The useful nature of the knowledge gathered through
conversation rendered it especially suitable for gentlemen and
was made much of by theorists, who carefully distinguished it
from book learning and the speculative erudition of the scholar.
Fordyce described the headmaster of his ideal academy as one
who had attained from conversation·"a more useful knowledge

than is acquired merely by reading."[5] Chesterfield was convinced that if a young gentleman was alert, no conversation could fail to impart useful information: "A good chemist will extract some spirit or other out of every substance; and a man of parts will, by his dexterity and management, elicit something worth knowing out of every being he converses with." He therefore exhorted his son, abroad on his travels: "For God's sake, my dear boy, do not squander away one moment of your time, for every moment may be now most usefully employed. . . . Every moment's conversation may, if you please, be of use to you."[6]

Most theorists, less sanguine on this point than Chesterfield, felt that a gentleman could not obtain much worthwhile information through conversation unless the persons with whom he talked were cultivated and intelligent. If they satisfied those requirements, however, he might perhaps derive more profit from them than he could from books. It was Burgh's opinion that the man who gathered around him a group of intelligent acquaintances, "with whom to converse freely, and without the trammels of systematic or academic rules," would "find more improvement, in a short time, from such a society, than from twenty years solitary study." "Reading," Burgh explained, "is necessary to get at the fundamental principles of a science. And the careful perusal of a few capital books is sufficient for this purpose. Afterwards to talk over the subject with a set of intelligent men, is the best method for extending one's views of it."[7] "That freedom of debate and diversity of topics, which adorn the conversations of men of rank and polite literature," another mid-century commentator affirmed, "will give his mind a generous enlargement, and open to him delightful scenes of knowledge, at once awakening the imagination and informing the understanding." In these conversations, the author added, "there are frequently such lucky hints thrown out, as prove a fruitful source of thoughts and imagination, which would never have occurred to him in the studious hour, or in the company of meaner spirits."[8] According to Fordyce's *Dialogues,* after a gentleman had spent some time at a university he should be sent to London, where he would continue his education by conversing with men of all sorts, from mechanics to members

of Parliament. "By spending his time in this manner for a
year or two in town," Fordyce stated, "and by an unlimited
commerce with men of business, as well as letters, I engage he
will learn more real useful knowlege [sic] than is to be acquired at any seat of learning whatsoever in double that time"
(II, 272-273).

Such remarks suggest the tendency in the eighteenth century to consider the world more valuable than books in gentlemanly education. It should be noted, however, that even writers
who placed so high an importance on conversation as opposed
to reading believed learning essential as a preliminary to worthwhile discussion, certainly for the gentleman and in most cases
for those with whom he conversed. Theorists would have been
unwilling to cut studies short merely in order to introduce him
into the world. Their comments had reference mainly to gentlemen who had already completed their period of formal study,
not to boys still occupied with textbooks. Even the warmest
advocates of learning would not have denied that for such men,
conversation was very beneficial.

The most important educational advantage accruing from a
participation in society was the one implied in the very definition of a knowledge of the world, "that [knowledge] which results . . . from the study and contemplation of men; as they
present themselves on the great stage of the world, in various
forms, and under different appearances."[9] It included not only
an understanding of human nature but, as a corollary to this,
the ability to deal adroitly and successfully with one's fellow
men. In the Elizabethan and early Stuart periods this dual
lesson of the world was viewed as indispensable to the gentleman
as a participant in the active life, and much attention was paid
to it by authors of courtesy literature—especially aristocratic
authors, as might be expected from the importance attached
to the world by persons of quality. Mention has already been
made of the book of prudential advice which, in the seventeenth
century, appeared alongside the moralistic advice book. The
former was practical and expedient in tone, often cynical, sometimes unscrupulous, and egregiously mundane, instructing the
gentleman in worldly wisdom and successful conduct. Repre-

sentative of this kind of courtesy literature were Burleigh's *Certaine Precepts or Directions* (first published in 1617 but written earlier) and Raleigh's *Instructions to his Sonne, and to Posterity* (first published in 1632). Continental works of the same order, influential in England, included Lorenzo Ducci's *Ars Aulica* (translated in 1607), Du Refuge's *Traité de la Cour* (translated in 1622), and Cardinal Sermonetta's *Instructions to His Cousin* (translated in 1633).[10] These books were related to treatises on policy; several of them fell directly under that classification. Seventeenth-century treatises on policy, written expressly for courtiers, statesmen, and diplomats, laid great stress on the necessity for understanding men, their typical actions and reactions, foibles and passions and dominant traits, if one was to shine at court and in a public sphere.

One might expect that with the decreased emphasis on the political role of the gentleman in the eighteenth century, the importance placed on a knowledge of man and of prudential conduct would also have decreased, but this was not the case— except, perhaps, toward the middle of the century, and then the reaction against a stress on worldly knowledge was largely attributable to other causes. Indeed, for the Augustans a knowledge of the world seems almost to have become an end in itself, "the proper study of mankind" in Pope's phrase. Its political value was less frequently mentioned in the eighteenth century than in the seventeenth; but the gentleman's sphere of activity was still society no matter whether he engaged actively in politics or not, and for this reason an understanding of human nature and the resultant skill in human relationships remained essential to him. Their eminently useful character, in fact, made them particularly appropriate for gentlemen.

Like the factual information gained from a participation in society, a knowledge of the world in its Restoration and eighteenth-century sense was sharply distinguished from the theoretical erudition of the scholar, and actual experience was said to be the only way to acquire it. "The scholar, who in the dust of his closet talks or writes of the world," Chesterfield maintained, "knows no more of it, than that orator did of

war, who judiciously endeavoured to instruct Hannibal in it"
(III, 1024). Therefore the Earl urged his son: "When you are
in company, learn (what company can only teach you) the
characters and manners of mankind" (IV, 1289). Fielding's remarks in *Tom Jones* (Book IX, chapter i) were typical; a
knowledge of the world, he said, was "beyond the power of
learning to bestow," and no men understood less about human
characteristics "than those learned pedants whose lives have
been entirely consumed in colleges and among books; for however exquisitely human nature may have been described by
writers, the true practical system can be learnt only in the
world." Even if one spent most of one's time in society, however, considerable perception and concentration were necessary
before one's experience could bear fruit. Chesterfield consequently informed his son:

> To know mankind well, requires full as much attention
> and application as to know books, and, it may be, more
> sagacity and discernment. I am at this time acquainted
> with many elderly people, who have passed their whole lives
> in the great world, but with such levity and inattention,
> that they know no more of it now, than they did at fifteen.
> Do not flatter yourself, therefore, with the thoughts that
> you can acquire this knowledge in the frivolous chit-chat
> of idle companies; no, you must go much deeper than that.
> You must look into people, as well as at them. (III, 779.)

If one did look deeply into people, the lessons learned were
legion. The comments of several courtesy writers will afford
some insight into the kinds of information about human nature
and successful social relationships which were considered most
valuable. Burnet mentioned, as elements of prudential conduct
taught by experience in the world, "discretion, to know . . .
how to converse, to be silent, to choose friends, to find out
peoples humours; and how to gain love, and the like."[11] The
ability to comport oneself well in diverse societies was important
for Gailhard; according to his *Compleat Gentleman,* a young
man should consort not only with persons of rank but also with

a "sort of choice persons, considerable, not so much for their birth and quality, as for their Virtue, Merits, Parts, and abilities," since from such people he would "learn how to carry himself well in all kinds of company . . . and learn how to comply with all manners of humours and tempers, yet excluding a vicious and sinful compliance" (Second Treatise, page 74). From his year or two at London, Fordyce declared in his *Dialogues,* a young man would "learn *life,* and discover on what hinges it turns; he will detect the arts and foibles of mankind, observe the genius of affairs; and know how to practise different characters." All this information, Fordyce thought, was indispensable to successful dealings with other human beings: "Thus he will enter upon the scenes of action properly armed and guarded; and consequently be better fitted to acquit himself wisely and worthily in every station" (II, 273).

Chesterfield, who considered a knowledge of the world essential to his son's success in a political sphere, furnished perhaps the most exhaustive analysis of the subject to be found among eighteenth-century authors of courtesy literature. A knowledge of the world consisted, in his view, of a comprehension of men's "prevailing weaknesses, their vanities, their follies, and their humours; with all the right and wrong, wise and silly springs of human actions, which make such inconsistent and whimsical beings of us rational creatures" (III, 1023). In the cynical tone of his remarks on human nature, Chesterfield is reminiscent of the Continental and pre-Commonwealth theorists who wrote books of prudential advice. At court, he said, self-interest was the primary motivation, women were to be flattered but not trusted, and a polite dissimulation concealed violent hatreds (IV, 1382-84). Vanity and love were the special passions of women, as avarice and ambition often were of men; persons who affected one certain virtue or who, early in one's acquaintance with them, made a great display of friendliness, should be the objects of particular suspicion (IV, 1469-71). An important aid to success in the world was the ability to discover a man's ruling passion and to govern one's relationship with him accordingly:

Almost all people are born with all the passions, to a certain degree; but almost every man has a prevailing one, to which the others are subordinate. Search every one for that ruling passion; pry into the recesses of his heart, and observe the different workings of the same passion in different people. And, when you have found out the prevailing passion of any man, remember never to trust him where that passion is concerned. Work upon him by it, if you please; but be upon your guard yourself against it, whatever professions he may make you. (III, 779-780).

Another extremely important aspect of a skill in human relationships, according to Chesterfield, was the ability to dissimulate—to control one's features and temper so that they did not betray the thoughts and feelings which it was advantageous to hide. "A man who has no *monde*," Chesterfield said, "is inflamed with anger, or annihilated with shame, at every disagreeable incident. . . . But a man who has *du monde* seems not to understand what he cannot or ought not to resent." Only those unacquainted with the world "have babbling countenances. . . . In the course of the world, a man must very often put on an easy, frank countenance, upon very disagreeable occasions; he must seem pleased, when he is very much otherwise; he must be able to accost and receive with smiles, those whom he would much rather meet with swords" (V, 1867-68). In his extraordinary emphasis on "that very sensible Italian saying, *Vuolto schiolto ed i pensieri stretti,* that is, close thoughts and an open countenance" (VI, 2914), Chesterfield was following a long tradition, represented in England by the late Elizabethan and seventeenth-century books of worldly advice and by such works as Bacon's essay on dissimulation and William de Britaine's *Humane Prudence* (1680). Though the tradition was less strong in the eighteenth century, it was by no means defunct. Puckle in 1711 had a wise old squire in *The Club* give his son the following counsel: "Keep your thoughts close, and your countenance loose; politicians are never more at a loss, than when they have to do with those who . . . are so much masters of their affections, that they do not appear in their countenances, words or actions" (page 80). And Fordyce in his *Dialogues* put ideas of a similar kind into the mouth of a father whom he called Urbanus: "A man of the world must wear a mask, and personate a character in public, which he not only may, but often must, lay aside behind the curtain, unless he means to pass for a fool or a madman. . . . In short, a man practised in affairs, must appear more or less than he is, and often disguise the sentiments he has, or assume those he is a stranger to, in a world where every man has a design upon every man, and uses his neighbour only to serve or raise himself" (II, 11-12).

There was, however, considerable reaction against such exhortations to hypocrisy, which were sometimes construed as instances of aristocratic immorality. Fordyce himself was not in sympathy with the attitude expressed here, and the reply to Urbanus suggested that honesty was, after all, the best policy. In 1720 the Scot Adam Petrie proclaimed: "It is undiscreet [i.e., ill-bred] to dissemble. A Dissembler imposes upon others who cannot suspect that a Person who smiles in their Face . . . can have any secret Poison in his Heart."[12] When Chesterfield's letters to his son were placed before the public in 1774, the criticisms leveled at them for advocating dissimulation clearly indicated that his strong recommendation of this aspect of prudential conduct was repugnant to many of his contemporaries.

Equally repugnant to them was the motive of self-advancement or self-aggrandisement which, unmitigated by any apparent public spirit, underlay Chesterfield's remarks not only on dissimulation but on other methods of comporting oneself in the world. Advice on ways to attain fame and power was, of course, not entirely absent from mid-eigtheenth-century instructions about how to act in society; but on the whole it received less mention that it had in the seventeenth century, since the gentleman was no longer viewed primarily as a politician and courtier, ambitious to win the favor of the king or his mistress and rise to a high office in the government. In large degree, prudential conduct had become no more than the means for making oneself agreeable and amusing, acceptable to fashionable society, respected by one's companions, offensive to nobody, the dupe of no designing persons, and the valued guest at brilliant entertainments. Chesterfield, on the other hand, fondly dreamed of his son as a political luminary.

Those many eighteenth-century authors of courtesy literature who wrote with a high moral purpose, furthermore, refrained from advocating the circuitious or unscrupulous practices, such as hypocrisy, flattery, forming connections with influential women, and playing upon a person's ruling passion, which Chesterfield considered so important. It was agreed that the gentleman should understand human nature and should know how to deal with his fellow men, but his actions as well as his motives had to be consistent with virtue. Even in the seventeenth century, we recall, the code later adopted by Chesterfield had run contrary to the pietistic courtesy books. In Chesterfield's own age, his doctrine was still less acceptable.

A third advantage of participation in the world was that if a young gentleman associated with virtuous companions he would be influenced toward virtue by their example. The converse was, of course, held to be just as true; if his friends were viciously inclined, he would be led to vice. Directions on choice of company were therefore frequent in courtesy literature of the Restoration and eighteenth century. Even the cynical Francis Osborn (e), a seventeenth-century Chesterfield in many of his attitudes, warned his son: "Be careful in the Choice of thy Company: As they are, so art thou: Let them be as thou wouldst be: Like will to like; Birds of a Feather, will Flock together: Associate thy self with such Society as are not past Shame . . . This is the Advantage of good Company, it will make thee good, or, at least, so esteemed."[13] More typical of late seventeenth-century instructions on choice of company, because less concerned with reputation, were Ayres' admonitions: "For the preventing this mischief of evil habits, and to further you in virtue and goodness . . . make your voluntary choice of the Society and Company of those that are good, that are Sober, Temperate and Vertuous." Occasionally, Ayres said, a young gentleman would "be cast into the Society of those that are evil"; in such a case the youth was told to "patiently dispence with [them] as well as you can, and stand upon your watch."[14]

Since the company a young gentleman kept was so instrumental a factor in his education to virtue, moralistic eighteenth-century authors such as Brokesby and Dykes held that intrinsic goodness rather than birth or fashion was the distinguishing feature of "good company,"[15] a term by which many aristocrats, Chesterfield among them, meant persons of quality. The same view was expressed by an anonymous mid-century author of a letter of advice, who informed a well-born youth: "You cannot be too careful in the choice of your company, for much every way depends upon it . . . let the modest, the virtuous, the studious, and above all, the religious, be your associates, without giving any preference to birth or fortune in the choice of them."[16]

If the importance of selecting good company was repeatedly asserted, the inadvisability of associating with wicked companions was mentioned even more often. The power of evil counsel to lead a young gentleman astray was sometimes illustrated by means of historical examples. "Alexander learned his drunkenness from Leonidas," Puckle said in *The Club,* "and Nero his cruelty from his barber" (page 83). Walker listed several characteristics by which vicious company could be recognized. A governor traveling with a young gentleman on the Continent, he declared, should beware of strangers consorting with his youthful charge *"if they be* extraordinarily officious without any reason; *if they* applaud whatever the young man saith, or doth; *if they* offer their service and assistance to all purposes: *if they* advise against the Governour, or to liberty, libertinisme, or idleness; *if they* railly, droll, and speak evil of others, especially of virtuous men, or such as the young man is recommended to; *if they* endeavour to draw him into unknown, obscure, or suspected places, or bring him into much company." Walker urged the governor to "get your charge out of their hands as soon as you can."[17]

The persuasion that irreligion was prominent in fashionable circles induced some commentators to caution young gentlemen with particular insistence to avoid the society of the impious.

Forming connections with disdainers of religion, Puckle thought, '
was the first step in a falling off from Christianity: "First, they
are corrupted by bad counsel and company, which the Psalmist
elegantly expresses, *by walking in the counsel of the ungodly*
. . . . . Next, they habituate themselves to their vicious practices, which is, *standing in the way of sinners* . . . . . And then,
at last, they take up and settle in a contempt of all religion,
which is, *sitting in the seat of the scornful.*"[18] Dykes too, shar-
ing the current belief that "some modish Gentlemen" spent
their time in "sporting with *Blasphemy* and ridiculing Religion," emphasized "the Keeping of better Company and Conversation, than that of profligate *Atheists,* foolish Deists, or
lewd Libertines,"[19] who, by their example, would turn innocent
youths into facsimiles of themselves.

Even Chesterfield, although he paid little regard to the efficacy of the world in helping to form a virtuous gentleman,
was worried about the influence of evil company on his son,
warning him not to model himself after the exponents of the
so-called "genteel vices" (gaming, drunkenness, and affairs with
low women) who were to be found in the most fashionable
society. Chesterfield did not recommend that young Philip shun
fashionable society, since it was the "best" company in his
opinion and conferred many benefits, such as giving a gentleman a knowledge of the court-world and a graceful, well-bred
air. Like Osborn, however, he was aware of the practical advantage of preserving a spotless reputation, and he therefore
advised his son to imitate the merits, not the follies, of his
companions:

When a young man, new in the world, first gets into that
company, he very rightly determines to conform to and
imitate it; but then he too often, and fatally, mistakes the
objects of his imitation. He has often heard that absurd
term of genteel and fashionable vices. He there sees some
people who shine, and who in general are admired and
esteemed; and observes that these people are whore-masters,
drunkards, or gamesters; upon which he adopts their vices,
mistaking their defects for their perfections, and thinking
that they owe their fashion and their lustre to those genteel

vices. Whereas it is exactly the reverse, for these people have acquired their reputation by their parts, their learning, their good breeding, and other real accomplishments; and are only blemished and lowered, in the opinions of all reasonable people, and of their own, in time, by these genteel and fashionable vices. (IV, 1241-42.)

At a university, where a youth met individuals of all sorts, he was inevitably exposed to vicious society. Theorists therefore took particular care to caution the university student against contracting friendships with fellow undergraduates of sinful tendencies. One is reminded of the Man of the Hill in *Tom Jones*, whose acquaintance with Sir George Gresham at Oxford led him into a life of debauchery. "I have known sundry young men sent up to the University," Grenville informed his nephew, "of very towardly Dispositions, and sweet Inclinations," youths who "might have become . . . considerable Instruments of good unto the World and great Props to Religion," but whose characters had been corrupted and destroyed by "Pernicious Example, and Diabolick Advice." In describing their decline, Grenville used the same Biblical allusions which Puckle was later to employ:

> [They] have been prevailed on at length to Enter into the ways of Darkness, and afterwards to *walk in the Counsel of the ungodly,* and at last to *stand* so boldly *in the way of Sinners* that they have in a short time Arrived to the Scorners Chair; that is, have become desperate Sinners, Villains of the first Magnitude, the very Pests of a Kingdom, open Opposers of Religion and Vertue, perfect Renouncers of God and goodness . . . in so egregious a manner, that it will be difficult to find out for them, in former Ages, even among Turks and Pagans, any Parallel.[20]

Bentham, though less violent in his terminology, warned the university student of quality that "a vicious man cannot be made an associate, without forfeiture of reputation, and danger to your virtue." He was especially concerned about the temptations offered to a well-born undergraduate by social inferiors who flattered him and catered to his vices from selfish ulterior motives. Such persons could ruin a genteel youth, for they were "ever ready to attend him in his diversions,—to encourage him in his follies,—to join in the ridicule of college-discipline, and to vilify the assertors of it as men of narrow thinking, low breeding, and ignorance of polite life."[21] The unknown author who wrote for the *Connoisseur* No. 82 (August 21, 1755) a supposed letter of advice to a gentleman entering a university provided a good imitation of actual letters of this kind. He graphically portrayed scorners of religion, gamesters, and drunkards as unsavory undergraduate types which should be the objects of particular avoidance.

The world as an aspect of education was thus viewed as entailing more threats to the gentleman's virtue than any other factor in his upbringing. Indeed, some theorists, especially from the mid-eighteenth century onward, maintained that the world characteristically made the young gentleman vicious rather than virtuous. "Gentlemen," said the anonymous author of *An Essay on Modern Education* (1747), ". . . vainly call the Ribaldry of a Debauch, Conversation, and the Ways of the Town, seeing the World" (page 7). According to Colman and Thornton in the *Connoisseur* No. 136 (September 2, 1756), "the knowledge of the world, as it is generally used and understood, consists not so much in a due reflection on its vices and follies, as in the practice of them." This attitude, of course, constituted the extremist position; as we have seen, many educational theorists, even in the mid-eighteenth century, contented themselves with merely cautioning the well-born youth to beware of the world's temptations. The view of the world as a predominantly evil influence was, nevertheless, the natural outgrowth of the common conviction that society *could* incline a gentleman to vice. It should not be supposed that the writers most aware of the world's perniciousness would have denied the young gentleman all worldly experience. Their moral objections to such experience, however, are significant of a reaction not only against the fashionable emphasis on a knowledge of the world but also against the importance accorded such knowledge by previous theorists.

They were particularly opposed to an early introduction to the world—to the aristocratic belief, voiced by Shaftesbury in Hurd's *Dialogues on the Uses of Foreign Travel*, that "so important a study [as the world] cannot be enter'd upon too soon, and that the rudiments at least of this science cannot be laid in too early" (pages 52-53). In their opinion, a participation in the world should be delayed until a gentleman was sufficiently mature and had acquired enough strength of character to prevent him from falling an easy prey to the evil examples and counsel he would encounter in society. Simply exhorting him to shun noxious company was not effectual, they felt; in the innocence of youth, he probably did not have the sagacity necessary to distinguish between company which was noxious and that which was not. Genteel parents were blameable, critics thought, for throwing their sons headlong into a world which would almost certainly corrupt them. J. A. Home complained in the *Mirror* No. 15 (March 16, 1779) that many youths were "introduced into the world almost from their very infancy," so that "the first knowledge they acquire is of the vices with which they are surrounded; and they learn what mankind are, without ever knowing what they ought to be." In such boys, he affirmed, "youth is not the season of virtue; they have contracted the cold indifference and all the vices of age, long before they arrive at manhood."

We saw in the preceding chapter that some commentators, especially those writing in the middle and later eighteenth century, considered learning more important than knowledge of the world. They sometimes did so from the persuasion that studies fortified a young gentleman against the wicked influence of the world and that if he was kept at his books long enough, the virtuous sentiments derived from them would help him to combat the temptations inevitable to social intercourse. Home, in the *Mirror* No. 15, relied on the moral efficacy of classical studies to support his claim that such studies were a necessary, though often vilified, part of education; they armed a young gentleman, he believed, against the world's enticements to sin. Colman and Thornton, speaking of learning in a broader sense, declared in the *Connoisseur* No. 136:

They, who have lived wholly in the world, without regarding the comments on it, are generally tainted with all its vices; to which the gathering part of their instructions from books would perhaps have proved an antidote. There, indeed, though they would have seen the faults and foibles of mankind fairly represented, yet vice would appear in an odious, and virtue in an amiable, light: but those, who unwarned go abroad into the world, are often dazzled by the splendor with which wealth gilds vice and infamy; and, being accustomed to see barefoot honesty treated with scorn, are themselves induced to consider it as contemptible.

Such a view was, of course, a direct contradiction of the theory, discussed earlier, that books could teach a man nothing about the world, that experience was the only tutor in worldly knowledge.

A high regard for study as an antidote to the immoral influence of society was evident in Johnson's disapproval of the fashionable mother who introduced her son into the world at a very early date because she did not wish him to acquire his tutor's awkward manners. As the tutor remarked in the *Rambler* No. 132, the young nobleman soon lost his taste not only for learning but for virtue. In No. 195 (September 2, 1751), the youth's opening adventures in the world were recounted. He consorted with a crowd of rowdy gentlemen, joined with them in creating so much disturbance at the theatre that they were beaten into silence by an irate audience, became intoxicated with his cronies at a tavern, took part in a drunken brawl and in an equally drunken battle against the chairmen, gambled recklessly, and incurred the sad consequences of gaming, until " 'he returned from a petty gaming-table, with his coat torn, and his head broken; without his sword, snuffbox, sleeve-buttons, and watch.' " In other words, he threw himself into the favorite diversions of fashionable young hell-raisers of the period, and he would probably progress from these to worse offenses. All of this could have been prevented, Johnson implied, if his studies had not been cut short prematurely in order that he might be made acquainted with the world.

Even when critics did not name study explicitly as a preserver of virtue, they painted a grim picture of the consequences of exposing a young gentleman to the world before he was adequately prepared for it. Chapman, for example, asserted that "before a boy be made acquainted with the sentiments and the manners of men, he should be taught how to estimate them. Without this preparation, he will be in danger of mistaking their follies for reasons." Lacking mature judgment, he was an easy convert to vice and, moreover, was deceived into a high admiration for mere exterior ornament and surface splendor: "If we would preserve a young man from a slavish attachment to show, and from the misery of a mistaken ambition, we should not carry him to brilliant assemblies, nor present to him the pomp of courts, or the magnificence of palaces, nor set before him the outside of things, till we have taught him how to estimate them; for that would be to deceive and corrupt him."[22] As will be demonstrated in Chapter VI, the strongest objection to the fashionable practice of sending youths abroad during adolescence was that a gentleman in his teens was too immature to resist the worldly temptations he would encounter on his tour.

Hurd was one of the most violent opponents of the aristocratic notion, expressed by Shaftesbury in the *Uses of Foreign Travel,* that an early initiation into the world was very desirable. Voicing his own opinions through the mouth of Locke, he described in detail what happened to the young gentleman whose early education had inspired him with virtuous sentiments but who, with no other preparation than this, was all at once exposed to the world. As an eloquent example of one point of view, the description deserves to be quoted in its entirety:

> Full of these sublime ideas, which his Parents, his Tutors, his Books, and even his own ingenuous Heart has rendered familiar to him, the fatal time is at hand, when our well-instructed youth is now to make his entrance into the world: But, good God, what a world! not that which he has so long read, or dreamt of; but a world, new, strange, and inconsistent with all his former notions and expectations.
>
> He enters this scene with awe; and contemplates it with

astonishment. Vice, he sees assured, prosperous, and tri-
umphant; Virtue, discountenanced, unsuccessful, and de-
graded. He joins the first croud, that presents itself to him:
a loud laugh arises: and the edge of their ridicule is turned
on Sobriety, Industry, Honesty, Generosity, or some other of
those qualities, he has hitherto been most fond of.

He quits this clamorous set with disdain; and is glad to
unite himself with *another,* better dressed, better manner'd,
in all respects more specious and attractive. His Simplicity
makes him for some time the Dupe of this plausible society:
but their occasional hints, their negligent sarcasms, their
sallies of wit, and polite raillery on all that he has been
accustomed to hold sacred, shew him at last that, tho' he
has changed his company, he has not mended it.

This discovery leads him to another. He attends to the
lives of these well-bred people, and finds them of a piece
with their manners and conversation; shewy indeed and,
on first view, decorous: but, in effect, deformed by every
impotent and selfish passion; wasted in sloth and luxury;
in ruinous play; criminal intrigues; or, at best, unprofitable
amusements. (Pages 132-134.)

The consequences of this disillusioning experience were either
that the young gentleman would become as contemptuous of
virtue as his associates or that, like Fielding's Man of the Hill,
he would turn into a misanthrope.

The alternative to so ill-advised an introduction into the
world was not only to "keep him out of that world, as long as
you can," but also, when he did finally enter it, to "let the
ablest friend or tutor lend him his best experience to conduct
him gradually, cautiously, imperceptibly into an acquaintance
with it." Hurd gave explicit directions as to the nature of the
guidance which was to be provided for the young gentleman
during the early stages of his participation in the world, instructing the friend or tutor

To take the veil off from some parts [of the world], and
leave it still upon others: To paint what he does not see,
and to hint at more than you paint: To confine him, at
first, to the best company, and prepare him to make allow-

ances even for the best: To preserve in his breast the love of excellence, and encourage in him the generous sentiments, he has so largely imbibed [from his earlier education], and so perfectly relishes; yet temper, if you can, his zeal with candour; insinuate to him the prerogative of such a virtue, as his, so early formed and so happily cultivated; and bend his reluctant spirit to some aptness of pity towards the ill-instructed and the vicious: By degrees to open to him the real condition of that world, to which he is approaching; yet so as to present to him, at the same time, the certain inevitable misery of conforming to it: Last of all, to shew him some examples of that vice, which he must learn to bear in others, tho' detest in himself; to watch the effect these examples have upon him; and, as you find his dispositions incline, to fortify his abhorrence of vice, or excite his commiseration of the vicious: In a word . . . to inform the minds of youth with such gradual intelligence as may prepare them to see the world without surprize, and live in it without danger. (Pages 139-141.)

Only when it was so treated could worldly experience be said to hold little hazard as a aspect of the gentleman's education. Otherwise, according to Hurd and many of his serious-minded contemporaries, a participation in society was likely to destroy all the good effects of his previous training in virtue.

Notes to Chapter IV

1. *Advices to a Young Man of Fortune and Rank,* p. 15.
2. *Uses of Foreign Travel,* p. 53.
3. *Thoughts on Education,* p. 70.
4. *Compleat Gentleman,* 2nd Treatise, pp. 1-2.
5. *Dialogues Concerning Education,* I, 18.
6. *Letters,* III, 1080, 1156-57.
7. *Dignity of Human Nature,* p. 166.
8. Nathaniel Lancaster, *The Plan of an Essay upon Delicacy* (London, 1748), pp. v, viii-ix.
9. Hurd, *Uses of Foreign Travel,* p. 52.
10. For further discussion, see Ustick, "Advice to a Son: A

Type of Seventeenth-Century Conduct Book"; Mason, *Gentle-folk in the Making*, pp. 61-63, 223-227; and Siegmund A. E. Betz, *Francis Osborn's "Advice to a Son,"* in *Seventeenth Century Studies*, 2nd Ser., ed. Robert Shafer (Princeton, 1937), pp. 54-56.

11. *Thoughts on Education*, pp. 68-69.

12. *Rules of Good Deportment, or of Good Breeding. For the Use of Youth*, in *Works* (Edinburgh, 1877), I, 55.

13. *Advice to a Son, Directing him How to demean himself in the Most Important Passages of Life*, 4th ed. (London, 1716), p. 138. 1st ed. was 1656-58.

14. *Vox Clamantis*, pp. 57-58.

15. See Brokesby's *Directions to Young Students* (subjoined to his *Letter of Advice*), p. 27, and Dykes's *Royal Marriage*, pp. 6-8.

16. *A Letter to a Young Gentleman upon his Admission into the University* (London, 1753), p. 11.

17. *Of Education, Especially of Young Gentlemen*, pp. 45-46.

18. *Club*, pp. 62-63. The consecutive periods are the text's, not mine.

19. *Royal Marriage*, pp. 7-8.

20. *Counsel and Directions*, pp. 56-57. See also Penton, *Guardian's Instruction*, pp. 55-56.

21. *Advices to a Young Man*, pp. 14-16.

22. *Treatise on Education*, pp. 172-173.

CHAPTER FIVE

Good Breeding as an Aim in the Gentleman's Education

A definition of what the Restoration and eighteenth century meant by good breeding is necessary before we consider this quality as an object in gentlemanly education. Good breeding embraced many diverse elements. The well-bred man, for example, had to possess the attributes mentioned in Steele's portrait of the ideal gentleman in the *Guardian* No. 34 (April 20, 1713): "When I view the fine gentleman with regard to his manners, methinks I see him modest without bashfulness, frank and affable without impertinence, obliging and complaisant without servility, cheerful and in good-humour without noise." He was also supposed to have correct table manners and graceful carriage; he was to employ the proper forms of address and to treat ladies with due honor; he was to show respect toward superiors, amiability toward equals, and graciousness toward inferiors; he was not to boast, talk lengthily or out of turn, discourse on topics alien or boring to his hearers (as a pedant might), utter coarse, obscene remarks, or repeat gossip and otherwise disparage persons not present. The multifarious instances of good breeding, however, shared one element in common, and it was upon this element that a definition of the quality was based.

The common denominator of all instances of good breeding was that they afforded pleasure to others. Profanity and obscenity were ill-bred because they were offensive; as Puckle said, "Such language grates the ears of good men."[1] A graceful air, on the other hand—Chesterfield's *"je ne sais quoi"*—was a component of good breeding because, embodying a certain beauty, it created a pleasing impression. Table etiquette, removing one's hat, making a leg, and the other conventions of politeness had as their *raison d'être* the fact that they were more agreeable than were boorish, awkward manners. The definition of good breeding given by Fielding in his *Essay on Conversation* (1743) was therefore the generally accepted one in the age: "In short, by good-breeding . . . I mean the art of pleasing, or contributing as much as possible to the ease and happiness of those with whom you converse."[2]

Chesterfield's conception of good breeding as "*l'art de plaire*" is well known. He was forever exhorting his son "to be very well bred; without which, you will be a very disagreeable, unpleasing man, though you should be an honest and a learned one."[3] By his predecessors as well as his contemporaries, good breeding was understood as the art of pleasing. Said Aurelia in Farquhar's *Twin-Rivals*: "I take good manners to be nothing but a natural desire to be easy and agreeable to whatever conversation we fall into; and a porter with this is mannerly in his way, and a duke without it has but the breeding of a dancing-master" (Act II, scene i). The very titles of works on good breeding indicate the widespread interpretation of the term as the process of rendering oneself agreeable or pleasing. For example, Colonel Forrester's *Polite Philosopher* (1734) was subtitled: *An Essay on that Art which makes a man happy in himself, and agreeable to others.* In 1736 John Ozell translated, as *The Art of Pleasing in Conversation,* an anonymous French treatise on good breeding, *L'Art de plaire dans la conversation* (Paris, 1688), an earlier translation of which had appeared in 1691. An anonymous English book about the conduct of the well-bred man in company appeared in 1738, bearing the title *The Conversation of Gentlemen considered In most of the Ways, that make their mutual Company Agreeable, or Disagreeable.*

Johnson preferred to alter the customary definition, stating in the *Rambler* No. 98 (February 23, 1751): " 'The true effect of genuine politeness seems to be rather ease than pleasure.' " Though Johnson obviously meant the two to be different, "ease" was apparently construed by most other writers simply as a form of pleasure, and the term was often used in conjunction with "pleasure" or "agreeableness" to define good breeding, as in several of the preceding citations. The distinction between promoting ease and promoting pleasure is too fine to be of much significance, and, Johnson to the contrary, most authors who spoke of good breeding as the art of setting people at ease merely had in mind one of its pleasurable effects.

Even cynical definitions of good breeding recognized it as the art of pleasing. According to Bernard Mandeville's sarcastic account of the origin of good breeding, primitive man discovered that society would be intolerable if each person demonstrated to the full his love for himself and his antipathy toward everybody else, and thus, in order to make his social environment more pleasant, he evolved the practice of concealing his self-liking and flattering others, on the assumption that his fellows would do the same. The custom became known as good breeding and was developed to its present "Pitch of Insincerity." It worked for the benefit of all concerned; by means of it, Mandeville declared, "we assist one another in the Enjoyments of Life, and refining upon Pleasure; and every individual Person is rendred more happy by it, in the Fruition of all good Things he can purchase, than he could have been without such Behaviour."[4] Horace Walpole's interpretation of good breeding, expressed in the *World* No. 103 (December 3, 1754), was equally cynical but relied just as much on the idea of pleasing: "It is not virtue that constitutes the politeness of a nation, but the art of reducing vice to a system that does not shock society. Politeness, as I understand the word, is a universal desire of pleasing others, that are not too much below one, in trifles, for a little time; and of making one's intercourse with them agreeable to both parties."

The second factor in a definition of good breeding, at least in the eighteenth century, was that well-bred actions were generally placed in one of two categories, which, for purposes of convenience, may be called ceremony and civility, terms which were often applied to them during the period under consideration. Ceremony comprehended the externals of politeness, such as table manners, forms of address, and the modes of conduct observed in a particular fashionable society. "For example," Chesterfield wrote to his son, "it is respectful to bow to the King of England; it is disrespectful to bow to the King of France; it is the rule to courtesy to the Emperor; and the prostration of the whole body is required by eastern monarchs" (V, 1938). People versed in this kind of good breeding, Johnson said in the *Rambler* No. 98, "know . . . at what hour they may be at the door of an acquaintance, how many steps they must attend him towards the gate, and what interval should pass before his visit is returned." The acts of ceremony were arbitrarily established; they "exist in form only," as Fielding declared, "and have in them no substance at all . . . being imposed by the laws of custom." Even so, however, they were necessary because they pleased; thus the forms of address "must be preserved by good-breeding, because . . . they raise an expectation in the person by law and custom entitled to them, and who will consequently be displeased with the disappointment."[5] Since they were dependent on custom only, they varied from place to place, "the good-breeding of Rome differing in some things from that of Paris," as Chesterfield explained: "that of Paris, in others, from that of Madrid; and that of Madrid, in many things from that of London" (IV, 1433). They also varied from age to age—so much, in fact, that "a man who travels," according to Swift, "must needs be at first a stranger to them in every court through which he passes; and perhaps at his return, as much a stranger in his own."[6]

Civility, on the other hand, was composed of those actions which a man performed not because the usages of a particular place and time told him that they would please, but because they were universally pleasing. They were permanent rather than transitory; they could be depended on to create an agreeable impression all over the world rather than just at a certain court or capital; they had their foundation in the laws governing human nature rather than in loco-temporal conditions. Demonstrations of amiability and affability belonged under civility as they were sure to please anywhere at any period. Boastfulness, obscenity, and captiousness were manifestations of incivility because they just as generally displeased.

The distinction between the two types of well-bred acts was

so common in the eighteenth century that writers employed quite similar terms to describe it. The "modes" or ceremonies of good breeding, Chesterfield asserted, "vary according to persons, places, and circumstances . . . but the substance of it [or civility] is everywhere and eternally the same" (IV, 1428). Reynolds remarked in terms reminiscent of Chesterfield: "The general principles of urbanity, politeness, or civility, have been ever the same in all nations; but the mode in which they are dressed, is continually varying."[7] Said Goldsmith in Letter No. 39 of his *Citizen of the World*: "Ceremonies are different in every country; but true politeness is everywhere the same."

In the Restoration the distinction appeared occasionally, though not nearly so often as in the eighteenth century. Walker in 1672 drew the following contrast:

> Civility is not . . . *punctuality of behaviour*: I mean that which consists in certain modish and particular ceremonies and fashions, in clothes, gesture, mine, speech, or the like; is not using such discourses, words, phrases, studies, opinions, games &c. as are in fashion in the Court; with Gallants, Ladies, &c. This is a constrain'd *formality*, not *civility;* a complying with the times, not with persons; and varieth with the age or season frequently . . . whereas the rules of *Civility,* founded upon Prudence and Charity, are to perpetuity unchangeable.[8]

Although Walker perhaps included more under ceremony than did later writers, his differentiation between ceremony and civility anticipated the remarks of eighteenth-century authors.

While there was thus no unwavering standard to which acts of ceremony could be referred, there definitely was one for acts of civility. Lancaster made this clear in 1748. In his dialogue between two philosophically inclined gentlemen, one of the gentlemen was disturbed because good breeding appeared to have no standard at all, seeming "to depend entirely upon prevailing customs, which are of so unsettled a nature, that they are ever varying with the complexion of times and climates. . . . How then," he asked, "can there be any settled principle, to direct our judgment concerning a thing so vague and incon-

stant?" The other speaker, however, assured him that he had
in mind only the kind of politeness which "relates . . . to
certain forms and ceremonies." Whereas he admitted that these
"have no other value but what they derive from the fashionable
world," other instances of good breeding, he held, must derive
from a universal standard, above and beyond the arbitrary forms
of etiquette. "If this were otherwise," he argued; "on what
principle do we claim a right to draw comparisons between the
politeness of different countries, and give the usages and customs of one, the preference to those of another?" In the usual
terms, he described the manifestations of civility as depending
"not on the caprice of fashion, or the varying complexion of
times and climates." The standard on which they were based
was "that universal humanity, common and natural to all mankind; which is the ground of our love and hatred, the guide
of our approbation and dislike."[9]

The concept of civility, with its recognition that all men,
despite individual differences, were governed in their reactions
of pleasure or displeasure by laws fundamental to human nature,
obviously bore a close relationship to the doctrine of univer-
sality or uniformitarianism which influenced so many areas of
thought in the eighteenth century.[10] It was also closely related
to the ideal of cosmopolitanism. The man who practiced civility
was a citizen of the world, equally polite at London and at
Lisbon. The man devoted to ceremony, on the other hand, was
exclusively a citizen of one particular country, and his forms of
etiquette served no function in other nations, where they might
even be considered very ill-bred. Civility was recognized as an
aspect of cosmopolitanism by many authors, as several of the
preceding citations may suggest. It was clearly regarded as such
by Goldsmith in Letter No. 39 of his *Citizen of the World*:

> Ceremony resembles that base coin which circulates through
> a country by the royal mandate: it serves every purpose of
> real money at home, but is entirely useless if carried abroad;
> a person who should attempt to circulate his native trash
> in another country would be thought either ridiculous or
> culpable. He is truly well-bred who knows when to value
> and when to despise those national pecularities which are

regarded by some with so much observance: a traveller of
taste at once perceives that the wise are polite all the world
over, but that fools are polite only at home.

Since civility embraced the essentials of good breeding whereas ceremony comprehended only its externals, commentators naturally inclined to place the former much above the latter. This
tendency, evident in the remarks of Goldsmith quoted above,
was particularly noticeable in Swift, who devoted much of his
Treatise on Good Manners and Good Breeding to ridiculing
"unfortunate proselytes to ceremony," such as the individual
who informed Prince Eugene, just arrived from abroad, that he
could not possibly be ushered into the presence of Queen Anne
"with a tied-up periwig." "I have seen a duchess fairly knocked
down," Swift observed, "by the precipitancy of an officious
coxcomb running to save her the trouble of opening a door."[11]
It was perhaps because of his extremely low opinion of the
externals of good breeding that in *Gulliver's Travels* he said
of the Houyhnhnms: "They preserve decency and civility in the
highest degree, but are altogether ignorant of ceremony" (Part
IV, chap. viii). Other writers, however, realized that although
ceremony was superficial, no one in fashionable society could
disregard it unless he was willing to acquire the reputation of
a boor. A nonconformity to the current modes of etiquette was,
in Fordyce's estimation, "no less folly than ill-manners," although marks of incivility were far more serious, approaching the
immoral.[12] Chesterfield's stress on ceremony was prompted by
an awareness that even though many of its customs were "bien
ridicules" and "inventées par des sots," those who did not
observe them would be pointed out as possessing "une singu-
larité affectée" (VI, 2867).

The particular modes of fashionable courtesy could, obviously,
not become known to a young gentleman except through training of some sort. Ceremony was therefore viewed as a product
of education; untaught peoples, such as the barbarians of Africa
and the New World, possessed little of it, although they very
likely had an essential civility. As a child, the young gentleman
could be informed of the fundamentals of ceremony by his

parents and governor; they could instruct him in how to act at the table, teach him the accepted formulas for expressions of gratitude or polite response to questions, tell him when to bow and when to remove his hat. These lessons could be commenced quite early; thus Petrie advised parents: "You may begin to teach Children from three Years old some easy Rules of good Manners; likewise . . . to make their Honours gracefully, &c."[13]

Directions on ceremony, furthermore, were often contained in courtesy books. Gailhard's *Compleat Gentleman* provided lessons in table manners, and Walker's *Of Education, Especially of Young Gentlemen* laid down rules for table etiquette and for visiting. There were, besides, treatises exclusively on good breeding which amounted to textbooks in the subject, such as *The Rules of Civility*[14] in the seventeenth century and, in the eighteenth, Petrie's *Rules of Good Deportment* (1720) and Nevelon's *Rudiments of Genteel Behaviour* (1737). Typical of the instructions in them were the following, issued by Petrie:

> In *France* it is ordinary to be covered at Meat, yet it is ordinary to discover when a Superior drinks to them, with a humble Bow; yet this Ceremony is not used with Equals, a Bow being sufficient.
> In *Britain* and *Ireland* it is usual to be uncovered at Table. (Page 83.)

> Some think it rude to sit with their Back towards the Picture of an eminent Person: For my part I see no Reason for that Fancy; for there are some Rooms that are surrounded with such Pictures, so as there would be no sitting in them. (Page 27.)

As a young gentleman grew older, he could learn the finer points of ceremony, such as the more complicated usages of a particular court, the ways for addressing persons of certain ranks, and the little politenesses to be observed towards ladies, through a participation in fashionable society. These refinements were acquired, in Chesterfield's terms, "by observation and experience" (V, 1428)—by watching what the most polished people did and following their example. The world was, in fact, by far the best educator in ceremony, as it afforded a youth living models after whom he could pattern himself and by whom mistakes in etiquette would not pass unnoticed. "Mothers . . . in *Italy*," Walker said with approval, ". . . send their Children frequently in errands, and visits to their kinred or neighbours; teaching them what to say, what titles to give, what answers to make to the demands most likely to be asked" (page 214).

The relationship of civility to an educative process is much less clear. One might assume that if civility concerned those reactions which all men shared in common, a gentleman needed only to rely on his own reactions of pleasure or displeasure in order to determine what would be universally pleasing and what would not. Indeed, this assumption was frequently made. In his *Plan of an Essay upon Delicacy,* Lancaster postulated an "internal sense of DECORUM" which corresponded with that of humanity at large. "The criterion . . . of DELICACY in any action," he maintained, ". . . is the sure feeling and consciousness of its conformity to a like natural sensation within us" (pages 68, 60). This is reminiscent of Shaftesbury's concept of "taste," or an inner sense by which men knew right from wrong; the inner sense in Lancaster's argument was that by which men knew what was most pleasing and decorous. Chesterfield clearly considered one's own reactions as the arbiter of the universally pleasing. "Un tel vous plaît par tel endroit," he told his son; "examinez pourquoi, faîtes comme lui, et vous plairez par le même endroit aux autres" (IV, 1743). The Golden Rule was thus most appropriate to civility. " 'Do as you would be done by,' " he declared to young Philip, "is the surest method that I know of pleasing. Observe carefully what pleases you in others, and probably the same things in you will please others" (III, 1035). Fielding similarly affirmed in his *Essay on Conversation*: "*Good-breeding* . . . is expressed two different ways, viz., in our actions and our words, and our conduct in both may be reduced to that concise, comprehensive rule in Scripture: *Do unto all men as you would they should do unto you.*"[15]

If this was true, it would seem that no education in civility was necessary.

Closely allied to a reliance on one's own reactions was a reliance on good sense, common sense, or reason to determine the universally well-bred. Indeed, if a man followed his own reactions on the matter, he was acting according to good sense. Lancaster therefore related comeliness of conduct "to common sense" (page 66) as well as to an inner recognition of decorum, and Chesterfield described civility as occurring "to every man of common sense" (IV, 1433). If modes of behavior conflicted with common sense or were unreasonable, they were not generally pleasing and, according to the more idealistic writers on good breeding, deserved little consideration; thus Steele declared in the *Spectator* No. 75 (May 26, 1711): "What is opposite to the general rules of reason and good sense, must be excluded from any place in the carriage of a well-bred man." Again, no education in polite conduct would seem to be necessary in order for a man to be universally well-bred; obeying the dictates of his reason was apparently sufficient. Swift referred to civility as "good manners" and called ceremony "good breeding," implying that ceremony was the result of training (or breeding) whereas civility arose naturally. He insisted that while "study and labour" were essential to the attainment of the former, "a tolerable degree of reason will instruct us in every part of good manners, without other assistance." Almost belligerent on this point, he announced: "I defy any one to assign an incident wherein reason will not direct us what we are to say or do in company, if we are not misled by pride or ill nature." A participation in society, so important to learning ceremony, was not educative to civility, he thought, for "no man will behave himself ill for want of experience; or of what, in the language of fools, is called knowing the world."[16] Courts, the centers of fashion and consequently the best places in which to become acquainted with ceremony, were in his opinion "the worst of all schools to teach good manners."[17]

It is surprising, in the light of such declarations as these, that civility was often regarded as the product of some educative process, as an acquirement for which some instruction was necessary beyond one's own reactions or the injunctions of reason. Yet such was undeniably the case. That it should have been true in the Restoration, when the distinction between the two types of good breeding was not clearly made, is not to be wondered at, but it was also true in the eighteenth century. Commentators on good breeding customarily provided directions for universally well-bred conduct as well as for etiquette, stating and restating the eternal rules—that a gentleman should avoid brusqueness and boisterousness, that he should suit his conversation to the tone and ability of the company, that he should not evince a critical, egotistical, or scandalmongering temper, that he should praise others rather than insult them. Such writers evidently assumed that an individual was not entirely capable of determining for himself the uniformly pleasing, or at least that outside aid could be advantageous to him. Even authors who stressed reliance on one's own reactions and on common sense considered education very important in the development of civility. Swift definitely did not, but Chesterfield and many others certainly did. Often, perhaps, they were unaware of any inconsistency between the theory that civility was of natural occurrence and the theory that education helped to form it. There were, however, several quite plausible reasons for assigning education a place in the fashioning of the universally well-bred gentleman.

One of these reasons involves an interpretation of civility not heretofore discussed. We noted earlier a couple cynical definitions of good breeding, ascribing it to selfish motives. The majority of commentators maintained, on the contrary, that good breeding, in its essential and universal aspects, originated in a sincere desire to make life pleasant for others—that it was, in fact, a manifestation of good nature. In Letter No. 39 of his *Citizen of the World,* Goldsmith termed genuine politeness "the result of . . . good-nature" as well as of good sense. According to Chesterfield, civility was "practised by a good-natured American savage as essentially as by the best-bred European" (IV, 1433). Addison, in the *Spectator* No. 169 (September 13, 1711), called good breeding "nothing else but an imitation and

mimicry of good-nature, or in other terms, affability, complaisance, and easiness of temper reduced into an art." For
that reason, he said, a man whose civility was not "founded upon
a real good-nature" was a hypocrite, and the discovery of his
hypocrisy would make him detested. Civility thus became a
byproduct of moral instruction. If a young gentleman's parents,
tutors, and governors made him good-natured by means of a
virtuous education, he would be motivated by the wish to
afford happiness to others through social intercourse, and he
would, in consequence, possess true civility. Without the heart-
felt desire to give others pleasure—with a primarily malevolent
disposition—his reactions and his reason would be of small use.
This view was current in the seventeenth century as well as in
the eighteenth. Thus Locke in *Some Thoughts Concerning
Education* said with reference to the young gentleman's education in civility: "Be sure to keep up in him the principles of
good-nature and kindness." A child, he believed, should be
taught little about "punctilios, or niceties of breeding," as the
more essential elements of courtesy were dependent soley on an
inbred good nature provided by virtuous training. He declared:
"Want of well-fashioned civility in the carriage, whilst civility
is not wanting in the mind (for there you must take care to
plant it early), should be the parent's and tutor's least care,
whilst they are young" (page 47).

Some authors did more than call good nature the fountain
of civility; they seemed to consider the civil act and the virtuous act as identical. Steele perhaps approached this attitude
in the *Spectator* No. 75, wherein he described a man who
passed for being very well-bred but who was actually very ill-
bred because his manners were not grounded in virtue. This
portrait was followed by a sketch of a truly well-bred gentleman, all of whose actions "have their rise in him from great
and noble motives." The conclusion was that "the more virtuous
the man is, the nearer he will naturally be to the character of
genteel and agreeable." One anonymous author stated flatly
that good breeding was " 'all moral virtues in epitome.' "[18] In
Petrie's *Rules of Good Deportment,* incivility and sinfulness
were synonymous. "It is sinful and ill Breeding," Petrie said,

"to lie." "It is unjust and uncivil in Magistrates to oppress their Subjects." "Gluttony is both a rude and uncivil Vice and Wickedness." Being of a somewhat Puritanical spirit, he even announced: "It is undiscreet [i.e., ill-bred] and sinfull to use such Plays and Recreations as the Community or Body of which we are Members look upon as sinfull" (pages 54, 115, 90, 103). According to such a view, all training in virtue was also training in civility. By recalling the moral and religious lessons which he had received as a child, and perhaps consulting his reactions or common sense in order to determine how best to apply them, a gentleman would be essentially well-bred. Petrie's advice on how to instruct children in good breeding therefore contained such exhortations as this: "Above all, let all Diligence be used to teach them the Fear of the Lord, and the Fundamentals of Religion." The Scottish theorist declared: "If Principles of Civility are timeously implanted in Children, the Practice thereof will be so far from being difficult and hard, that it will be familiar and connatural to them. I wish Parents, from whom they have derived their Corruption and Irregularity of their Morals, would use their uttermost Endeavours to sow the Seeds of Virtue in their Souls" (pages 4, 2-3).

Petrie's position, however, represented an extreme. According to a far greater number of commentators, the world was at least as significant an agent in education to civility as was moral and religious training. The notion that a participation in society was educative to true good breeding was quite characteristic of the Restoration. Gailhard counseled the young gentleman on his travels to associate with persons of rank, "of whom he will learn a gentile, and a good behaviour."[19] A gentleman's civility had to be refined upon, carried to the highest degree of politeness. It had to be, in Panton's words, "this polished Civility that gives us the reputation of being Gentlemen" and that was to be encountered "only in tractable spirits that have been carefully cultivated, and educated, thereby being furnished with those precepts to live in the World."[20] Since most Restoration authors did not define civility exactly as did eighteenth-century theorists, their emphasis on learning it through worldly experience did not pertain entirely to learning the universals.

Walker, however, who did anticipate the eighteenth-century definition, referred to civility as one of "the most usual occurrences in *Active life*. Such as enter not into any Art or Science, but are the result of experience in the conversation and affaires of this World" (page 209).

The assumption that civility was acquired by means of a participation in a polite society was inherited by the eighteenth century from English courtesy writers of the preceding age and also from French authors, such as Bellegarde, whose *Reflexions upon Ridicule* was translated into English six times between 1706 and 1764, usually together with his *Reflexions upon the Politeness of Manners*. Certain writers, of course, questioned the contribution of worldly experience to true civility; Swift, we remember, firmly denied that the world, and courts in particular, could teach anything about good manners. Perhaps more typical of eighteenth-century opinion, however, was Colonel James Forrester's pronouncement, with reference to good breeding, that "the World is a great School, wherein Men are first to learn, and then to practice."[21]

A high regard for society as educative to civility did not entirely conflict with the conception of civility as natural to all men and as ascertainable by the use of one's reactions or reason. Even though the fundamentals of courtesy belonged to both an American savage and a French courtier, the courtier had made his courtesy wellnigh infallible by spending his life in polite circles. Civility was, after all, a social phenomenon. The reactions on which one relied to determine the universally pleasing arose in company; a man secluded from society had little opportunity to consult them or to put his good sense to use. Chesterfield therefore urged his son to look for the laws of good breeding "in company, and renounce your closet till you have got them" (IV, 1740). Participation in society required the unremitting performance of acts of civility, so that universally pleasing conduct gradually became habitual to a gentleman and he no longer had even to pause and consider what would be agreeable and what would not. "As soon as we have gained Knowledge [of civility]," Forrester affirmed, "we shall find the best way to improve it will be *Exercise*." Through frequentation of company, *"Politeness,* by an imperceptible gradation, will enter into our minutest Actions, and give a Lustre to every Thing we do." In addition to "exercise" (or practice), careful observation of the reactions of those about him to certain kinds of behavior also helped a gentleman to arrive at a notion of invariably pleasing conduct. Having described many acts which were instances of incivility rather than of mere unceremoniousness, Forrester declared: "I have explained *Politeness* negatively: If you would know it positively, you must seek it from Company and Observation."[22] Common sense in itself was not sufficient; a man had to take scrupulous note of what everybody around him did and felt before he could attain the highest reach of civility. "Good-sense can only give you the great outlines of good-breeding," Chesterfield told his son; "but observation and usage can alone give you the delicate touches and the fine colouring" (IV, 1488).

Observation partook in eminent degree of that primary aim of a participation in the world, the study of human nature. The better acquainted a gentleman was with the characteristics of mankind, the more adept he would be at pleasing. "In the common manners of social life," Chesterfield explained, "every man of common sense has the rudiments, the ABC of civility; the means not to offend; and even wishes to please." More than the rudiments, however, were necessary to make a gentleman not only "received and tolerated in good company" but "desired," "loved," and "courted," as a gentleman should be. The successfully polite man was one who, through observation of human nature, knew "the various workings of the heart, and artifices of the head; and who by one shade can trace the progression of the whole colour; who can, at the proper times, employ all the several means of persuading the understanding, and engaging the heart" (V, 1849-50).

Courts were the best places in which to learn good breeding, according to Chesterfield, who was thus at the farthest remove from Swift. At Dresden, the first court which Chesterfield's son visited on his tour, the youth evinced a tendency to speak impudently and derogatorily about various professions and nationalities—a clear mark of incivility. But his father assured him:

"The frequentation of Courts checks this petulancy of manners; the good-breeding and circumspection which are necessary, and only to be learned there, correct those pertnesses. I do not doubt but that you are improved in your manners, by the short visit which you have made at Dresden; and the other Courts, which I intend that you shall be better acquainted with, will gradually smooth you up to the highest polish" (III, 1147).

The good breeding practiced at courts was, in Chesterfield's view, often a mask for feelings of animosity, and he adjured his son to watch courtiers closely in order to see "how politely they can differ, and how civilly they can hate" (V, 1703). For Chesterfield, therefore, good breeding involved that dissimulation which he considered so important a lesson of the world. He was thus at odds with theorists who ascribed more significance to the notion that true good breeding originated in good nature, in an unselfish desire to please. Furthermore, his recommendations of good breeding, whether they entailed dissimulation or not, had a basis in self-interest, in a recognition that charming manners were indispensable to success at court. "You must be sensible that you cannot rise in the world," he informed his son, "without forming connections and engaging different characters to conspire in your point. . . . Those necessary connections can never be formed or preserved but by an uninterrupted series of complaisance, attentions, politeness" (IV, 1435). This utilitarian conception of good breeding was undoubtedly one reason why Chesterfield's letters were so severely condemned, in the late eighteenth century, by men more idealistic than he.

We have so far been dealing exclusively with the well-bred act. Also included under good breeding, however, was a genteel and pleasing demeanor. Petrie in his *Rules of Good Deportment* described this demeanor in its rudimentary aspects:

A Gentleman ought not to run or walk too fast in the Streets, lest he be suspected to be going a Message; nor ought his Pace be too slow; nor must he take large Steps, nor too stiff and stately, nor lift his Legs too high, nor stamp hard on the Ground, neither must he swing his Arms backward and forward, nor must he carry his Knees too close, nor must he go wagging his Breech, nor with his Feet in a straight Line, but with the In-side of his Feet a little out, nor with his Eyes looking down, nor too much elevated, nor looking hither and thither, but with a sedate Countenance. (Pages 6-7.)

Be careful what Gestures or Motions of the Body you use, especially in speaking; see that it be decent, not accompained [sic] with nodding, shaking of the Head, or looking a skew, or wry Mouth'd, moving the Hands, &c. (Pages 58-59.)

The well-bred demeanor was an esthetic way of doing everything, a graceful air, a comeliness of execution—the "graces" or the "je ne sais quoi" of which Chesterfield so often spoke. It was to be a part of every action of the gentleman and was to be observed even when he was in a state of inaction, simply standing in a room or sitting in a chair. It was a decorative quality, rendering more attractive the solid merit which it adorned. In fact, beauty of performance set off to advantage even a gentleman's virtue and knowledge. "Without it," Hurd remarked, "his improvements of other sorts would be almost thrown away; nay his virtues themselves would be offensive and unlovely."[23] Although a man might have correct sentiments as to the conduct of life, Lancaster maintained in his *Plan of an Essay upon Delicacy,* "something still is wanting; some additional grace, to make truth and virtue operate with full success." Correct sentiments could not "gain us the love of mankind, without AN HAPPINESS OF MANNER" (page 80). Chesterfield was well aware of this, and consequently of the practical advantages of the well-bred air. He counseled his son: "Adorn yourself with all those graces and accomplishments, which, without solidity, are frivolous; but without which, solidity is, to a great degree, useless." The man possessing "a very moderate degree of knowledge" but a graceful bearing would be much more successful than the man possessing "sound sense and profound knowledge" but little grace (IV, 1493). If an exquisite demeanor embellished virtue and learning, it also embellished the very act of civility or ceremony. A farmer or shopkeeper who performed such an act was in essence well-bred, but a courtier was much better bred because he performed it with a charm which made it infinitely more pleasing.

Many theorists did not, of course, draw any explicit distinction between the matter and the manner of good breeding, and their usage of such terms as "air," "polish," "politeness," "behavior," "demeanor," "conduct," and "manners" was so broad and ill-defined that it is impossible to determine precisely what they were referring to, if, indeed, they themselves had any clear notion. Often, however, a distinction was implied in their remarks, and some writers did differentiate lucidly between the two elements of good breeding. In *Some Thoughts Concerning Education,* for example, Locke described the well-bred manner as "that decency and gracefulness of looks, voice, words, motions, gestures, and of the whole outward demeanour which pleases in company," and termed such demeanor "the language whereby that internal civility of the mind is expressed" (page 111). Although Chesterfield was not always unambiguous on the subject, he made the difference most intelligible when he informed his son: "The worst-bred man in Europe, if a lady let fall her fan, would certainly take it up and give it to her; the best-bred man in Europe could do no more. The difference, however, would be considerable; the latter would please by doing it gracefully; the former would be laughed at for doing it awkwardly. I repeat it, and repeat it again, and shall never cease repeating it to you, air, manners, graces, style, elegancy, and all those ornaments, must now be the only objects of your attention" (IV, 1680). With Chesterfield, as, perhaps, with others who associated good breeding principally with courts, the well-bred manner at times assumed so much importance as to render the matter negligible.

Graceful, exquisite manners were the peculiar mark of a gentleman, setting him apart from the unpolished multitude; they were, as Chesterfield said, "the distinguishing characteristics of men of fashion; people of low education never wear them so close but that some part or other of the original vulgarism appears" (IV, 1254-55). They constituted the aspect of good breeding in which a dancing master provided such useful instructions. Even more valuable than a dancing master's lessons, however, was a participation in society. Through watching and imitating the carriage of others, the young gentleman could acquire a finish of execution. The graces were, said Puckle, "attainable only by company and conversation, and," he added "chiefly by that of ladies: by observing the care and pains they take to please, only to out-shine each other."[24] Locke, whose conception of a polished air as the superficial manifestation of internal civility seems to have led him to identify it with what the Augustans termed ceremony, declared that this beauty of manner, "being very much governed by the fashion and custom of every country, as other languages are, must, in the rules and practice of it, be learned chiefly from observation, and the carriage of those who are allowed to be exactly well-bred" (page 111). The assumption, denied by no one, that a comely air could be attained only in the world provides another reason why many theorists considered civility in its highest form as the result of some educative process. Even if a young gentleman's own reactions or common sense dictated the act of civility, he could not perform that act in the most graceful and pleasing way until experience and observation had taught him how to do so.

The more fashionable a young gentleman's associates were, the more charm of execution he would learn from them. Thus Locke said it was "impossible, that any one should come forth well-fashioned out of unpolished, ill-bred company" (page 78). "Such as is his company," Locke affirmed, "such will be his manners. A ploughman . . . that has never been out of his parish . . . will be as soon in his language, as his carriage, a courtier; that is, in neither will be more polite than those he uses to converse with" (page 112). For this reason as for others, Chesterfield thought experience at court essential to the education of his son. "You want nothing now, thank God," he told young Philip, "but exterior advantages, that last polish, that *tournure du monde,* and those Graces which are so necessary to adorn and give efficacy to the most solid merit. They are only to be acquired in the best companies" (IV, 1529).

The scholar's awkwardness in society was largely attributable to the fact that, secluded as he was from the world and particularly from courts, he had little chance to observe the manners of fashionable people. Untutored by polite company, he was *gauche* rather than graceful; his performance of good breeding was ludicrous rather than elegant. The "cloistered pedant," Chesterfield remarked in the *World* No. 148 (October 30, 1755), necessarily possessed little polish of bearing, and the "most ridiculous and most awkward of men are . . . the speculative well-bred monks of all religions and all professions," who theorized about good breeding without having seen it in practice. Lancaster advised the learned man to associate with persons of quality, as he would learn "from their demeanor, which is comely in manners," and would gain "that genteel graceful dignity of expression, which is peculiar to those who move in the higher spheres of life."[25]

It was sometimes believed that the country gentleman as well as the scholar was deficient in a refined and elegant air. Living in the rural retirement of his provincial seat, and perhaps consorting mainly with his fox-hunting, hard-drinking, coarse-mannered neighbors, he could scarcely be expected to possess the exquisite mien of those who moved in the *beau monde* of the town. This assumption was evident in the contrast between the rude Squire Western and his sister, who prided herself on courtly refinement. Steele, in the *Spectator* No. 240 (December 5, 1711), portrayed a country gentleman who was essentially well-bred but did not have the delicate manner, and a London gentleman who had acquired at court and in fashionable society " 'a soft air' " and " 'a grace and assurance.' " The country gentleman and his friends found themselves unable to compete with such a fine-mannered person for the favor of the ladies. Steele, however, valued the genuine civility of the rustic gentleman much more than the polished veneer of the Londoner, and his attitude was shared by those who had idealistic notions of good breeding and who emphasized its relationship to good nature and to virtue. It was evident, for example, in Johnson's description, in the *Rambler* No. 147 (August 13, 1751), of the visit of a fine gentleman of London to his nephew, the elder

son of a country squire. The uncle, as a result of his acquaintance with fashionable society in town, was well versed in " 'all
the strategems of endearment,' " but he practiced the manner
of good breeding to the exclusion of the matter. His nephew
observed with considerable despair:

"I soon discovered that he possessed some science of graciousness and attraction which books had not taught, and of
which neither I nor my father had any knowledge; that he
had the power of obliging those whom he did not benefit;
that he diffused, upon his cursory behavior and most
trifling actions, a gloss of softness and delicacy by which
every one was dazzled; and that by some occult method
of captivation, he animated the timorous, softened the
supercilious, and opened the reserved. I could not but
repine at the inelegance of my own manners, which left
me no hopes but not to offend, and at the inefficacy of
rustic benevolence, which gained no friends but by real
service."

Johnson seemed to consider fine manners, in such a man as the
uncle, an excrescence of good breeding, if not a hypocrisy.

Notes to Chapter V

1. *Club,* p. 44.
2. *Works,* ed. William E. Henley (London, 1903), XIV, 249.
3. *Letters,* II, 505.
4. *The Fable of the Bees,* ed. F. B. Kaye (Oxford, 1924),
II, 145, 147; see 127-149.
5. *Essay on Conversation,* in *Works,* XIV, 252-253.
6. *A Treatise on Good Manners and Good Breeding,* in
Prose Works, XI, 84.
7. *Discourses* (London, 1924), p. 125. From Discourse No.
VII.
8. *Of Education, Especially of Young Gentlemen,* p. 212.
9. *Plan of an Essay upon Delicacy,* pp. 65-68. See also Fordyce,
Dialogues Concerning Education, I, 46-47.
10. For a discussion of this relationship, see George C. Brauer,

Jr., "Good Breeding in the Eighteenth Century," Univ. of Texas *Stud. in Eng.,* XXXII (1953), 25-44. This article contains much of the illustrative material used in the present chapter.

11. *Prose Works,* XI, 81-83.

12. *Dialogues Concerning Education,* I, 47.

13. *Rules of Good Deportment,* ed. cit., pp. 3-4.

14. This book was a translation of a French work. For discussion of it see Mason, *Gentlefolk in the Making,* pp. 261-263; Virgil B. Heltzel, "*The Rules of Civility* (1671) and its French Source," *MLN,* XLIII (1928), 17-22; and W. L. Ustick, "Seventeenth Century Books of Conduct: Further Light on Antoine de Courtin and *The Rules of Civility,*" *MLN,* XLIV (1929), 148-158. Ustick relates the book to treatments of forms and ceremonies rather than to treatments of true civility.

15. *Works,* XIV, 249. See also *Covent-Garden Journal* No. 55 (July 28, 1752).

16. *Treatise on Good Manners and Good Breeding,* ed. cit., pp. 83, 79.

17. *Hints on Good Manners,* in *Prose Works,* XI, 87.

18. "Thoughts on Education, by Way of Introduction," in *The Pleasing Instructor: Or, Entertaining Moralist,* 6th ed. (London, 1768), p. ii, n.

19. *Compleat Gentleman,* 2nd Treatise, p. 74.

20. *Speculum Juventutis,* pp. 149-150.

21. *The Polite Philosopher: Or, An Essay on That Art, Which Makes a Man happy in Himself, and agreeable to Others,* in *The Magazine of History with Notes and Queries,* XXI, Extra No. 83 (Tarrytown, N. Y., 1922), 123.

22. *Ibid.,* pp. 123-124.

23. *Uses of Foreign Travel,* p. 47. Hurd put this statement into Shaftesbury's mouth rather than Locke's; with his stress on the intrinsic value of virtue and learning, he probably wished that the observation had less point.

24. *Club,* p. 82.

25. *Plan of an Essay upon Delicacy,* pp. v, vii.

CHAPTER SIX

The Place of Travel in the Education
of the Gentleman

The aims of the gentleman's education have now been set forth. This and the succeeding chapter will treat, from the standpoint of educational theory, certain educational practices in their relationship to those aims.

Among the most significant of these practices was that of sending the young gentleman on a tour of the Continent as part of his training. Men of rank in the Restoration and eighteenth century, like their Renaissance ancestors,[1] deemed the grand tour an invaluable aspect of their sons' upbringing. Ramesey, a courtesy writer of good family, affirmed in 1672 that "Travel . . . will be requisite to experience, and accomplish a *Gentleman*."[2] The esteem which Chesterfield had for the tour is demonstrated by the fact that he kept his son abroad from 1746 to 1751. Shaftesbury, whom Hurd employed to express the genteel attitude, was made to say that " 'FOREIGN TRAVEL is, of all others, the most important and essential part of Education.' "[3] The tour of the Continent grew increasingly popular throughout the eighteenth century, until the sons of squires as well as of noblemen customarily went abroad and until even the sons of merchants, in imitation of those persons of quality with whom they wished to be identified, visited the nations of Europe. Most educational theorists, including many who were not well-born, endorsed the fashionable opinion that travel was necessary to the finished gentleman. Its educational advantages were many.

Because the young tourist associated with a wide variety of people, foreigners and fellow travelers alike, a voyage to the

Continent was lauded as an introduction to a knowledge of the world, providing those lessons which participation in society was peculiarly constituted to teach. Gailhard's belief that young gentlemen should learn "how to know the world" prompted him to advise parents to "send them into Foreign parts." On his tour, Gailhard said, a well-born youth would acquire an understanding of mankind and of prudential conduct: "When a man is abroad, he studies the temper of men, and learns their several fashions; he becomes a fit companion for every one, he observes the good and evil of others, he knows how to avoid tricks put upon men."[4] Although Locke viewed "the knowledge of men" as "so great a skill, that it is not to be expected a young man should presently be perfect in it," he nevertheless declared that "his going abroad is to little purpose, if travel does not somewhat open his eyes, make him cautious and wary, and accustom him to look beyond the outside."[5] A similar attitude obtained in the eighteenth century; the perceptive man, as Burgh remarked, "returns from foreign parts improved . . . in useful knowledge of men and manners."[6]

With many aristocrats, the acquisition of a knowledge of the world was a strong motive for sending sons abroad. One essayist, for example, described a fashionable mother who, under the persuasion that her son already had a " 'comprehensive knowledge of all book-learning,' " decided " 'that it was now high time he should be made acquainted with men and things; that she had resolved he should make the tour of France and Italy.' "[7] Chesterfield was perhaps the most enthusiastic exponent of this aristocratic attitude. Nearly all his remarks to his son on a knowledge of the world were written while young Philip was making the grand tour. In a letter wherein Chesterfield listed the purposes of travel, he informed his son: "The characters, the heads, and the hearts of men are the useful science of which I would have you perfect master."[8]

As an aspect of worldly experience, travel taught good breeding. On the grand tour the young gentleman was supposed to visit courts and associate with the "best" or most fashionable company, from which he could learn foreign ceremonies, the highest civility, and a graceful air. The ideal gentleman, Steele averred in the *Guardian* No. 34 (April 20, 1713), "must travel . . . to fashion and polish himself." An admiration for France as the seat of politeness was already prominent in the Restoration and, of course, continued through the eighteenth century. Gailhard in 1678 praised "that French Breeding so much approved of" and said that other countries sent their young gentlemen to France in order that they might acquire this elegance of manners.[9]

Since Gailhard was a Frenchman by birth, he may conceivably have been prejudiced in favor of the manners of his homeland, but even native Britons affirmed that the average Frenchman possessed more polish than the average Englishman. In fact, the Englishman who had not traveled was often viewed as egregiously boorish, perhaps not lacking in an essential civility but devoid of that pleasing comeliness of demeanor which should accompany the well-bred act; he was, as one seventeenth-century author observed, "supposed to be . . . *Rough* in *Address*, not easily acquainted, and *blunt* even when he obliges."[10] This assumption was not uncommon among persons of quality, who hoped that in foreign countries, France above all, their sons would lose their national clumsiness and take on a refined air. In his *Uses of Foreign Travel*, Hurd put into Shaftesbury's mouth the disparaging remark that Englishmen were "considered by the rest of *Europe*, as proud, churlish, and unsocial. . . . And if . . . we cherish, and not correct, those manners . . . let us not take it amiss that foreigners distinguish us by such names." The only means of correction, Shaftesbury implied, was a tour of the Continent; in fact, "it seems . . . to be an inevitable consequence of what has been said, that we of this country have a more than ordinary occasion for the benefits of *foreign travel*" (page 36). Although Hurd himself did not approve of the view expressed here, he evidently considered it typical of English aristocrats. It was certainly held by Chesterfield. "How many men have I seen here [in England]," he wrote his son, "who, after having had the full benefit of an English education, first at school and then at the university, when they have been presented to the King, did not know whether they stood upon their heads or their heels!" (III, 1151). The French, unlike the English, had attained to the highest degree of polish, in his opinion. "There is hardly a French cook," he announced, "that is not better bred than most Englishmen of quality" (II, 526). He trusted that travel would rid his son of "the English crust of awkward bashfulness, shyness, and roughness" (III, 877).

A visit to the nations of the Continent also gave a young gentleman a facility in the modern languages. He was not to rely exclusively on his native tongue in his conversations with foreigners, but to use German with Germans and French with Frenchmen. One author in the Restoration even specified that a language should be learned in the particular city where it was spoken most correctly, recommending Valladolid for Spanish, Florence or Siena for Italian.[11] In the seventeenth century this fluency in foreign languages was viewed as part of the preparation for a political career. "The Languages he hath learned in his travels," Gailhard said in his *Compleat Gentleman*, "I would have him not to forget, but rather to practice upon all occasions, both by reading and speaking; for they are . . . qualification necessary to a Statesman, or to any employed in publick Affairs" (Second Treatise, page 177). During the eighteenth century, when political service was less strongly emphasized for gentlemen, a knowledge of the modern languages, French in particular, seems to have been valued by persons of quality chiefly as a fashionable acquirement, and young gentlemen who had been abroad adorned their conversation with French phrases as a mark of having received a genteel education. But the desirability of a skill in the modern languages for a career of statesmanship was not entirely forgotten. Thus Chesterfield told his son: "You cannot conceive what an advantage it will give you, in negotiations, to possess Italian, German, and French, perfectly, so as to understand all the force and *finesse* of those three languages" (IV, 1538). Hurd, however, who disputed the value of travel on nearly all counts, questioned the importance of learning foreign languages abroad. Although he conceded that it was usually an object of the grand tour, he felt that it left the young gentleman little time "for accomplishing himself in those other studies, which . . . are of much greater importance." Languages, in Hurd's opinion, belonged among "such things as he may very well do without, or, at best, are of an inferior and subordinate consideration: While the branches of learning, he must neglect for these, are of the most constant use and necessity to him in the commerce of his whole life" (pages 88-89).

Travel widened the scope of the young gentleman's practical knowledge, affording him much information of a factual and useful nature by acquainting him with the customs, characteristics, and cultures of various nations, their politics, forms of government, military establishments, religious beliefs, educational facilities, trade, and manufactures. The acquirement of this timely kind of information was reckoned the principal aim of travel for young gentlemen during the Renaissance, when its obvious appropriateness to future service of the state was stressed.[12] It received somewhat less attention after the Renaissance, but it was still an important aim of travel during the Restoration, and courtesy writers of the period discussed it in detail. Leigh, for example, said in the first of his *Three Diatribes* that the gentleman touring a foreign country should observe its geographical features, commodities, products, and defects, "the Manners, Shape, Language and Attire of the People, their Building, their Havens and Harbours, the Religion and Government, the History of the Countrey and Families," the courts of princes, the courts of justice, "Libraries, Colledges, Disputations and Lectures where they are, Shipping and Navies . . . Exchanges, Burses, Ware-houses . . . Training of Soldiers, and the like" (pages 7-8). A list comparable to that of Leigh was provided in 1672 by Ramesey, who deemed it advisable for the gentleman-traveler to "keep an account in writing, of every dayes Observation, wherever he goes,"[13] a practice advised by later writers also. Walker, in the same year, called it an advantage of travel "to *learn* the . . . Laws, Customes, and understand the Government, and interest, of other Nations,"[14] and Gailhard's *Compleat Gentleman* gave the following

directions to the youth abroad who had just entered a town
strange to him:

> When you walk up and down the streets, if any remarkable
> thing be obvious, desire to be informed of it, enquire about
> the most potent Families, whether noble or not, of their
> Charges, Estates, and Interest in the place; then ask by what
> Trade or other means the Town or City doth chiefly sub-
> sist, and what are the customs and temper of the Inhabi-
> tants; afterwards of the policy, and of the way and form of
> Government; not forgetting to know how far doth reach the
> power and authority of the Clergy, what are the Priviledges
> of the City and Citizens, what difference is amongst them,
> and what are the Prerogatives of the Nobility and Gentry.
> (Second Treatise, page 36.)

Theorists in the Restoration did not always mention how
advantageous this kind of information would be to the gentleman as statesman, although writers such as Walker and Gailhard, who made much of the gentleman's obligation of serving
his nation in a public capacity, must have had its political
usefulness in mind. During the eighteenth century the gathering
of factual data about foreign countries was still less frequently
given a political significance, but authors apparently felt that
even if a gentleman never exploited it in a career of statesmanship, it at least contributed to make him well-informed, to
furnish him with the unscholarly kind of knowledge which
he was to possess. Besides, advocating it had been a tradition
for so long that commentators on travel were reluctant to omit
all reference to it from their directions to young tourists. It
therefore continued to be named as one of the most important
objects of the tour. " 'Certainly,' " said the author of the
Spectator No. 364 (presumably the Earl of Hardwicke), " 'the
true end of visiting foreign parts is to look into their customs
and policies, and observe in what particulars they excel or
come short of our own.' " Puckle, Dr. John Hawkesworth, and
Burgh, the last of whom recommended keeping a travel notebook, were among those eighteenth-century writers who deemed

making sucn investigations a very significant duty of the young gentleman abroad.[15] Fordyce's instructions to the traveler illustrate the strength of the tradition as late as the mid-eighteenth century:

> Let him study . . . chiefly the natural, political, and commercial state of countries: let him inspect their manufactures, magazines, arsenals, work-houses, and their special regulations; examine their natural produce and foreign import, the price of their markets, the rise, fall, and revolutions, or [sic] their trade . . . let him, in short, if he has leisure or abilities for it, study the improvements they have made in arts, sciences, and in any part of government or trade.[16]

Some eighteenth-century authors, like earlier writers, must have valued the acquirement of this information for its political usefulness. It certainly had a political purpose with Fordyce, who considered public spirit so important an object of education, and also with Priestley,[17] whose system of education was in large degree designed to equip young gentlemen for service of the state. Chesterfield, reminiscent of a prior period in many of his beliefs, clearly regarded travel as preparation for a political career because it afforded a factual knowledge of the Continental nations. "Your destination is political," he told his son; "the object, therefore, of your inquiries and observations should be the political interior of things; the forms of government, laws, regulations, customs, trade, manufactures, etc., of the several nations of Europe" (IV, 1756). When Philip entered a new country, his father specified the particular information he should seek there. At Berlin, he should investigate "the present state of the civil, military, and ecclesiastical government of the King of Prussia's dominions," inquire into the strength and composition of the army, and acquaint himself with Frederick's legal reforms (IV, 1294). In order to stimulate his son to make such investigations, Chesterfield frequently demanded reports on what he had discovered, questioning him, for example, as to the government of Switzerland and the church, government, and military establishment of Saxony.[18] Like other commentators, he thought a travel notebook very useful, and he explained in detail what this notebook should contain:

> You will . . . do well, while you are in Germany, to inform yourself carefully of the military force, the revenues, and the commerce of every Prince and State of the Empire, and to write down those informations in a little book kept for that particular purpose. To give you a specimen of what I mean:
>
> THE ELECTORATE OF HANOVER
>
> The revenue is about £500,000 a year.
>
> The military establishment, in time of war, may be about 25,000 men; but that is the utmost.
>
> The trade is chiefly linens, exported from Stade.
>
> There are coarse woollen manufactures for home consumption.
>
> The mines of Hartz produce about £100,000 in silver, annually. (III, 1111-12.)

Travel permitted the young gentleman to view antiquities, relics, curiosities, and works of art, and examining such objects was held to be a subsidiary purpose of his tour, helping to render him a man of cultivation. An interest in this kind of sight-seeing arose, of course, in the late Renaissance, when the cities of Italy were admired as the repositories of ancient art and when gentleman-connoisseurs such as the Earl of Arundel and Sir Kenelm Digby brought classical works of art back to England. Examining ruins, monuments, sculptures, paintings, and even collections of coins and gems continued to be recommended for the tourist in the Restoration and eighteenth century,[19] though with progressively less force and frequency than in the Renaissance. The author of the *Spectator* No. 364 put unusual emphasis on investigating the places in which classical authors lived and wrote, believing that the spots would inspire young minds to emulate the virtues of these authors. Chesterfield called to his son's notice the "many valuable remains of the remotest antiquity, and many fine pieces of the *antico moderno*" (IV, 1360) which were to be found at Venice. The attitude of many fashionable travelers, however, probably re-

sembled that of the young gentleman in an anonymous poem
entitled "Dialogue *between a* Beau *and a* Scholar." Here the
scholar, with the enthusiasm of one in his profession, asked the
beau, just returned from abroad:

> But tell me, (since you've seen each foreign coast,)
> What precious stores can learned Gallia boast?
> Or say what treasures Italy imparts,
> The mother and the nurse of social arts?
> What brass or Parian statues noblest shine?
> What ancient tomb, or consecrated shrine?
> What stately column, scorning vales below?
> What animated scenes on canvas glow?

But the beau, whose time abroad had been amorously employed,
replied with considerable scorn:

> A comfortable task for youthful Squires—
> To view the crest-fall'n remnants of their sires?
> . . . .
> Can proud antiques, those dear-bought, trifling toys,
> Resemble happier youth's substantial joys?
> . . . .
> 'Tis strange that men of greatest learning prize
> A face adorn'd with neither nose nor eyes.
> . . . .
> No charms like these my soaring genius sought;
> Far different scenes engag'd my every thought.[20]

The author of this poem was non-committal on the issue,
simply remarking at the end: "Caetera desunt." And, indeed,
the scholar's emphasis on viewing relics of antiquity and other
artistic masterpieces was as liable to criticism, according to
eighteenth-century commentators, as the beau's utter contempt
for this pursuit. In his *Dialogues Concerning Education,* Fordyce made it clear that "the principal aim of going abroad . . .
is not, in my opinion, to traverse countries in search of curiosities, antiquities, or other monuments of learning; or to improve
one's taste by studying the most elegant and finished models
of art, either ancient or modern" (II, 274). This kind of sight-

seeing was valuable in moderation, but, like the polite accomplishments, it was in the main a diversion, and indulging
in it to excess detracted from the more useful and important
objects of travel, such as gathering timely information. Chesterfield therefore cautioned his son, who was about to visit Rome:
"When you are there, do not imagine that the Capitol, the
Vatican, and the Pantheon are the principal objects of your
curiosity. But, for one minute that you bestow upon those,
employ ten days in informing yourself of the nature of that
government, the rise and decay of the Papal power, the politics
of that Court . . . and, in general, everything that relates to
the interior of that extraordinary government" (IV, 1416).

The young English gentleman was thought by some commentators to be not only unpolished in his manners but also
insular in his ideas, the victim of many national prejudices
which resulted in an extreme narrow-mindedness and short-
sightedness. The grand tour was often viewed as the corrective
to his insularity. By visiting foreign countries and mingling
with their citizens, the Briton could broaden his mind and
become a cosmopolitan. Thus Puckle in *The Club* suggested
that those who passed their lives in one place were provincial
but that travel "enlarges all the faculties, and takes off that
narrowness of mind" (page 47). In laying down the requirements for the ideal gentleman in the *Guardian* No. 34 (April
20, 1713), Steele specified that he "must travel . . . to get
clear of national prejudices, of which every country has its
share."

Eighteenth-century men of fashion were particularly prone
to extol travel for cosmopolitanizing the gentleman. Fordyce
therefore had Eugenio, an aristocratic student, express the view
that there were "national . . . prejudices, to be rooted out,"
an "attachment to our own manners and customs . . . which
savours something of antient barbarity" and which must be
destroyed before one could approach "the true standard of a
fine gentleman." A man could do away with his provincialism,
Eugenio said, only by "enlarging his views beyond his own
country, studying foreign manners, and conversing with men
of different nations and interests, in those places where they

are to be seen in their truest lights" (II, 273-274). Hurd made
Shaftesbury, spokesman of the aristocracy, argue for the necessity of travel on these grounds. Shaftesbury regretted the tendency of all the inhabitants of one country to acquire "one
uniform prevailing character," spoke contemptuously of "the
idiot PREJUDICES of our home-bred gentlemen," and lauded
travel for acquainting them with "other combinations and
societies; that so, as their views enlarge, they may be enabled
to shake off their local, as we may say, and territorial prejudices."[21] One of Chesterfield's motives for sending young Philip
abroad was to cosmopolitanize him. Through traveling, and
through "frequenting good company in every country," Chesterfield held, a young gentleman "himself becomes of every
country; he is no longer an Englishman, a Frenchman, or an
Italian, but he is an European" (V, 1939).

Notwithstanding all the praise of travel as an aspect of
gentlemanly education, there was considerable awareness of its
defects. Adverse criticism of travel was, of course, not new
with the Restoration; the Circe passages in Ascham's *Schole-
master* and Bishop Joseph Hall's *Quo Vadis?* are perhaps the
best known but certainly not the only serious attacks on travel
produced in the Renaissance. In some respects, then, Restoration
and eighteenth-century objections to touring Europe were a
continuation of a long-established tradition, though with changes
of direction and emphasis.

Most critics of travel were not gentlemen themselves but
rather members of the middle class, often educators or clergymen. To a degree, therefore, their views may be regarded as
illustrating the conflict between gentlemanly ideals and the
ideals proposed for gentlemen by other orders of society, a conflict already evident with respect to learning. As the preceding
pages have indicated, however, a great number of non-aristo-
cratic commentators were conscious of the benefits of travel;
and very few of them condemned it on all counts, even though
they may have attacked certain aspects of it. Furthermore,
gentlemen themselves sometimes animadverted against elements
in the tour. Consequently, the disparity between men of quality

and critics, while it no doubt existed, must not be overestimated.

The first body of criticisms to be examined consists of those leveled at young travelers themselves rather than at the institution. They did not constitute objections to travel *per se* but merely to its abuses. According to some authors, the young gentleman abroad was frequently very negligent of what was still one of the most important purposes of his tour, gathering timely, factual information about foreign countries. He possessed little more knowledge at his return, they said, than he had at setting out. It may be conjectured that some parents of rank, who sent their sons to the Continent largely because it was fashionable to do so, were not especially disturbed if the tour contributed little to the youths' store of information. Others, however, who held a more serious view of travel, were probably dismayed to find their sons not profiting intellectually from the years on the Continent. Thus Chesterfield concurred with non-genteel commentators in deploring such abuse of the tour.[22]

The young traveler who returned in a state of comparative ignorance was much satirized. Boyer, for example, included in his *English Theophrastus* a sketch of a beau who brought back from the Continent no more than "the nicest cut Suit, and the prettiest Fancied Ribbands for Sword-Knots." His stay in France was exceedingly uninformative: "All the knowledge he has of *France*, or Manners in it, consists in an imperfect Idea of *Versailles*, St. *Cloud, Fountainbleau*, St. *Germains*, and the *Louvre*, and in the keeping of the Valet that follow'd him hither" (page 52). Puckle in *The Club* described a tourist who, although he had been abroad for seven years, came back to England supplied only with superficial platitudes about foreign countries and cities—that "Constantinople was the storehouse of Greece, Paris the metropolis of France, Venice the eye of Italy, Florence the seat of beauty." He had been told that "the Low Countries, for war, traffic, and learning, were all Europe in Amsterdam print: but, confound Mars, Mercury, and Minerva"—in other words, confound all investigation of military affairs, trade, and learning. His seven years abroad had been wasted in drinking and carrying on amours: "Bacchus and Venus were his delight" (pages 45-46).

Despite the popularity of the cosmopolitan ideal among men of fashion, a great many young eighteenth-century English gentlemen had a contempt for everything foreign, an unalterable conviction that nothing on the Continent was worthy of notice. They traveled with closed minds, scornfully refusing to concern themselves with Continental ideas, politics, economics, and religions, "insolently despising foreign manners and customs, merely because they are foreign," as an unknown author declared in the *World* No. 22 (May 31, 1753). Most in need of the cosmopolitanizing influence of travel, they resisted it most strongly and, in the process, sacrificed the opportunity of gaining useful, practical knowledge of the countries of Europe.

Thomas Gordon wrote for his *Humourist* an essay entitled "Of Travel, misapply'd," which presented a vivid picture of such a tourist. This prejudiced traveler, appropriately named Oliver Gape and supposed to be the son of a country squire, went abroad accompanied by a servant from home called John, who was a victim of the same prejudice and who fortified him in it. In a letter to his father, Oliver had little to say about Holland except that England possessed more timber than the Netherlands and "sweeter Butter, especially in the *May*-Month, and our *John* says the same." He assumed that the Dutch were not Christians because, unlike the English, they had no bishops; but he made no effort to examine the Dutch church since it was "all Dissenters and Presbyterians, and so I did not go to church because they be all *Scismaticks,* which is as bad as *Popish Idolatry,* and our *John* don't like either of them." When he reported on France, his antipathy toward foreigners and his consequent lack of all real knowledge about them were revealed even more clearly. He disliked the French because "our Beef is fatter than theirs by at least an Inch on the Rib, and they never make any Pudding at all. But they eat Frogs like any mad, and the Devil and all of Onions. Our *John* is heart-sick of their Diet." Having tried no harder to inform himself of religion in France than in Holland, he dismissed Catholicism with the words: "Tho their churches be very brave and neat, yet I likes nothing in them, but the Organs and the Ring of Bells; all the rest is *Popish Idolatry.*"[23] When Oliver's remarks are contrasted with Chesterfield's injunctions to his son, it may be seen how flagrantly the young squire was abusing travel: "Now that you are in a Lutheran country [i.e., Germany], go to their churches, and observe the manner of their public worship; attend to their ceremonies, and inquire the meaning and intention of every one of them. . . . Do the same thing when you are in Roman Catholic countries; go to their churches, see all their ceremonies, ask the meaning of them, get the terms explained to you" (III, 1103-04).

Closely related to a prejudice against foreigners was the practice of associating exclusively with one's fellow countrymen abroad. Obviously, this practice prevented a young gentleman from realizing the principal aims of travel. It was through association with foreigners that a gentleman acquired the ability to speak foreign languages fluently, learned an elegant, polished manner, rid himself of his provincialism, and gained information about the nations of the Continent. In the Restoration, therefore, the young gentleman-tourist was warned to "consort but little with thy own Country-men."[24] If fellow Englishmen on the Continent were "sober and civil Gentlemen," Gailhard said, they "may well be frequented; yet," he added, "with moderation: for one must not be too often with them, which is a hinderance to the end for which we travel abroad."[25] In the eighteenth century, the youthful Briton on the Continent underwent much satire for making few acquaintances except other Britons. Chesterfield, in the *World* No. 29 (July 19, 1753), pictured a young nobleman who, considering the Romans "a parcel of thin-gutted, snivelling, cringing dogs," and disgusted that "none of those Signors speak English," flatly refused to consort with them. Unlike Oliver Gape, this biased aristocrat was accompanied not by an ignorant servant from home but by a conscientious Swiss governor who tried to persuade him to mingle in the Continental society he so much detested, but the youth called him an "impertinent *mounseer*" and complained bitterly that he was "always plaguing me to go into foreign companies, to learn foreign languages, and to get foreign manners; as if I were not to live and die in Old England, and as if good English acquaintance would not be

much more useful to me than outlandish ones." In Chesterfield's opinion, far too many English gentlemen on the Continent were guilty of this attitude. They "go abroad, as they
call it," he told his son; "but, in truth, they stay at home all
that while; for . . . they go into no foreign company, at least
none good; but dine and sup with one another only, at the
tavern" (III,1148). Fearful lest his son thus abuse travel, he even
invented a dialogue showing young Philip the proper way to
decline invitations from other Englishmen to join their groups.[26]

Hurd, violent opponent of the grand tour, tried in his
satirically entitled *Uses of Foreign Travel* to indicate the profit-
lessness of travel by affirming that when young Englishmen took
up residence for a while in some foreign city, their "usual way"
was "to keep at distance from the better company of the place,
and to flock together into little knots and clubs of their own
countrymen" (page 103). Hurd's claim was perhaps not much
of an exaggeration. Dr. John Moore, who in the late 1770's
accompanied the young Duke of Hamilton on the Continent,
estimated that "many English travellers remain four or five
years abroad, and have seldom, during all this space, been in
any company, but that of their own countrymen." Their custom,
he said, was to "form societies or clubs of their own," and in
these exclusive groups they would "confirm each other in all
their prejudices, and with united voice condemn and ridicule
the customs and manners of every country but their own."
Moore entirely agreed with other commentators that "by this
conduct the true purpose of travelling is lost or perverted."[27]

Some young travelers committed their first mistake before
they ever left England. This was the error of neglecting to
acquire a knowledge of their native land, especially of its laws
and constitution. If they did not go abroad equipped with such
knowledge, they would have little basis for comparison when
they came to consider the legal and political institutions of
foreign nations, and consequently their investigation of these
matters would be of small advantage to them. To seek information from travel without first having become acquainted with
British institutions was, according to the author of the *Spectator* No. 364, " 'to build a gaudy structure without any founda-

tion; or . . . to work a rich embroidery upon a cobweb.' "
Priestley demanded: "How can . . . comparison be made, or
any judgment formed of the constitution and laws of other
countries with respect to our own, when that constitution, and
those laws with which they are to be compared, are unknown."[28]
Travel, therefore, afforded an additional reason for the desirability of legal training in the young gentleman's curriculum.
Yet the knowledge of England requisite for travel was not to
be restricted to law and related sciences; Fordyce in his *Dialogues* mentioned as well the "interests, or the manners of his
countrymen" (II, 274), and Sheridan suggested that young
gentlemen "should begin their travels with seeing every thing
that is curious at home," which "would not only enable them
to form a better comparative judgment of things in other
countries" but, by providing them with the conversational
topics in which foreigners were most interested, "would be the
surest means of recommending them to the best society every
where."[29] As a preliminary to travel, however, legal knowledge
was advised more often than information of any other kind.

The most serious abuse of travel, in the eyes of many commentators, was one attributable to fashionable parents rather
than their sons—the custom of sending youths to the Continent
in their middle or later teens, perhaps just after they had completed their training at a public school or had obtained some
learning from a tutor. A number of parents, of course, delayed
the grand tour until a later period, but early travel was very
common. Chesterfield himself endorsed it; his son was only
fourteen when he commenced his travels. "It is evident," Thomas
Sheridan announced, "that there can be no greater evil than
the sending our youth abroad at so improper and dangerous a
season."[30] Sheridan was voicing the opinion of a great many
theorists, for few practices in gentlemanly education were so
unfavorably regarded by the critics. In condemning the custom,
they were not condemning the theory of travel itself, since they
usually admitted that a journey through the Continent could
be valuable if it was made at the right period. They were, however, disparaging travel as actually undertaken by perhaps the
majority of young gentlemen.

A common objection against visiting the Continent during adolescence was that the gentleman in his teens was too young to profit mentally from his tour. His travels should be deferred until "a mature age," as one seventeenth-century author maintained, "when by the help of his foregoing education his Judgment is setled and qualified to make useful observations."[31] "Having no knowledge or experience," Walker pointed out, young gentlemen "cannot advantage themselves abroad, but are there in a kind of amazedness; variety of objects, which they neither understand, nor value, confounding rather than edifying, them."[32] Here, then, was another explanation of why British travelers so often returned from the Continent without having acquired worthwhile information. Even if they did not despise foreign ways and mingled in foreign company, they could not be expected to benefit by their experiences because they were intellectually unable to appreciate or interpret the unfamiliar sights, events, and ideas which crowded upon them. According to the *Spectator* No. 364, the typical English gentleman of sixteen on the Continent spent " 'his time as children do at puppet-shows, and with much the same advantage, in staring and gaping at an amazing variety of strange things; strange indeed to one that is not prepared to comprehend the reasons and meaning of them.' " As Sheridan remarked, "to collect valuable stores of knowledge, and to treasure up wise observations, demands the skill and experience of more advanced years."[33]

Another and perhaps a more important objection to an early grand tour repudiated the fashionable argument that travel was to be commended as an introduction to the world. Social intercourse on the Continent at the age of fifteen or sixteen was held liable to the same kind of criticism leveled in general at a premature exposure to the evils of society; in fact, it was even more censurable because of the circumstances under which the young gentleman abroad entered into company. As an impressionable adolescent, not yet settled in his principles, new to the ways of the world, suddenly placed in strange lands far away from the counsel of his parents, dazzled by meretricious allurements of many varieties, and directly responsible for his conduct to no one except a tutor or governor who might be negligent or even profligate (like the Monsieur Creutzer in Letter XLVII of *Sir Charles Grandison*), the immature gentleman in foreign countries was thought to be an easy prey to temptation. Travel posed no serious threat to virtue, critics believed, if a tourist had already attained moral wisdom and integrity, but, unfortunately, these attainments were beyond the grasp of the youth in his teens. Thus the author of *The Gentleman's Calling*, who fully approved of travel for adult gentlemen, asserted that "the negligence of Governours, or their own headiness, when they find the rein thus slackned," caused adolescent travelers to "run a full career in all debaucht pleasures" (pages 38-39). They lived "licentiously, and not according to the best examples abroad," Walker affirmed; they associated with undesirable company, from which they learned " evilness of manners."[34]

Pope in the *Dunciad* described the youthful British traveler as indulging in vice but assigned no definite cause for his conduct except possibly the carelessness or collusion of his tutor:

Led by my hand [the tutor said], he sauntered Europe
   round,
And gathered every Vice on Christian ground;
. . . .
The Stews and Palace equally explored,
Intrigued with glory, and with spirit whored
                   (IV.311-316.)

Whereas Pope did not explicitly blame the immaturity of the tourist or demand that the adolescent gentleman be kept at home, other eighteenth-century authors were more direct. They did not simply describe; they propagandized. Clergymen were especially vehement. Brown declared that travel was inevitably an invitation to vicious living for the young tourist because his inexperience made him unable to distinguish the admirable from the reprehensible: "For as the uninstructed Youth must needs meet with a Variety of Examples, good and bad, vile and praise-worthy, as his Manners are childish, and his Judgment crude, he will naturally imbibe what is most consentaneous with his puerile Habits. Thus, while Wisdom and Virtue can find no Place in him, every Foreign Folly, Effeminacy, or Vice, meeting with a correspondent Soil, at once take Root and flourish."[35] The central point of Hurd's *Uses of Foreign Travel* was that "so long as *travel* is considered as a part of early tutorage and education, I see nothing but mischiefs spring from it" (page 9). Hurd was firmly convinced that letting unwise, headstrong, and impressionable youths journey away from home and from the guidance of their parents was fatal to their virtue. He put into the mouth of Shaftesbury the view that since vice was to be encountered everywhere it might just as well be encountered on the Continent as in England, but, knowing that Locke had himself written against sending adolescents abroad, he gave Locke the following reply: "Allowing that vice were of every clime, the same every where, and equally malignant, I should still imagine your youth to be safer from the infection at home, under the eye and wing of their own parents or families, than wandering at large in foreign countries, with as little respect of others, as prudence of their own, to guard them from this danger."[36]

Although Leigh in his *Three Diatribes* stipulated that the gentleman should not travel before the age of eighteen or twenty, he did admit that "the years of 14 or 15 are more proper for learning the true accent of any language, and all exercises belonging to the body" (pages 4-5). Grenville was satisfied that his nephew had seen France and Italy at the age of twelve or thirteen.[37] Gailhard too "would have Gentlemen young when they begin to Travel abroad"; he approved of an early tour from the same motives that led other writers to condemn it, thinking that a young traveler would learn more (at least about foreign languages) and would acquire less vice than an older person.[38] Indeed, in the Restoration early travel met with somewhat more approval from theorists than it did in the eighteenth century. It is probable, however, that Gailhard had in mind an age prior even to adolescence, and if this is so, his views, like those of Grenville, were less opposed to the opinions of later commentators than might appear. The worst age for travel was, according to critics, the middle and later teens. If a son was still a child and not yet a youth when he visited the Continent, his tour could not be expected to do much harm to his virtue. Locke in *Some Thoughts Concerning Education* therefore disapproved of making the tour between the ages of fifteen and twenty-one but recommended travel for the boy of from seven to fourteen as well as for the mature man. The earliest period, he believed, was the best in which to learn foreign languages, and at this time also "the tutor may have some authority; neither the stubbornness of age, nor the temptation of examples of others can take him from his tutor's conduct, till fifteen or sixteen." In the latest period, a gentleman was "of age to govern himself, and make observations of what he finds in other countries worthy his notice." It was only in the middle period, when gentlemen were headstrong and uncontrollable youths, that they should not be sent abroad: "To put them out of their parents' view, at a great distance, under a governor, when they think themselves too much men to be governed by others, and yet have not prudence and experience enough to govern themselves: what is it, but to expose them to all the greatest dangers of their whole life, when they have the least fence and guard against them?" (pages 175-176).

In the eighteenth century, however, the earliest period for travel was less frequently taken into consideration by theorists. Even if a pre-adolescent might acquire foreign languages more readily than an older person, the common attitude, as we have seen, was that no immature gentleman could learn a great deal from a visit to the Continent. In fact, critics tended to postpone travel to a later and later date. An anonymous author writing in 1704 considered the age of twenty still too early for travel and was worried about young gentlemen who went abroad at this age to study medicine and law, for, he said, "they acquire neither Virtue nor Learning, but Habits of all sorts of Debauchery, as we are taught by every day's experience."[39] Costeker's *Fine Gentleman* (1732) did not advise the grand tour until a gentleman had been taught at home under a master, attended an academy, gone to a university, and received additional training at a post-university academy (page 50). Fordyce in 1745 wished the tour delayed till a university graduate had spent a year or two in London, where he would gain enough worldly experience to prevent him from erring when he was exposed to the world on the Continent.[40] In 1769, Sheridan proposed an academy for gentlemen who had finished their university studies or who did not plan to attend a university, hoping that such an institution would provide an alternative to making the tour before they were old enough for travel.[41]

Although the foregoing remarks illustrate a conviction on the part of many authors that the grand tour could be unbeneficial and perhaps extremely harmful, even animadversions against travel during adolescence were not, strictly speaking, attacks on travel itself. They did not invalidate the theory that if a visit to the Continent was postponed until adulthood, it could be immensely profitable to a gentleman. There were, however, other criticisms of travel which seemed to strike at the heart of the institution and which may consequently be viewed as the most serious of all objections to the tour.

The mildest of these denied that travel was necessary or useful for obtaining a knowledge of mankind. Hurd was perhaps the most outspoken exponent of this attitude. "If," he said, "by a knowledge of the world, be meant only a knowledge of the external modes and customs of it," it could be learned through travel. But an understanding of the fundamental laws of human nature was usually not a product of the tour, especially when the tourist was still a youth. "He has not so much as the idea of what constitutes *Man*," Hurd argued. "How then should he obtain any real and useful knowledge of the human character?" Travel mught supply him with "matter, at his return, for much unprofitable babble in conversation: But, that he should come back fraught with any solid information concerning men and things . . . is what I can never promise myself from this fashionable mode of Education."[42]

Even if a tourist was mature enough to look deeply into the human heart, the uniformitarian conception of human nature as essentially the same all over the world rendered the study of man a poor excuse for travel; it suggested that a gentleman could discover just as much about mankind in England as on

the Continent. Eighteenth-century novels reflected this conclusion. Harriet Byron's view in Letter XXIII of *Sir Charles
Grandison* surely impressed many of Richardson's contemporaries as a logical one:

> Is not human nature the same in every country, allowing
> for only different customs?—Do not love, hatred, anger,
> malice, *all* the passions in short, good or bad, show them-
> selves by like effects in the faces, hearts, and actions of the
> people of every country? And let men make ever such
> strong pretensions to knowledge from their far-fetched and
> dear-bought experience, cannot a penetrating spirit learn
> as much from the passions of a Sir Hargrave Pollexfen in
> England, as it could from a man of the same, or the like ill
> qualities, in Spain, in France, or in Italy?

The Man of the Hill in *Tom Jones* expressed a similar idea,
declaring that " 'those who travel in order to acquaint themselves
with the different manners of men might spare themselves much
pains by going to a carnival at Venice; for there they will
see at once all which they can discover in the several courts
of Europe' " (Book VIII, chapter xv). His misanthropic conviction that " 'human nature is everywhere the same, everywhere the object of detestation and scorn,' " did not obviate
the attitude that travel was far from indispensable for obtaining
a knowledge of the world.

Fellow Englishmen on the Continent were sometimes thought
to be bad influences, and travelers were counseled to avoid
them for this reason. The Frenchman Gailhard subscribed to
the notion that drunkenness was the peculiar vice of Englishmen abroad,[43] as did also Chesterfield, who described their
alcoholic brawling and riotous conduct.[44] Smollett, in Chapter
XLIV of *Roderick Random,* mentioned a young English lord
abroad who "was so unfortunate as to meet with three of his
own countrymen on their travels, in whose company he committed such excesses, that his constitution failed, and he fell
into a consumption." Far more common, however, was the
view that foreigners constituted the principal source of temptation.

The wide concern over the susceptible English adolescent who was exposed to Continental ways is, in some degree, a testimony to the fear that foreigners provided evil examples. A sizeable body of writers seems to have laid the blame for the contraction of vice not so much on the immaturity of British travelers as on the wickedness of the Continent itself. The relative importance of immaturity and Continental viciousness as alleged factors in the traveler's loss of virtue is, of course, impossible to determine, but a conception of foreign nations as inimical to virtue strongly influenced many theorists. Possessed of a deep distrust for foreign manners and practices, they appear actually to have assumed that the Continent was a more immoral and irreligious place than England. Although any participation in society was viewed as entailing dangers to morality and religion, the dangers were multiplied many times, in the eyes of these authors, if the society was composed of foreigners. Like objections to travel during adolescence, their attitude denied the fashionable theory that the tour was valuable for furnishing worldly experience. Their picture of foreigners was perhaps inherited from the Renaissance, when Italy in particular gained an unsavory reputation among Englishmen, but in the eighteenth century France more often than Italy was regarded as notoriously sinful. Ruin of character was predicted with grim certitude when the corrupting influence of the Continent joined forces with the youthfulness of the traveler; and some commentators evidently felt that the Englishman would be better off if, instead of merely postponing his tour until maturity, he did not make it at all. In grave language they described the bad effects of an association with foreigners—the undermining of virtue, the indoctrination into sin and impiety. Typical of their remarks were the following, made by Burnet, who was probably alluding to France: "As for the corruption of their [i.e., young English travelers'] manners, why sould not that be looked upon as assured, among a people who have made their greatest study, ane unmanly idolising of women, and where uncleanness is thought but a sport; neither is a man judged in fashion if he keep not a courtisan, and where the dialect of speech is to sweare with open mouth; and by all, even those who are not atheists in principle, a sense of God and piety is hissed at and forgotten."[45]

Burnet wrote this blast early in the Restoration; the succeeding years saw no diminution in the attitude he expressed. "Follies, fopperies, vices and luxuries" were so prevalent on the Continent, Sheridan implied in his *British Education,* that they were "to be found in the streets, and on the high-ways; and to be picked up riding post" (page 32). According to Hurd's *Uses of Foreign Travel,* there were "degrees in vice, as well as varieties of it," and youthful gentlemen grew more proficient in it or adopted "new species of it" as a consequence of "rambling into countries where it may chance to rage with greater virulence, or where such modes of it, at least, prevail as are luckily unknown to us" (page 23). Despite Hurd's concession toward the end of his book that a Continental tour could be of value for certain well-qualified gentlemen whose education proper was already completed, one has the feeling that he would have been satisfied if no gentleman ever traveled at all.

Some critics were afraid that the returned English tourist would inseminate in his own country the wicked ways of foreigners, "bringing home," as Grenville said in his *Counsel and Directions,* "no more considerable Remarks, than some noted Vices of a Forein Nation, to Transplant, and Propagate in his own Country, and among his own Kind" (page 91). Hurd had recourse to history on this point. He made Shaftesbury assert in support of the grand tour that the Stuart courtiers had imported polish into England from France, but Locke's reply cut Shaftesbury short: "As to the worthies of CHARLES' court . . . if they brought any thing with them from *France,* besides it's follies and vices . . . it is a secret which it has not been my fortune to be apprized of" (pages 19-20). In 1722 Dykes branded foreign nations as the sources of the evils which infested England. Britons went abroad, he said, "to get ill Habits or foul Diseases . . . to bring home ill Manners or worse Languages; and to fall at last into ill Company or the worst Corruptions of all Virtue." He thoroughly regretted "the fond Vagaries of leaving our own native Climate for new

Fangles, and Foreign Fanfarons."[46] Here was a condemnation of travel *per se*. It may be assumed that Dykes would have preferred English gentlemen, mature as well as youthful, to remain in their native land.

The corruption of religion as well as of morality was ascribed to travel. Critics were apprehensive that an English gentleman's religious principles would be affected by Catholicism, and the freethinking associated with France and Italy loomed as an even greater menace. Jenyns portrayed a young man who, having traversed the nations of Europe and "Glean'd all their follies," came under the influence of both Catholicism and freethinking, so that he returned to England as

A monster of such complicated worth,
As no one single clime could e'er bring forth;
Half atheist, papist, gamester, bubble, rook.[47]

The unknown author of the *World* No. 205 (December 2, 1756) was especially concerned over the atheism resulting from an exposure to French freethinkers, for "the majority of our young travellers return home entirely divested of the religion of their country, without having acquired any new one in its place." This author made the ironic suggestion that since travel to France was currently rendered impossible by the war, young gentlemen visit China instead; then rather than acquire French atheism, they might adopt Confucianism. Hurd again employed historical example. When in his *Uses of Foreign Travel* Shaftesbury claimed that the Elizabethans had gained enlightenment from Italy, Locke responded that they "had done better to stay at home," since "it is no secret that the civility, we thus acquired, was dearly paid for; and that Irreligion and even Atheism, were, by mistake, packed up with their other curiosities; and shewn about, at their return, as choice things, which could not but very much enhance the consideration of those who had been to gather them beyond the mountains" (pages 18-19).

An equally strong criticism of travel, but one grounded in patriotism rather than in an anxiety for virtue, involved the removal of English provincialism and, incidentally, the acquirement of French polish as objects of the grand tour. In the Restoration Gailhard characterized the true gentleman as one who toured the Continent "not forgetting himself to be an Englishman, nor with becoming a Frenchman, an Italian, or a German, but building upon the true foundation of an Englishman, and making use of the different ways of those several Nations, as Ornaments only, and not as a bottom."[48] Notwithstanding the widespread popularity of the cosmopolitan ideal among both gentlemen and theorists in the eighteenth century, many authors subjected this ideal to severe qualifications. Even some of those who endorsed it stipulated that becoming a citizen of the world should not entail the loss of British attributes or of love for one's native country. Sir Charles Grandison, whose heart was "generously open and benevolent to people of all countries," was described in Letter CXLI as "in the noblest sense, a citizen of the world; but see we not," Richardson added, "that his long residence abroad has only the more endeared him to the religion, the government, the manners of England?"

Sir Charles managed to balance cosmopolitanism and patriotism nicely, but a host of gentlemen, according to the critics, did not. Imbued, perhaps, with the same prejudice against the Continent for which other critics reprimanded young travelers, these writers maintained that the process of cosmopolitanizing often went too far, turning an English gentleman into a foreigner. Moore, it is true, believed that Britons who tried to pattern themselves after the Continentals were generally unsuccessful and that, in any case, it was "much more natural to the English character to despise foreigners than to imitate them,"[49] but a large number of commentators were decidedly less disposed than he to minimize de-Anglicization. In their opinion, the Englishman abroad, taking a course directly opposite from that of his fellow countrymen who scorned everything foreign, often hastened to exchange his native customs and attributes for alien ones, particularly those of the French, whose influence on national character was as strongly feared as the Italian influence had been during the Renaissance.[50]

There was, of course, considerable pro-Gallic feeling in England throughout both the Restoration and eighteenth century, one manifestation of which was the admiration for French polish discussed previously. Yet anti-French feeling was a powerful counter to this pro-Gallic sentiment. The declaration of the Man of the Hill, " 'I had infinitely rather pass my life with the Hottentots than set my foot in Paris again,' "[51] was not entirely an instance of eccentricity. In the later eighteenth century, opposition to Frenchification had grown so strong that Moore was able to write:

> A prejudice against French manners is not confined to the lower ranks in England:—It is diffused over the whole nation. Even those who have none of the usual prejudices;— who do all manner of justice to the talents and ingenuity of their neighbours;—who approve of French manners in French people; yet cannot suffer them when grafted on their countrymen. . . .
>
> I can scarcely remember an instance of an Englishman of fashion, who has evinced in his dress or style of living a preference to French manners, who did not lose by it in the opinion of his countrymen.[52]

It should not be inferred that critics objected to Frenchification alone; other nations were thought to contribute their share in de-Anglicizing the traveler. Richardson's remarks in *Sir Charles Grandison* had reference mainly to Italy, and Alexander Abercromby was speaking generally when, in the *Mirror* No. 57 (August 10, 1779), he called it "a misfortune for a private gentleman, who means to pass his days in his native country, to become attached to foreign manners and foreign customs, in so considerable a degree, as a long residence abroad, in the earlier period of life, seldom fails to produce." But France was regarded as the principal threat. And here many commentators found themselves in conflict with theorists and men of fashion who, viewing the attainment of the well-bred air as an important aim of travel, praised the French for their polished manners and urged young Englishmen to adopt these manners.

French polish was treated by the more patriotic commentators as superficial, hypocritical, and frivolous—as an elegant veneer for insecurity and as related in no way to an inner civility.

They therefore denied that the acquirement of the well-bred air was a legitimate object of the tour; English manners might be ungraceful, but at least they were genuine. Thus one Restoration author, despite his awareness of the alleged boorishness of the untraveled English, thought this boorishness preferable to French polish, which was "not worth the Charge the *Gentleman* is at, that travels for it." He was, in fact, "sorry for the poor Returns many make, that import hither the *Air* and *Carriage,* and *Assurance* of the *French,* therewith quitting their own staple native Commodities of much greater Value, *viz.* the *Sincerity* and *Generosity* of the *English Disposition.*"[53] This opinion was more frequent in the eighteenth century. As Moore (who himself had a high respect for France) pointed out in his *View of Society and Manners,* "What Frenchmen consider as common good manners, many Englishmen would call flattery, perhaps fawning" (I, 67). Smollett ridiculed French polish when, in Chapter L of *Roderick Random,* he described Banter's barber as "an exceeding coxcomb, lately come from Paris, whose absurd affectation and grimace would easily pass . . . for the sprightly politesse of a gentleman improved by travel."

Again, some authors, in rejecting the elegant air as an aim of the tour, were not thinking exclusively of France. Fordyce, at least, did not refer specifically to that country when he cautioned the traveler that "the principal aim of going abroad . . . is not . . . to polish and refine one's manners . . . and thus to learn a shrewdness, circumspection, and certain versatility of address."[54] But Fordyce probably had France in mind more than any other country, and Hurd almost certainly did when, in his *Uses of Foreign Travel,* he stipulated that the young gentleman-traveler should not occupy himself with "that excessive sedulity about Grace and Manner." The pursuit of a graceful bearing "would dissipate the young mind too much," he felt, "and take it off from those other more important pursuits, which are proper to that age" (pages 114-115). As an aim of travel, good breeding belonged among "such things as he may very well do without, or, at best, are of an inferior and subordinate consideration" (page 88).

Hurd, however, was somewhat inconsistent as to the attainment of a comely demeanor through travel. He maintained at one point that travel was ill-constituted to improve the gentleman's manners, since most Englishmen abroad did not mingle with the best-bred foreign society (page 102), but elsewhere he held that travel could refine young gentlemen too much, producing "I know not what varnish of manners and good breeding . . . and other trappings and shewy appendages of education," and, as he commented sarcastically, "tricking out a set of fine *Gentlemen*" (pages 70-71). He even ventured the opinion that this excessive foreign polish or delicacy of breeding rendered gentlemen unfit for fulfilling their national obligations, tending "to cramp their faculties, effeminate the temper, and break that force and vigour of mind which is requisite in a man of business for the discharge of his duty, in this free country." "The day may come but too soon," he morosely predicted, "when . . . politeness shall be fatal to ability of every kind; and, at least in the higher ranks of life, when our countrymen shall be too well bred to be good for any thing" (pages 115-116).

The reaction against de-Anglicization had reference to much more than mere polish, however. The youthful traveler, critics said, adopted French mannerisms, fopperies, and foibles, sprinkled his conversation with French phrases, enthusiastically endorsed the French cuisine, and dressed in conformity to the French mode, until he was, like Jenyns' *Modern Fine Gentleman,*

Now quite a Frenchman in his garb and air,
His neck yok'd down with bag and solitaire.
                                        (*Works,* I, 66.)

Such a creature was a citizen of England in name only, or, at best, a preposterous hybrid, the product of two opposing cultures but the member of neither.

The mid-eighteenth century was especially full of satiric treatments of the Englishman Frenchified by travel, one of the best known of which is probably Fielding's portrait of Bellarmine in *Joseph Andrews.* The unknown author of the *World*

No. 22 (May 31, 1753) facetiously proposed that gentlemen be whipped for traveling, just as schoolboys at Eton were whipped for rambling through the surrounding countryside. This satirist suggested that a board be established, "the president and principal members of which are to be chosen out of the laudable society of Anti-Gallicans," in order to examine and sentence travelers. Among the crimes which deserved flagellation were "debasing the purity of the English language, by a vile mixture of exotic words, idioms, and phrases . . . the frequent use of the word *canaille*, and the least contempt wantonly cast on the roast beef of Old England." It is possible that this writer considered the anti-French prejudice of his countrymen excessive and that he was satirizing it as well as Frenchified travelers. Not so, however, the unidentified author of the *World* No. 205 (December 2, 1756), who pretended to regret that the current war between England and France prevented young English noblemen from visiting the latter country. The admiration for France on the part of many aristocrats was suggested by mention of a gentleman who, with regard to his son, "most pathetically lamented his ill-fortune, that the doors of France should be so critically shut against a lad formed, by nature, for all the accomplishments which so eminently distinguish that polite nation." The writer's ironic proposal that gentlemen visit China rather than France was intended to ridicule the introduction of French fashions and customs into England by returned tourists; he even professed to envision a day when not only in their religious beliefs but in their dress and cuisine too, Englishmen of quality would imitate the Chinese instead of the French.

Quite possibly the young English traveler even developed a violent prejudice against the land of his birth, as did the nobleman whom Thomas Gordon depicted as coming home "quite out of Conceit with *Old England,* his own native Country . . . but full of the Finery of the *French* Court, and of the Praises of its Government."[55] Gilbert West, whose Spenserian imitation *On the Abuse of Travelling* (1739) painted Versailles in most opprobrious terms, was gravely concerned lest this glittering but rotten court should turn the traveler against his homeland:

To that seminary of fashions vain
The rich and noble from all parts repair,
Where grown enamour'd of the gaudy train,
And courteous haviour gent and debonair,
They cast to imitate such semblaunce fair,
And deeming meanly of their native lond
Their own rough virtues they disdain to wear,
And back returning drest by foreign hond
Ne other matter care, ne other understond.[56]

A number of critics feared that a young gentleman's politics
would be poisoned by a residence abroad and that he would
exchange his faith in British liberty and in the British constitution for despotic notions obtained in absolute monarchies,
particularly France. The tourist, Fordyce said in his *Dialogues
Concerning Education,* should remember to "despise chains and
the servile pageantry of life, however they may be gilded"
(II, 276). The author of the *World* No. 22 ironically described "such young patriots who make the tour of Europe from
a laudable desire of discovering the many imperfections of the
English constitution, by comparing it with the more perfect
models which are to be found abroad."

Hurd did not treat the matter so humorously. It will be
recalled that he had Shaftesbury speak with disdain of "the
idiot PREJUDICES of our home-bred gentlemen" in favor of their
native land—prejudices which, in Shaftesbury's aristocratic opinion, should be rooted out through travel. But Hurd's own
view, expressed later through Locke, was that such prejudices
were very desirable and should by no means be destroyed, even
if they entailed "honest errors" and an "extravagant conceit"
as to the merits of "the soil and climate of *Old England.*" For,
Hurd asked: "What if the ideas of Liberty chanced to be closely
connected with those of *Old England*; so as, by the magic of
this union, to convert her rude heaths and barren mountains
into pleasurable landskips; Would you be forward . . . to dis-
solve this charm, and, by setting those objects in their true
and proper light, disenchant the mind, at the same time, from
the idea, or warm love at least, of English liberty?" (pages
95-96). Hurd believed that despotic governments obliged men

to practice flattery and hypocrisy, which, he thought, were what French politeness often amounted to. He contrasted "the more absolute monarchies of *Europe*," where "all are Courtiers," with "our freer monarchy," where "all should be Citizens. . . . We have a country to embrace," he said proudly, "not a court to adore." Waxing still more eloquent, he exclaimed: "Let our countrymen then be indulged in the plainness, nay the roughness of their manners: But let them attone for this defect by their useful sense, their superior knowledge, their public spirit, and above all, by their unpolished integrity." He was afraid that if Englishmen adopted the insincerities, dissimulations, and adulations necessary to the subjects of tyrannical governments, then Britain was doomed, just as Athens had been doomed when it relinquished "the simplicity and manly freedom of it's antient character, for the fopperies and prostrations of the Asiatic courts" (pages 159-160). The parallel drawn here was an expression of the apprehension that must have possessed many patriotic Englishmen when they saw their well-born countrymen return from the Continent fully equipped with French manners and ideas.

The seventeenth-century custom of sending young gentlemen to French academies for their education has been referred to in Chapter III. This custom continued to be observed by some families in the eighteenth century, as did the practice of having youths educated at the academies and universities of the other Continental nations. Such measures are, of course, not directly related to the grand tour, except that training at Continental institutions was often combined with travel, as in the case of Chesterfield's son, who attended academies in Italy and France. Objections to educating young Englishmen at foreign institutions were especially prevalent in the middle and later eighteenth century, when the reaction against de-Anglicization in general perhaps reached its height. These seminaries, critics declared, undermined the young Englishman's national character and love for his country and engrained into him beliefs antithetical to British political principles and the doctrines of the Church of England. The unknown author of the *World* No. 61 (February 28, 1754) even accused the French government of dispatching Irish officers to its academies in order to instruct the British students there and thus "gradually instil into their vacant minds the poisons of popery and disaffection."

The charge was perhaps not entirely groundless, but most other critics, without being quite so explicit, were content simply to enumerate the undesirable consequences of academic training abroad. Thus Richard Davies, in his *General State of Education in the Universities* (1759), spoke against sending young British noblemen to foreign universities because "it is a great national inconvenience to weaken the Affection, which in the course of Education is riveted to our native Soil; and to trust to Virtues of a foreign growth for the support of the British Constitution" (page 7). As a critic of the English universities, Davies, like others before him, felt that an awareness of the shortcomings of Oxford and Cambridge prompted aristocratic parents to send their sons to Continental institutions. The anonymous author whose *Observations on the Present State of the English Universities* (1759) was a reply to Davies ascribed the custom to "that universally adored phantom, *fashion*," and his view was probably closer to the truth. He agreed, however, that the practice resulted in "the no small detriment of the publick" (page 25).

Hurd, as might be expected, shrank with horror from the notion of sending young Englishmen to French institutions. His objection was grounded partly in religion. "High as their reputation is," he had Locke remark to Shaftesbury, "you would hardly advise the breeding of our *English* youth in the colleges of the Jesuits." Possible alternatives on the Continent were the Protestant universities in Germany, the Netherlands, and Switzerland, but Hurd disapproved of these as well. The state of learning at them, he argued, was no higher than that at the English universities, and they were inferior with respect to discipline. Most important of all, they did not teach a young English gentleman a proper regard for the political and religious principles of his own nation. "Is it all one," he demanded, "whether a young Boy, who is destined to be a subject to the Crown, and a member of the Church of *England*, be inured to the equality of Republican governments, and of Calvinistical Churches? . . . would you train up your son in a way that is likely to indispose him, right or wrong, to the institutions of his own country?"[57]

Even Moore, who as governor to the young Duke of Hamilton abroad did not object to the grand tour *per se,* was opposed to sending Britons across the Channel for their academic training: "The most important point, in my mind, to be secured in the education of a young man of rank of our country, is to make him an Englishman; and this can be done nowhere so effectually as in England." Only in his native land could a well-born youth "acquire . . . that particular taste and turn of mind, which will make him prefer the government, and relish the manners, the diversions, and general way of living, which prevail in England." Only there, furthermore, could he "acquire that character, which distinguishes Englishmen from the natives of all the other countries of Europe." Moore recognized the claim that education abroad was valuable for checking the growth of undesirable English prejudices, "but," he countered, "other prejudices, perhaps as ridiculous, and much more detrimental, will be formed"—prejudices which "may render the young people unhappy in their own country when they return, and disagreeable to their countrymen all the rest of their lives."[58]

Since views on travel in the education of gentlemen during the period under consideration were widely divergent and often contradictory, it may be well to summarize them here.

By fashionable parents, the grand tour was regarded as an essential part of education. Many theorists shared their attitude, in degree if not in entirety. Travel was said to bestow several important benefits on the gentleman. It supplied him with a knowledge of the world. It gave him a facility in the modern languages. It polished his manners, especially if he sojourned long in France, the recognized arbiter of elegance, whose citizens were praised for their graceful demeanor whereas, according to one point of view, Englishmen were inherently loutish and ungainly. Very desirable in the eyes of all commentators was the practical, factual, timely information about the nations of Europe which an attentive journey through them provided. In the Renaissance, acquiring this kind of information had been valued chiefly as preparation for political service; in the Restoration and eighteenth century it seemed to be valued more for its own sake, although its appropriateness to a career of statesmanship was sometimes mentioned. A lesser advantage of the tour was the opportunity to examine and appreciate ancient relics, curiosities, works of art, and other items of esthetic or historical interest. Travel also rid the Englishman of his native prejudices and provincialism, cosmopolitanizing him and making him a citizen of the world. Thus a visit to foreign countries could be a most profitable aspect of education if it was rightly pursued.

Certain authors, however, criticized the genteel order for abusing the tour. One of the abuses, that of neglecting to acquire a knowledge of English laws and institutions before going abroad, left a youth with no basis for comparison when he encountered the laws and institutions of foreign nations. Some young gentlemen, besides, were said to have such a strong prejudice against everything alien to England that they traveled with closed minds, declining to learn anything about the Continent. Many of these, according to the critics, associated as much as possible with their fellow countrymen abroad. By so doing, they denied themselves the advantages which resulted from mingling with foreigners; they might just as beneficially have remained in England.

Sending gentlemen abroad during adolescence was an abuse of travel for which parents were to blame. A gentleman in his teens was thought to be too young to learn much from the grand tour; only at a later stage of mental development could he understand the unfamiliar habits and concepts which he encountered on the Continent. In addition, the adolescent gentleman, impetuous, impressionable, far from the watchful eyes of his parents, and under no authority except that of his tutor or governor, was described as readily susceptible to unsavory influences; he was exposed too soon to the evils of the world, and the consequence was serious damage to his moral character. Some writers in the Restoration condoned travel at an age prior to adolescence, as a boy of ten or twelve was still amenable to his governor's injunctions and was not old enough to be much tempted by vicious example. In the eighteenth century, however, travel for pre-adolescents was seldom referred to; critics devoted their efforts to demanding that the tour be delayed until a gentleman was definitely a mature man.

Sometimes the advisability of travel was flatly denied. For example, the view that human nature conformed to the same essential principles all over the world invalidated the claim that a tour was desirable for giving a gentleman a knowledge of mankind. Extremists seem to have felt that the nations of the Continent were by nature more wicked than England; they asserted that a residence abroad almost inevitably corrupted an English gentleman's morals and religion, especially if he was not yet an adult, and they saw no necessity for even the mature man to visit foreign countries. Travelers, they feared, would bring back to England the sinful ways of foreigners, which would take root and spread there. Critics of a patriotic turn of mind and with a strong anti-Gallic bias disputed the desirability of cosmopolitanizing a gentleman and polishing his manners through travel. The graceful demeanor of the French, they said, was frivolous and hypocritical; English manners were to be preferred even if they were rough. Many young men of rank, they complained, were converted into foreigners abroad, especially in France; the youths returned home thoroughly Frenchified with regard to dress, language, custom, and even choice of food, despising England and perhaps admiring absolutist principles of government rather than British liberty. The practice of sending well-born youths to foreign academies and universities for their education was also decried on patriotic grounds.

The extent to which criticism of travel was an attack on the gentry and nobility may be conjectured from the following facts: (1) the grand tour was a favorite fashionable mode of education, (2) censure of travelers for learning little and for declining to mingle in foreign company was directed almost exclusively at the sons of gentlemen, (3) censure of sending sons abroad during adolescence was directed at fashionable parents, among whom the custom was common, and (4) the denial that travel was valuable for introducing a young gentleman to the world, giving him a polished air, and destroying his English provincialism constituted a rejection of what were, with many persons of quality, three of the most essential objects of the tour. Those who criticized travel in practice or in theory held to the view that among the most important products of gentlemanly education were practical knowledge, virtue, and patriotism; in so far as the grand tour did not help to supply these, it was considered blameworthy, no matter what noblemen and country squires might think. As has been remarked before, however, some men of rank joined with nongenteel commentators in writing against particular factors in the tour. Besides, many authors admitted that travel had certain advantages while condemning it in other respects, and almost no one said that it was entirely bad.

Notes to Chapter VI

1. See Kelso, *Doctrine*, pp. 142-146; Howard, *English Travellers of the Renaissance*, pp. 7-11; Watson, *Beginnings of the Teaching of Modern Subjects*, pp. 128-130; Woodward, *Studies in Education*, p. 131; and Bacon's influential essay *Of Travel*.

2. *Gentlemans Companion*, p. 55.

3. *Uses of Foreign Travel*, p. 35.

4. *Compleat Gentleman*, 2nd Treatise, pp. 2, 4.

5. *Some Thoughts Concerning Education*, p. 177.

6. *Dignity of Human Nature*, p. 156.

7. *Spectator* No. 364 (April 18, 1712), attrib. to the Earl of Hardwicke, who, however, did not approve of the lady's decision. See also Costeker, *Fine Gentleman*, p. 13.

8. *Letters*, IV, 1416.

9. *Compleat Gentleman*, 2nd Treatise, p. 75.

10. Lingard, attrib., *Letter of Advice*, p. 22.

11. See Edward Leigh, *Three Diatribes or Discourses. First of Travel* (London, 1671), p. 11.

12. See E. S. Bates, *Touring in 1600* (Boston and New York, 1911), pp. 25-26, 38-39; Einstein, *Italian Renaissance in England*, pp. 123-128; Howard, *English Travellers of the Renais-*

sance, pp. 30-38; Mason, *Gentlefolk in the Making,* pp. 31, 53, 128; and George B. Parks, "Travel as Education," in *The Seventeenth Century: Studies in the History of English Thought and Literature from Bacon to Pope* (Stanford, Calif., 1951), pp. 265-272.

13. *Gentlemans Companion,* p. 57; see pp. 56-57.

14. *Of Education, Especially of Young Gentlemen,* p. 192.

15. See *Club,* p. 47; *Adventurer* No. 17 (Jan 2, 1753); and *Dignity of Human Nature,* p. 156.

16. *Dialogues Concerning Education,* II, 275-276.

17. See *Course of Liberal Education,* pp. 90-91.

18. See III, 773-774, 788, 1112, 1117-18, 1128.

19. See Leigh, *Three Diatribes,* p. 8; Ramesey, *Gentlemans Companion,* p. 57; Gailhard, *Compleat Gentleman,* 2nd Treatise, pp. 36, 185; Puckle, p. 47; and Burgh, p. 156.

20. *Gentleman's Magazine,* XLIX (1779), 464.

21. *Uses of Foreign Travel,* pp. 38, 32.

22. See III, 1046-47, and V, 1809.

23. I, 184-186. For further instances of the anti-foreign prejudice, see William Edward Mead, *The Grand Tour in the Eighteenth Century* (Boston and New York, 1914), pp. 124-125, 131-132, 404.

24. Osborn, *Advice to a Son,* p. 21.

25. *Compleat Gentleman,* 2nd Treatise, p. 86.

26. See IV, 1394-97.

27. *A View of Society and Manners in France, Switzerland, and Germany* (London, 1779), I, 72-73.

28. *Course of Liberal Education,* p. 91. See also Higford, *Institutions,* p. 63; Costeker, *Fine Gentleman,* p. 50; Fordyce, *Dialogues Concerning Education,* II, 274; and Burgh, *Dignity of Human Nature,* pp. 155-156.

29. *Plan of Education,* p. 144.

30. *British Education: Or, The Sources of the Disorders of Great Britain* (London, 1769), p. 33. 1st ed. was 1756.

31. Allestree, attrib., *Gentleman's Calling,* p. 39.

32. *Of Education, Especially of Young Gentlemen,* p. 195.

33. *British Education,* pp. 32-33.

34. *Of Education, Especially of Young Gentlemen,* p. 194.

35. *Estimate,* pp. 34-35.

36. Pp. 23-24. As will appear later, Hurd was actually unwilling to grant that vice was "the same every where."

37. See *Counsel and Directions,* pp. 143-145.

38. See *Compleat Gentleman,* 2nd Treatise, pp. 18-20.

39. *Proposals For the Reformation of Schools & Universities,* p. 10.

40. See *Dialogues Concerning Education,* II, 274.

41. See *Plan of Education,* pp. 118-119, 144.

42. *Uses of Foreign Travel,* pp. 122-123, 128.

43. See *Compleat Gentleman,* 2nd Treatise, p. 88.

44. See IV, 1394, 1397, 1532-33.

45. *Thoughts on Education,* p. 79.

46. *Royal Marriage,* p. 200.

47. *Modern Fine Gentleman,* in *Works,* I, 65.

48. *Compleat Gentleman,* 2nd Treatise, p. 4.

49. *View of Society and Manners,* I, 73-74.

50. See Mead, *Grand Tour,* pp. 380, 382-385, 396-398.

51. *Tom Jones,* Book VIII, chap. xv.

52. *View of Society and Manners,* I, 289. See also Mead, pp. 229-231.

53. Lingard, attrib., *Letter of Advice,* pp. 22-23.

54. *Dialogues Concerning Education,* II, 274.

55. *Humourist,* II, 72.

56. *Poetical Works* (Edinburgh, 1781), pp. 16-17 (stanza xxvii).

57. *Uses of Foreign Travel,* pp. 177-180.

58. *View of Society and Manners,* I, 287-289.

CHAPTER SEVEN

Public Versus Private Education

In the preceding chapters, occasional mention has been made of both the public and the private modes of bringing up the gentleman. Either method could be followed exclusively, according to the inclination of a boy's parents. If the parents so chose, the two methods could be combined in any of several ways. For example, a young gentleman might be instructed at home under a tutor during childhood and adolescence and sent to a university to complete his education. He might be given a combination of public and private training even during his boyhood, as was Chesterfield's son, who received lessons from both a tutor and the masters at Westminster. His tutor might go with him to a school or university, in order to help him with his studies. Or he might, immediately after attending a public school, proceed to the Continent, where his further education was conducted by the governor who accompanied him on his travels.

The evidence indicates that, on the whole, families of quality preferred the private to the public method. There was a long tradition behind this preference. In the Middle Ages the sons of noblemen and gentlemen were privately educated, at their own houses or the residence of some great lord or church dignitary; the monastic and cathedral schools seem to have been designed for the lower orders of society, and although endowed grammar schools existed, not until after 1450 were the gentry and nobility often taught at them.[1] The Tudor period saw the founding of many public grammar schools, but most well-born youths continued to be brought up privately, despite the objections of men such as Mulcaster. During the

eighteenth century the public schools were regarded by a large
number of people as unfashionable. Thus a mid-century novel-
ist portrayed the wife of a prosperous merchant's son as employing a tutor for her offspring "because she had heard it
was genteel to educate young Gentlemen at home."[2] Defoe had
one man of rank remark to another that eldest sons were
customarily " 'bred at home,' " to which the other, an eldest
son himself, replied: " 'They are bred like gentlemen.' "[3]

Aristocratic parents evidently felt that to subject their sons
to the domination of a schoolmaster and the harsh controls
of a grammar school was demeaning to their dignity. A fashionable mother, according to Defoe, might reason as follows: " 'Shall
my son be sent to school to sit *bare headed* and say a lesson
to such a sorry, diminutiv rascall as that, be brow beaten and
hector'd and threatn'd with his authority and stand in fear
of his hand! *my son!* that a few yeares after he will be glad to
cringe to, cap in hand, for a dinner! no, indeed, *my son* shall
not go near him. Let the Latin and Greek go to the D --- l.
My son is a *Gentleman,* he sha'n't be under such a scoundrel
as that.' "[4] "Indeed," Priestley commented a third of a century
later, "the severe and proper discipline of a Grammar-school
is become a common topic of ridicule; and few young gentlemen,
except those who are designed for some of the learned professions [i.e., medicine and divinity], are made to submit to
the rigours of it."[5]

Educational theorists were divided into two hostile camps
on the question of private as opposed to public education.
Some of them, especially during the Restoration, apparently
assumed that private training was the only kind conceivable
for the sons of persons of quality. This assumption underlay
Burnet's *Thoughts on Education,* Gailhard's *Compleat Gentleman,* and Locke's *Some Thoughts Concerning Education.* Although during the eighteenth century the weight of approval on
the part of theorists shifted from private to public upbringing, a
great many commentators adhered to the older preference, in
some cases perhaps because they were tutors themselves. Law
in his *Serious Call* evidently expected that if a child was a
gentleman he would receive his education at home "from

virtuous and sober parents, and learned tutors and governors" (page 231). The anonymous pamphlet *Of Education* (1734), written for "the Sons of Gentlemen of moderate Fortunes" rather than for the sons of great noblemen, did not consider public education for even these less eminent youths until they were seventeen, when their parents were advised to send them to a university (pages 2, 22). Influential theorists continued to raise their voices in defense of the private method, while their adversaries were fully as vociferous in support of the public method. Thomas Sheridan's remark that "there have been many altercations about the different excellence of public and private education, and each have had their warm advocates,"[6] was a gross understatement of the situation. A few authors, such as Sheridan himself and Eustace Budgell, could see the merits and defects of both systems; a few others, such as Walker in the seventeenth century and Clarke and Burgh in the eighteenth, were equally opposed to training at home and training at the great public schools, favoring a small private boarding school,[7] and may therefore be said to have reached some sort of a compromise between the two extremes; but most writers were adamantine in their partisanship of one method or the other.

Advocates of private education claimed that their system was more conducive to virtue than was public schooling. The notion that unless a young gentleman's associates were carefully chosen they would exert an injurious influence on his moral character has been indicated in Chapter IV. Champions of private tuition availed themselves of this notion, maintaining that at a public school, where an impressionable boy came into contact with a wide variety of students at an age when he was not yet wise enough to avoid the undesirable ones, the infection of vice was almost inevitable. "I judge the morals of a child," Burnet announced, "to be that which deserves the chieffe care, and the great dissoluteness that must needs be in a rabble of base ill-bred boys, doth much scare me from school education."[8] Gailhard believed that at the schools a boy would "fall into a disorderly course of life." Much as he admired the universities for their learning, he held that the same danger was characteristic of them, as "there is often so much corruption, by reason of the great concourse of Scholars, who debauch one another . . . that . . . when they should improve themselves in Vertue . . . they abjure all good manners, and become proficient only in Vices."[9] The universities, however, were only incidentally concerned in the dispute over public and private education; most writers centered their attentions on whether a boy should be sent to a school or brought up at home.

More forcefully than Burnet and Gailhard, Locke argued that the public schools ruined a youth by exposing him to evil company. A gentleman's son, according to him, should not leave "the shelter of his father's house" until he was "sufficiently acquainted with the dangers of conversation, and has steadiness enough not to yield to every temptation." Prematurely exposed to ill-assorted company at school, he was in imminent peril of losing his virtue forever. In fact, Locke asserted, "it is impossible to keep a lad from the spreading contagion, if you will venture him abroad in the herd, and trust to chance, or his own inclination, for the choice of his company at school."[10]

Locke's influence may be detected in later writers. Clarke, for example, devoted several pages of his *Essay upon the Education of Youth in Grammar-Schools* to quoting Locke's attacks on public education. As a schoolmaster rather than a tutor, Clarke was not in favor of training at home, but he was even less in favor of training at a large public institution. He confessed himself unable to understand why any parent who could afford a private education should choose to have his son brought up "in a promiscuous numerous Herd of rude wild Boys, many of them very vicious (for it is impossible it should be otherwise in a *great School,* especially in a populous place) where if he scapes without the loss of his Innocence, or without a strong Infection from the foulest of Vices, it must be next to a Miracle."[11] At a small and select private school, Clarke believed, a boy retained his virtue.

A second reason why public schools injured moral character, according to proponents of the private system, was that the schoolmaster, who normally had a great number of pupils under his care, could not devote individual attention to any particular one. A schoolmaster's duties were so multifarious that a boy was necessarily left without the proper counsel and moral guidance and thus fell a prey to vicious examples. At home, or at a small private school, his preceptor had the leisure to watch over him and to correct him if he went astray. The majority of students in a public school, Burnet complained in his *Thoughts on Education,* "are much neglected, and the most considerable are less looked too [*sic*] by one who hath perhaps a hundred others to divide his care amongst, than by one whose only and entire work it is to see to him" (page 22). Locke made much of this argument:

> Till you can find a school, wherein it is possible for the master to look after the manners of his scholars, and can show as great effects of his care of forming their minds to virtue . . . as of forming their tongues to the learned languages; you must confess, that you have a strange value for words, when preferring the languages of the ancient Greeks and Romans, to that which made them such brave men, you think it worth while to hazard your son's innocence and virtue for a little Greek and Latin.[12]

In the *Spectator* No. 337 (March 27, 1712), Budgell repeated Locke's very words on the issue. Percival Stockdale, perhaps the most outspoken defender of private education in the late eighteenth century, pointed out, in addition, that the size of a public school meant that despotism had to be substituted for individual encouragement in virtue; the students, "almost universally ruled by the rational and odious *fiat* of arbitrary power," were punished with the same severity for failure to learn their lessons and instances of incipient vice, so that their conceptions of virtue became confused indeed.[13]

The aim of Thomas Sheridan was to strike a compromise between public and private education, removing the faults and incorporating the merits of both methods. He recognized it as a defect of public schools that the students' "morals are liable to be corrupted by an imprudent choice of companions," but this defect would be eliminated, he felt, if a schoolmaster's duties were reduced. His proposal was therefore "to increase the number of tutors in proportion to the number of pupils; and never suffer any one to have more intrusted to his charge, than he can with ease attend . . . with respect to morals." With this increase in tutors, it would be possible to divide each class into a number of smaller classes and to put a special master in charge of each division, the conduct of whose few members he would be able to oversee adequately. This was tantamount to employing private tutelage in a public school; indeed, Sheridan declared that if his plan were followed, "each boy will reap every benefit which might be expected from a private tutor."[14]

Even authors wholly in favor of the public schools were forced to concede that the charge of damaging moral character was in some degree justified. Chapman, for instance, confessed that "children at public schools, are often . . . corrupted in their morals." He maintained, however, that a remedy could easily be effected by raising the salaries of schoolmasters. Were teachers paid higher wages, he thought, not only would more and better-qualified men be attracted into the profession, but schoolmasters would not have to take on so many pupils in order to earn a decent living; and as a result, the proportion of masters to pupils would be increased. Chapman's solution was therefore similar to that of Sheridan. He implied that the plan was already in operation in his own school at Dumfries, where "a greater number of teachers" was employed than was ordinarily the case, and where, consequently, the lower forms had "been reduced to more moderate numbers, so as seldom to exceed ten or twelve boys." At Dumfries, therefore, "a tendency in the mind to whatever is vicious or hurtful to society, is . . . corrected with the greatest attention," and the methods of correction could be made to vary in accord with the personalities of particular students.[15]

The lack of attention to individual pupils at schools not only permitted the growth of vice, according to opponents of public education, but also rendered it impossible for the pupils to make as much intellectual progress as they could under a tutor. At a large school and at a rural grammar school, all the boys were necessarily taught the same lessons. Critics who objected to this situation because it did not provide adequate vocational training have been discussed in Chapter III. Some critics also pointed out, however, that it left a student's particular ability undeveloped; a boy who had a special aptitude for history was given no more instruction in history than a boy whose talent was Latin grammar. Education under a tutor or at a small private school produced better results because it could be adapted to a boy's individual genius. If the efforts of an instructor were to "be effectual upon a young Scholar," the tutor Gailhard stipulated, it was "very necessary for him to understand his genius and inclination." Gailhard based his argument on the theory of humors, explaining that a certain intellectual faculty was incident to each humor, listing the branches of learning comprehended under each intellectual faculty, and stressing the advantages of assigning studies according to the peculiar humors of one's pupil.[16] In the *Spectator* No. 307 (February 21, 1712), Budgell told the story of Christopher Clavius, who, after nearly being dismissed from a college of Jesuits as a hopeless blockhead because he seemed to understand nothing, was discovered to be proficient in mathematics, was trained in his special talent, and became a celebrated mathematician. " 'How different from this manner of education,' " Budgell exclaimed, " 'is that which prevails in our own country, where nothing is more usual than to see forty or fifty boys of several . . . inclinations, ranged together in the same class, employed upon the same authors, and enjoined the same tasks.' " Although there were not many boys " 'to whom Nature has been so unkind that they are not capable of shining in some science or other,' " the public schools made little effort to help a boy advance in the field of learning in which he was most competent: " 'Instead of adapting studies to the particular genius of a youth, we expect from the young man that he should adapt his genius to his studies.' "

The pedagogical technique at a great school, moreover, was the same for all the students in a class, though it suited the personalities of some much better than it suited the personalities of others. "Hence different, hence opposite dispositions . . . are tortured and depressed," Stockdale observed, "or emboldened and made abandoned by a sameness of discipline, which is really melancholy to humane and philosophical reflexion."[17] By using the pedagogical method most appropriate for his pupil, a tutor could make him learn the most from his studies. This was one of Gailhard's main arguments in support of the private system. Instruction acording to the moods and temperaments of individual boys, he affirmed in his *Compleat Gentleman,* "is better done by a Preceptor in a House, than by a Master in a publick School. He, who at once hath but one or two to mind . . . hath more leisure to study his or their temper, and accordingly order or alter his method; but he who hath many to look to, hath generally one common way . . . and certainly this cannot be alike fit for every Scholar" (First Treatise, pages 21-22).

Furthermore, in a large class the quick-witted and the slow-witted were taught at the same rate. The most intelligent were consequently retarded in their studies by the mediocrity of the class as a whole, and the most stupid, unable to keep pace with the average students, were left in "absolute ignorance," as Sheridan declared in his *Plan of Education.* According to Sheridan, the solution of this situation was obvious. The classes at his proposed school would be determined by intellectual capacity rather than by age, and the pupils' rise from class to class would depend on their ability to learn, not on their birth dates. As for the public schools already in existence, they should raise the salaries of their teachers. The root of the whole trouble was "the low prices at first established, and still continued, to the masters of schools for the instruction of each boy," prices which necessitated a master, in order to gain a livelihood, "to take more boys under his care than it is possible for him to give a proper attention to" (pages 46-47). Budgell, notwithstanding his attack on the public schools in the *Spectator* No. 307, took the stand in No. 313 that the great schools were already adequately staffed; it was only in the rural grammar schools, he said here, that the masters had too many students to instruct. Chapman, however, was less sanguine. Convinced though he was that children profited most by a public education, he was conscious of the ill effects of "crouding them into few classes or forms, and jumbling the diligent and the idle, the sprightly and the slow, promiscuously together." This system, he said, was bad not for the dull-witted and the clever alone but for pupils of average intelligence as well, since even if the master tried to steer a middle course the spirit of emulation, so useful in prompting the average boy to study diligently, would receive little encouragement. Chapman's answer to the problem already discussed, was that of Sheridan—to create small classes by offering higher salaries, as he claimed to have done in his own school at Dumfries.[18]

The public schools were often criticized for subjecting the students to corporal punishment, "the slavish Discipline of the Rod," as Clarke termed it in his *Education of Youth in Grammar-Schools*. Clarke admitted that it was advisable for the correction of flagrant vices (especially contumacy), but he thought that schoolmasters used it too frequently and unwarrantably. The fact that they had to resort to flagellation in order to make their pupils learn was, in his opinion, an indication that their pedagogical techniques needed much improvement (pages 132-133). Sheridan cried histrionically: "Away with the rod - - - - away with corporal punishment - - - - away with servile fear!" He considered whipping the natural result of the understaffed condition of the public schools. "When the number of boys is out of all proportion to the number of masters," he observed, "nothing short of despotism can establish their government, no principle but fear can support it. Thus the torturer rod is introduced."[19]

Even more extravagant in his terminology than Sheridan was Gilbert West, whose poem *Education* (1751), an allegory in imitation of Spenser, attacked the application of the rod. West represented the course of instruction at a school by means of a raging river, difficult of passage and "stain'd with infants' gore." Conveniently situated on its bank was "a birchen grove." To this river the schoolboys were brought, "helpless, meek, and innocent of wrong," and by "faitours strong" (the cruel schoolmasters) they were "driv'n with furious rage, and lash'd into the tide." The terrified children looked around in hope of escape, but close behind them "With secret scourges arm'd those grisly faitours press." The spectacle then became one "Of tender striplings stain'd with tears and blood" (stanzas xiv, xxviii-xxix).

An important objection to corporal punishment was that it, like the evil company encountered at school, produced vicious young gentlemen. It destroyed the students' sense of shame, hardened them against all correction, and beat their innocence and virtue out of them. Steele in the *Spectator* No. 157 (August 30, 1711) severely censured the "stupid tyrants" who brought about such results. After describing an intrinsically virtuous lad who went to school only to be punished and humiliated, he remarked: "I would fain ask any reasonable man whether this lad, in the simplicity of his native innocence, full of shame, and capable of any impression from that grace of soul, was not fitter for any purpose in this life, than after that spark of virtue is extinguished in him, though he is able to write twenty verses in an evening?" The birchrod, Clarke maintained in his *Education of Youth in Grammar-Schools,* had the most injurious effects on the moral characters of "Boys of Courage and Spirit," as they would "be hardened by it, and grow up into an habitual Contempt, and Defiance of Correction; a terrible Disposition of Mind, that leads naturally to the most audacious and profligate Villany" (page 140).

An equally telling argument against corporal punishment was that it broke a young gentleman's free and independent spirit, making him servile and easily cowed, and killing his initiative. Clarke thought that this was especially true with respect to boys "of a soft and timorous Disposition." What little spirit they had would be destroyed by a whipping. They would "be dispirited, and moaped, and the Spring of the Mind quite broke in them by it; and then the Danger is of their becoming lifeless, unactive, good-for-nothing Creatures, all the Days of their Lives after" (page 140). Stockdale did not omit this point from his attack on the public schools. "If we rule *boys* with the discipline of *slaves,*" he exclaimed, "should we wonder that they are never *men*?" A tutor, he felt, could assign subtler punishments, which would appeal to a youth's reasoning powers, heart, and sense of honor.[20]

Perhaps because a free and independent spirit was cherished by persons of quality as the distinctive birthright of a British gentleman, or perhaps because fashionable parents were loath to subject their sons to the indignity of being beaten by a lowly schoolmaster, the prevalence of corporal punishment at the schools often influenced the upper classes to have their children brought up at home. The "current opinion" among the nobility, Swift averred, was that "whipping breaks the spirits of lads well born."[21] He himself was not in sympathy with the attitude; nor was Hurd, who, however, let Shaftesbury deliver the aristocratic charge that the punishment characteristic of public institutions was to be condemned because it rendered young gentlemen humble and spiritless.[22]

Even Chapman, opposed to private tuition on all counts, did not deny in his *Treatise on Education* "that a public education by accustoming children to an implicit obedience, tends to depress their spirits, to inspire them with slavish notions, and thus to prepare them for absolute subjection to their political governors." He maintained, nevertheless, that tyranny at school "ought not to be charged to the account of a public education: it can arise only from the unskilfulness of the teacher, and his unpardonable abuse of the authority with which he is invested." Where public education was carried on as it should be, he asserted, "the obedience of the learner will be voluntary, pleasant, and healthful" (page 48). This attempt to excuse the schools no doubt struck many fashionable readers as most inadequate.

There were two arguments against public education which were even more characteristic of persons of quality than the fear that whipping extinguished a young gentleman's spirit. One was the claim that a boy educated at home acquired good breeding, whereas a boy educated at school did not. In his home a young gentleman could attain a graceful air by emulating his parents and well-bred visitors; he could gain the principles as well as the particulars of politeness by the same means, and his tutor could help to teach him etiquette. Since a school was in some sense an introduction to the world, removing a boy from domestic seclusion, one might expect that it would have been thought to provide desirable training in courtesy, but such was not the case. From the standpoint of good breeding, especially its ceremonies and an elegance of demeanor, a public school was the worst kind of "world." A young gentleman's associates there, far from being well-mannered people, were rude, rowdy, and unrefined schoolboys, whose influence on his manners could be as deleterious as their influence on his morals. Thus many fashionable parents subscribed to the belief of Locke and Budgell that a private training, in contrast to a public one, assured good breeding.[23] Their attitude, in some cases, was similar to that of the aristocratic mother depicted by Johnson in the *Rambler* No. 109 (April 2, 1751). When she and her husband discussed whether their son should be brought up publicly or privately, she advocated a public education because " 'she never knew any boys at a grammar school that could come into a room without blushing, or sit at the table without some awkward uneasiness.' " As her husband agreed that " 'he had known very few [public school] students that had not some stiffness in their manner,' " the noble couple determined upon a private education for their offspring.

Hurd had Shaftesbury, exponent of the fashionable attitude toward schooling as toward other matters in the *Uses of Foreign Travel,* refer disdainfully to the "clownish, coarse, ungainly demeanour" of the products of public institutions. "Bring but one of these grown boys," Shaftesbury remarked, "into a circle of well-bred people, such as his rank and fortune entitle him, and in a manner oblige him, to live with. And see how forbidding his air, how imbarassed all his looks and motions! His aukward attempts at civility would provoke laughter, if, again, his rustic painful bashfulness did not excite one's pity" (pages 44-45). This aristocratic contempt for the public schools as centers of ill breeding was shared by Chesterfield. Although he sent his son to Westminster for a few years, he viewed that institution as anything but beneficial to the boy's manners. "Westminster School," he informed young Philip, "is, undoubt-

edly, the seat of illiberal manners and brutal behaviour."
Afraid that his son would acquire vulgar habits there, he demanded: "Are you sufficiently upon your guard against awkward attitudes, and illiberal, ill-bred, and disgusting habits;
such as scratching yourself, putting your fingers in your mouth,
nose, and ears? Tricks always acquired at schools, often too
much neglected afterwards; but, however, extremely ill-bred
and nauseous."[24]

The other largely aristocratic objection to the public schools
was that they obliged young gentlemen to mingle with social
inferiors. In the eyes of some persons of fashion, we recall, the
only "good" company, the only portion of the world in which
young gentlemen should participate, consisted of other persons
of fashion. Parents hesitated, therefore, to expose their progeny
to contact with the low-born boys who were often admitted to
the schools. A lady of rank portrayed in Defoe's *Compleat
English Gentleman* said of her son: " ' No, indeed, he shan't go
among the rabble of every trades-man's boys and be bred up
among mechanicks. No, no, my son is a gentleman; my son,
is he not a baronet by his blood? and he is born a gentleman,
and he shall be bred like a gentleman' " (pages xv-xvi). This
way of thinking, mentioned by Swift as common among the
nobility in his age,[25] persisted throughout the century.

Perhaps some parents blamed the low-born boys in particular
for the bad manners which they thought a young gentleman
acquired at school. Others may have seen indignity if not danger
in their sons' forming friendships with boys who, as Stockdale
remarked in his *Examination,* "are to inherit inferior fortunes;
or . . . those who must be adventurers in life." Stockdale supposed that "the grandees of our realm" would take no pleasure
in the reflection that their sons at school "will be so situated
as to be apt to make many humble friends and dependents, at
an unsuspecting and imprudent age. Nay, the idea will suggest
to them much future prejudice to the interest and pride of
their family" (pages 16-17). Hurd made Shaftesbury cite the
complaint of aristocratic parents that their sons, "in their
passage thro' our public and vulgar schools," contracted, "together with many illiberal habits . . . many low and illiberal

friendships, which are, in all reason, to be shaken off; That these unworthy companions follow them to the University, and are, if not the bane, yet the dishonour and incumbrance of their future lives." Such "hasty and ill-timed connections," Shaftesbury inferred, were inappropriate to a young gentleman's "birth and quality" (pages 143-144).

Several other criticisms of public training, treated in Chapter III, should be briefly mentioned here. They were the objection to emphasizing Latin at the expense of more immediately useful branches of learning, the reaction against teaching Latin principally by means of grammar, the disapproval of Latin theme-making and versifying, and the accusation that the gentleman's usual course of studies did not prepare him in any way for a future profession or career. Such criticisms, it is true, were not always offered with a view to illustrating the superior advantages of private upbringing. They were, furthermore, not leveled entirely at the public method; sometimes they were stated in general terms, so as to include private education as well. The public method, nevertheless, received the brunt of the attack. Stockdale's *Examination* (see pages 44-55) was to a considerable degree an assault against the old stress on Latin and the old ways of teaching the language as typical of the public schools and as advocated by Knox in his *Liberal Education*, which was written in defense of public institutions. Private upbringing, as has been demonstrated, was a flexible entity and could vary in accord with the particular preferences of tutors and parents; but public education was fixed by tradition and hostile to change, following a rigid and uniform pattern. Thus all tutelage at home was not censurable for the above alleged failings whereas all public schooling was.

Proponents of public education, like proponents of private education, tried to claim virtue as the result of their system. Maidwell, in support of this claim, cited Quintilian's *Institutions,* a favorite with champions of the public method, "in which . . . He gives ample Satisfaction to the Cavils of some *Parents,* that in a Crowd of Boys at a Public Schole the Manners of their Sons are Corrupted, and a *Tutor* more at leasure to improve One, than the Ablest Schole-Master can pretend to win a Number."[26] Chapman, we remember, attempted in his *Treatise on Education* to repudiate these "cavils" by asserting that if the schools employed more teachers than was sometimes the case and paid them higher salaries, the students would be so well supervised that they would not be corrupted by their fellows. He insisted that basically the schools were much better constituted to inculcate morality than was private training. "Can any virtues, or any good habits," he demanded, "be taught by private instruction, that cannot be more successfully taught by public education, when properly conducted?" (page 55). Uncomfortably conscious that the objections to the schools had some justification, Vicesimus Knox said that unfortunately a number of public institutions had deteriorated; but, he implied, there were others "where the intention of the founder is not quite forgotten, and where a degree of the more practicable part of the original discipline is still retained." At such schools, he maintained, there was not "more danger of a corruption of morals than at home." He was, he affirmed, "well aware that boys contribute greatly to each others corruption." On the other hand, the boy brought up at home might "associate with menial servants, from whose example, especially in great and opulent families, he will not only learn meanness, but vice." More important, he would realize that he was being held back from a participation in the world and would consequently be impatient for release; and when the release came, his passions would "break forth with an additional violence, as the waters of a stream when they have long been confined. In the course of my own experience, I have known young men nearly ruined at the university, who attributed their wrong conduct to the immoderate restraint of a domestic education."[27]

Tutors were sometimes accused of encouraging viciousness in their pupils or at least doing nothing to prevent its spread. Defoe, for example, affirmed that the aims of young gentlemen's tutors were " 'to teach them to be wicked, instill the love of their pleasures into them very early, teach them to wast their first houres in which the mind is most capable of improvement till at last 'tis too late.' "[28] The tutors were often young college

graduates or clergymen, but fashionable families would sometimes engage educators from France. Swift deplored "that pernicious custom in rich and noble families, of entertaining
French tutors in their houses," as a result of whose efforts a
"young gentleman is, in every article, as fully accomplished at
eight years old, as at eight and twenty, age adding only to the
growth of his person and his vice."[29] Stockdale was equally
severe against the kind of clergyman sometimes employed as a
tutor—the "ecclesiastical coxcomb," as he called him. Despite
his warm championship of private training, Stockdale was forced
to admit: "*Private* education, as it is in general conducted, is,
perhaps, worse than *public*. You may as well leave you [*sic*] son
to himself, and to the seduction of the devil, as pretend to
educate him under the auspices, of a *fashionable priest*."[30]

In addition to showing why private training resulted in vice,
commentators advanced reasons why public training led to
virtue. According to Swift, who thought that gentlemen educated under tutors read very little, the textbooks studied at
public institutions promoted morality, being full of passages
which stimulated the boys to virtue.[31] Coventry approved of
whipping and intercourse with schoolfellows as aids to virtue.
In *Pompey the Little* he portrayed a brother and sister who,
having been brought up at home by their parents and tutors,
were "proud, selfish, obstinate and cross-humoured." Their
parents, he suggested, should have sent "them to Schools, where
they would have been whipt out of many of their Ill-tempers,
and perhaps by Conversation with other Children, might have
learnt a more open generous Disposition" (page 79). Association with schoolfellows was also praised by Moore as affording
valuable lessons in morality. His statements were a direct re-
pudiation of the charge that mingling with all sorts of company
at school corrupted a young gentleman's character:

> A boy perceives, that courage, generosity, gratitude, com-
> mand the esteem and applause of all his companions. He
> cherishes these qualities in his own breast, and endeavours
> to connect himself in friendship with those who possess
> them.—He sees that meanness of spirit, ingratitude, and
> perfidy, are the objects of detestation.—He shuns the boys

who display any indications of these odious qualities. What is the object of applause or contempt to his school-fellows, he will endeavour to graft into, or eradicate from, his own character, with ten thousand times more eagerness than that which was applauded or censured by his tutor or parents.[32]

It was an important point of educational theory throughout the Restoration and eighteenth century that parents should not be indulgent toward their children. No one, indeed, questioned this principle. Among Restoration writers, Ramesey discussed ways in which parental leniency could ruin a child,[33] and Walker devoted almost a whole chapter to the ills that resulted from coddling children and raising them delicately.[34] Chesterfield, cognizant of the bad consequences of catering to children's wishes, fancied himself a demanding father rather than a lenient one. "I indulged no silly womanish fondness for you," he remarked to his son: "instead of inflicting my tenderness upon you, I have taken all possible methods to make you deserve it." Having mentioned young acquaintances of Philip who had been spoiled by pampering, he wrote confidently: "However you may turn out, you can never make me any of these reproaches" (V, 1861). Proponents of public education used the dangers of indulgence to good effect in arguing that boys should be sent away to public schools. Before we investigate their claims, however, a survey of the general treatment of parental leniency, by writers who supported the private system as well as by others, is desirable. These writers were often referring to the very early rearing of children, which occurred before they were old enough to attend school or be tutored at home; but the evils of indulgence which they described were equally incident to a later period of education.

The most serious effect of pampering children was thought to be the fostering of vice rather than virtue. Doting parents, Gailhard affirmed, could spoil their offspring so thoroughly as to bring them at last to the gallows.[35] We remember from Chapter I that according to most commentators, a virtuous education consisted in large degree in training a boy to control his passions by use of his reason. If a parent catered to the whims and fancies of his child, he was obviously accustoming the boy to the gratification of his passions, so that when the boy grew to manhood his reason would be too weak to prevent him from satisfying his vicious appetites. As Locke observed in *Some Thoughts Concerning Education,* "he that is not used to submit his will to the reason of others, when he is young, will scarce hearken or submit to his own reason, when he is of an age to make use of it." Thus affectionate parents, "by humouring and cockering them when little, corrupt the principles of nature in their children, and wonder afterwards to taste the bitter waters, when they themselves have poisoned the fountain" (pages 29-30). Penn admired the ancients for establishing virtue in their young by the use of severe discipline.[36] Authors throughout the eighteenth century continued to point out that raising children tenderly enslaved them to their physical passions and pleasures.[37]

A second unfortunate consequence of indulgence toward children, commentators said, was that of rendering them unfit to cope with the problems and hardships of adulthood. Delicately reared gentlemen, it was felt, were incapacitated for playing an active and prominent role in the business of life; indeed, men born into adversity often made much more of themselves. In illustration of this point, Dykes included in his *Royal Marriage* the following graphic passage, adapted with minor changes from Penton's *Guardian's Instruction:*

> *Give me a curl-pated Boy from a Beggar's Side, (the phleg-matick Offspring of Butter-milk and sour Cheese) who runs bare-headed all Day, and snoars all Night upon a Bag of Straw. Take this rational Clod, I say, and spirit him into Turkey: And after a Course of Hardship, in the Compass of Thirty or Forty Years Travel, you may, perhaps, meet him at the Head of an Hundred Thousand Men, matching Politicks with all the witty and civiliz'd World. Certainly Gentlemen are born with better Blood, Spirits and Parts, than such a Fellow of mean Extract: But thus you see what Wonders good Discipline can do with such an one; while by too much Warmth, Laxity or Luxuriousness, the very Soul of the other transpires and wasts through the Softness of his Skin.* (Pages 336-337.)

Among eighteenth-century theorists who shared the sentiments of Penton and Dykes was Burgh. No folly, he exclaimed,
"goes to more extravagant lengths, or proves more fatal, than
that which appears in the partiality of fond parents for their
children." Its effect was "to effeminate and enervate their spirits
by fondling them," so that they accomplished little throughout
life. "Natural sons, foundlings, and out-casts," Burgh maintained,
"often make their way better in the world, by their own industry, with little or no education, than those who have been
brought up in effeminacy and extravagance."[38] Chapman in
his *Treatise on Education* approached the matter from a slightly
different viewpoint. Pampering children, he thought, gave them
an unrealistic outlook on life; their failure to perform worthwhile acts in maturity came about because they could not
reconcile themselves to the buffets of fortune which inevitably
accompanied adulthood. Parents were to be blamed for not
"teaching them patiently to endure pain and disappointment,
and the other evils of life, which cannot be altogether avoided,"
and for allowing "them to contract an impatience under misfortune, and an impetuosity of spirit when thwarted, which,
gathering strength from indulgence, are often productive of
trouble to others, and of misery to themselves" (pages 22-23).

An awareness of the dangers of indulgence induced some
authors who preferred private education to qualify their preference. Convinced as he was of the advantages of private tutelage, Burnet wished a young gentleman to be brought up at a
house other than his own, so that the boy would not come under
the influence of his doting parents.[39] Although Burgh despised
the public schools, he recommended a small private boarding
school rather than training at home, for at such an establishment, "instead of an indulgent parent, who might fondle or
spoil the youth, there is . . . an impartial and prudent governor, who, not being biassed by paternal weakness, is likely to
consult, in the most disinterested manner, their [i.e., the
pupils'] real advantage" (page 123). Stockdale was too firmly
convinced of the value of tuition at home to recommend even
a private school, but he made the stipulation "that unlimited
power shall be given to the tutor over his pupil. If this article

is not fulfilled, while he is forming his young mind to simplicity and virtue, the rising moral fabric may be demolished by the fashionable prejudices, and destructive indulgence of his parents."[40]

In the hands of proponents of public education, the indulgence frequently concomitant with training at home became a powerful argument against the private system. Critics often cited the theory that as a result of pampering a boy would grow vicious, spoiled, egocentric, and obnoxious, like the son of the Baynards in *Humphrey Clinker* (letter of September 30th, Matthew Bramble to Dr. Lewis), or like the boy in Fordyce's *Dialogues Concerning Education* who, if he was defeated in games with his playmates, "cried and stormed, and bullied like a petty tyrant" (I, 159). They expanded on the notion that gentlemen shielded by loving parents were unfit for active participation in the great world, and, as will appear later, they asserted that the public schools were the ideal places for preparation for a life of affairs and service of the nation. They added the further point that even a boy who had been unduly coddled during his infancy could still be made virtuous if he was later sent to school and subjected to the severe discipline of a public pedagogue, whereas if his education was carried on under a tutor at home, his virtue was irrecoverable. Unlike a schoolmaster, they said, a tutor in a wealthy house was powerless to apply corrective measures to his pupil. Since he was entirely dependent on the fond parents for his livelihood, he feared to protest when, in the excess of their affection, they forbade him to reprimand or punish their darling child. The servile position of the tutor was made clear in the following remarks by Costeker:

> He is generally a young Collegian on his Preferment, who hardly dares exert the Authority he is invested with over his Pupil in the manner his Judgment would permit him, lest the Animadversion (when culpable) be thought by her Ladyship either too strict or severe; then he endangers his Place, and so necessarily lies under so great a Restraint betwixt the Execution of his Duty, in respect to his Pupil, and the regard of his own Interest, that our

young Nobleman falls far short of those Advantages he
might reap from a greater Authority in his *Praeceptor*.[41]

Should the tutor be of a somewhat higher station than the
one described by Costeker—should he, for example, be an educator from France—his place in the household was still tenuous,
so that when the parents acted too leniently toward their son,
he still had to hold his tongue or face possible dismissal. Indeed, critics affirmed, no gentleman educated at home had
much opportunity to be taught virtue unless his parents were
wise enough not to interfere with the methods of the tutor they
had hired; and wise parents, according to these writers, were
not numerous. Chapman, bewailing "the dependence of tutors
on the parents of their pupils," made much of "the risk a boy
thus [privately] educated, runs of being perverted in his temper . . . by undue indulgence from his parents."[42] Coventry
in *Pompey the Little* used the subservience of tutors to their
employers as an explanation for the ill nature of the brother
and sister who, he thought, should have been sent to school.
Since their tutors "never opposed any of their Humours, for
fear of offending their Parents" (pages 79-80), the children were
allowed to become as spoiled and wicked as they liked.

Fond parents were said to interfere not only with the moral
education of their sons under tutors, but also with the boys'
lessons, with the result that young gentlemen brought up at
home exemplified the lack of learning attributed to the genteel
orders. Gailhard himself, although as a tutor he was devoted
to private education, conceded that parents who did not permit a preceptor unhampered surveillance of his pupil's studies
constituted a menace to the private system: "At home often
the fondness of a Mother will spoil all, accusing the Tutor
one time of too much severity, another of neglect, and another
time for giving too hard tasks; so that a young Boy who is not
willing to be tied to his Book, perceiving this, abuses it, and
then there is no dealing with him."[43] Swift, who labeled the
whole of private education "the gulph of ignorance," pictured
a fashionable mother as enjoining the tutor that her son "be
not kept too long poring on his book, because he is subject

to sore eyes, and of a weakly constitution."[44]

It has been remarked that the noble parents described by Johnson in the *Rambler* No. 109 (April 2, 1751) decided to have their son educated at home because, as the mother maintained, public schools produced bad manners. In the remainder of this essay Johnson demonstrated the unwisdom of the decision. The mother took it upon herself to interfere in the tutor's province, and the tutor, perhaps even more servile than some, obeyed her ill-judged dictates without the slightest protest. Her son wrote later that under the mother's directions " 'he frequently took away my book, lest I should mope with too much application.' " A tutor named Eumathes, to whom Johnson devoted the *Rambler* No. 13. (June 22, 1751), encountered a similar attitude on the part of the aristocratic parents by whom he was employed. His pupil was at times markedly inattentive, but instances of inattention, Eumathes complained, would have occurred less frequently " 'had not his mamma, by entreating at one time that he should be excused from a task as a reward for some petty compliance, and withholding him from his book at another, to gratify herself or her visitants with his vivacity, shown him that everything was more pleasing and more important than knowledge.' " Less inclined toward obsequiousness than some tutors, Eumathes ventured to object to the mother's intereference; but he met with a curt reply, and his hands were tied.

Even when indulgent parents did not, like the mothers portrayed by Gailhard, Swift, and Johnson, actively interfere in their sons' learning, they could cause as much harm by simply not supporting a tutor in his efforts to make the children study. A young gentleman could easily see that his tutor was in a subordinate position and that, whatever commands or threats the man might issue, punishment for failure to learn his lessons would not be forthcoming without his parents' approval. "Simple Admonition, without Authority," Costeker explained in *The Fine Gentleman,* "makes him not dread, but despise Correction at the Hands of him he knows dares not proceed to Execution." It was because of this situation that "whilst a Youth's educated at Home, (which I by no means

approve of) instead of pursuing his Studies, and bringing them
to that Perfection he ought, he comes into the World with the
bare Name of them only" (pages 11-12). A spoiled boy and girl
mentioned by Fordyce knew that they were protected by their
doting parents against their tutor's injunctions and indignation.
They consequently "go to learn, as to some terrible task, are
restless and impatient till it is over, and mind their tutor
almost as much as the maid that puts them to bed." In such
a situation, Fardyce thought, a man "must have . . . almost
the capacity of an angel, to shape and improve them into any
tolerable figure: though with the genius and temper they have,
they might be taught any thing . . . were they under the influence of proper discipline and authority."[45]

Sometimes, without even laying the blame specifically on
the foolish indulgence of fond parents, commentators accused
private education of teaching the young gentleman much less
than the public method could. The very tutors employed, they
thought, had little learning or were neglectful of their duties.
"The young gentleman has a tutor," Defoe said, "that is, a
playfellow." While the boy was yet a child, his preceptor might
"learn him his letters and to read English, and indeed, *this
but sorryly* too sometimes, and very seldome to spell it." Later
on, "with some difficulty, he is taught his accidence, which he
can rather say than understand, and this carryes him on to 12
or 13 years old, perhaps farther, according as he is dull or
quick."[46] Such training obviously included less than the bare
minimum of what a gentleman ought to know, but Defoe
considered it characteristic of education at home. In *Pompey
the Little* Coventry described a tutor who, for somewhat different reasons, taught his pupil almost nothing. This individual,
Mr. Jackson by name, "had been dragged out of a College-
Garret at Thirty," and he "soon grew to despise the Books he
had read at the University, and affected a Taste for polite
Literature—that is, for no Literature at all." His pupil's mother,
a very ignorant woman, readily believed the ill-qualified preceptor's extravagant asseverations that the boy was making great
strides in his studies and was, in fact, something of a prodigy.
The results were ludicrous. When company came to the home,

the mother attempted to parade her son's learning in front of the guests, saying: " 'What is the *Syntax,* my Dear? Tell the Ladies what the *Syntax* is, Child!' 'Why, Mamma, cries the Boy, the *Syntax* is—it is at the End of the *As in Praesenti,* and teaches you how to parse.' 'Ay, ay, said the Mother, I thought so, my dear; 'tis some very good Book I make no doubt, and will improve your Morals as well as your Understanding. Be a good Boy, Child, and mind what Mr. *Jackson* says to you, and I dare say, you'll make a great Figure in Life' " (pages 80-82).

Clarke unwillingly admitted that adverse criticisms of tutors had some validity. Trying to ascertain why gentlemen ever sent their sons to public schools, he suggested: "The Inducement to this odd kind of Conduct in Gentlemen . . . is, I suppose, a Presumption, that such Schools are the best provided with able Masters: and it must be acknowledged, they generally are so." As a defender of private education, he went on to say that even if "a young Gentleman could not get so much Latin and Greek in his Father's House, or a Boarding-School," as he could at a public school, the more important consideration was virtue, which only a private training could supply. He added that if parents were willing to pay larger salaries to tutors, thereby encouraging the best-qualified educators to enter the private field, "they might have their Sons much better instructed in a private way, than it is possible they should be in a great School."[47] The implication, however, was that such was rarely the case.

It was often said that a public education prepared a young gentleman for an active participation in the world, especially in politics. Even when theorists were not writing with the specific intention of disparaging private education, we recall, they remarked that a boy whose parents were guilty of over-fondness would not be likely to distinguish himself in maturity. When commentators were demonstrating the advantages of the public system, they carried the argument farther than this, availing themselves of the belief that a knowledge of the world was to be gained only through experience in society. At home, they declared, a young gentleman was to a considerable extent secluded from society and could thus acquire little understanding of human nature, so that he emerged "vastly unknowing in the World."[48] He relied on his parents to a deleterious degree if they pampered and protected him, and to an unfortunate degree even if they did not. He learned little about how to deal cleverly and successfully with others.

On the other hand, by mingling with scores of students at school he received an early indoctrination into the ways of the world. He lost his former bashfulness and gained self-confidence, till he could act with bold assurance among his fellows and make his own decisions; and his ability to do these things would be invaluable to him in later life. "I have perceived a certain hardihood and manliness of character," Moore affirmed, "in boys who have had a public education, superior to what appears in those of the same age educated privately." The schoolmaster's inability to look after his pupils individually, so lamented by proponents of private tutelage, was called an advantage by Moore, since it threw a boy on his own resources and forced him to learn how to act in the world: "His reputation among his companions depends solely on his own conduct. This gradually strengthens the mind, inspires firmness and decision, and prevents that wavering imbecility observable in those who have been long accustomed to rely upon the assistance and opinion of others."[49] Since Chapman wished the proportion of masters to students to be increased, he could not offer Moore's argument, but he did make the point in his *Treatise on Education* that "if a boy is accustomed to associate with others of the same age, and under the same regulations with himself, he will more effectually get the better of that rawness, and that aukward bashfulness, which are so remarkable in those who have been late in entering into society." A school, furthermore, taught that primary lesson of the world, essential to all successful dealings in it—an understanding of human nature. "Boys who are educated at a public school," Chapman said, "being placed in circumstances similar to what they will experience in their progress through life, will learn to examine the characters of their companions, and derive advantage from the experience of others, as well as their own" (pages 46-47).

The likelihood that training at home would not provide

adequate preparation for the world was one of the factors inducing Clarke and Burgh, both of whom were firmly opposed to the public schools, to recommend a small private boarding school rather than tuition under the parental roof. "It is . . . obvious," Burgh thought, "that by a home-education youth misses all the advantage of being accustomed to the company of his equals, and being early hardened by the little rubs he will from time to time meet with from them." Having faced those "little rubs," he would later be able to face the greater hardships of the world at large, eventualities "which a youth, who goes directly out of his mother's lap into the wide world, is by no means prepared to grapple with." This latter youth, Burgh announced in extravagant terms, was not even able "to bear the sight of strange faces, nor to eat, drink, or lodge differently from the manner he has been used to at his father's house."[50] Clarke was aware that in the eyes of some people, even education at a small private school did not furnish adequate worldly experience: "What, will some say, are young Gentlemen to be entirely sequestred from the World, and not suffered to converse with any but such as themselves, a small number of School-fellows, till they arrive at the Years of Manhood? What strange kind of aukward ill-fashioned Creatures must they needs be, when they come first to make their Appearance in the World, and how unfit either for the Business or Conversation of it?" But Clarke defended the private school against these charges. Young gentlemen educated at such an institution were not "wholly sequestred from Company," he said, and therefore "would not come into the World, such meer Novices and Strangers to it." A master at a private school, moreover, was able to select virtuous, innocent company for his pupils, so that they would not be exposed to the contagion of vice. "There is, I presume," Clarke remarked, "more useful Knowledge of the World . . . to be learnt, from such kind of Company, than any, Youth educated in a publick Way, have usually the Advantage of, or care much to converse with, if they have."[51]

The knowledge of the world acquired at a public school was thus, according to Clarke, the wrong kind of knowledge, since it did not provide virtue. Clarke may have adopted this view from Locke, whose educational writings he so admired. Locke admitted that there was some justice to the claim that training at a public school gave a young gentleman a knowledge of how to get along in the world. "Being abroad, it is true," he conceded, "will make him bolder, and better able to bustle and shift amongst boys of his own age." But he emphasized that this ability was not virtue-forming—"that those misbecoming and disingenuous ways of shifting in the world must be unlearned, and all the tincture washed out again, to make way for better principles, and such manners as make a truly worthy man." Forcing a boy to fend for himself by throwing him among schoolfellows could only injure his moral character. Anyone who took into consideration the "malapertness, tricking, or violence, learnt among schoolboys," all of which were "opposite the skill of living well, and managing, as a man should do, his affairs in the world," would prefer a private education for his son. Boldness and self-confidence, far from being valuable products of public education, were inappropriate to boys of school age. "Boys will unavoidably be taught assurance," Locke maintained, "by conversation with men, when they are brought into it; and that is time enough. Modesty and submission, till then, better fits them for instruction; and therefore there needs not any great care to stock them with confidence beforehand."[52] Locke did not even mention a private boarding school as a compromise; he approved only of upbringing at home, where a boy would not learn reprehensible methods of making his way in the world.

Although Budgell agreed with Locke that the ways of the world acquired at a public school were not virtue-forming, he believed they were a necessary part of education because their very cynicism and utilitarianism equipped a young gentleman for playing a successful role in the active life which he would enter as an adult, particularly public service. Locke's view was, in Budgell's opinion, unrealistic. In the *Spectator* No. 313 (February 28, 1712), he said that whereas a private education " 'would furnish out a good subject for Plato's republic,' " a public one would furnish " 'a member for a community overrun with artifice and corruption.' " Since the actual world contained a great deal of artifice and corruption, an introduction to it through the miniature world of the public school was most practical. " 'A boy who forms parties, and makes himself popular in a school or college,' " Budgell suggested, " 'would act the same part with equal ease in a senate or a privy council.' " He cited the observation of the Commonwealth courtesy writer Francis Osborn " 'that the well-laying and carrying on of a design to rob an orchard trains up a youth insensibly to caution, secrecy, and circumspection, and fits him for matters of greater importance.' " Thus the very reason for which Locke condemned the schools, their effect on character, led Budgell to recommend them. Budgell also contested Locke's claim that adequate assurance or acquaintance with the world could be gained from conversation with friends of one's parents. " 'Conversation is not the only thing necessary,' " he pointed out. Unless a boy conversed with others of his own age, his social intercourse would be of little practical advantage to him.

Notwithstanding his respect for "the judicious Locke," Sheridan too questioned his views on these matters. Young gentlemen brought up under the private tutelage which Locke advised, he thought, "might be made sober, peaceable, and inoffensive members of society, but they would not be qualified for the active sphere of life." Like Budgell, he stressed the gentleman's duty of serving the state. Privately educated youths "might make good men, but not good citizens. And as there is no constitution in the world which requires more activity in its members [than the British], nothing could be more unsuitable to it than such a mode of education."[53]

In addition to the practical preparation for an active life afforded by the public schools, there were other reasons, according to proponents of public education, why their system best equipped a gentleman to serve the state. Fordyce, for example, believed that as a school was a society, it endowed a boy with public spirit. Students at a great school looked upon themselves as members of a definite community, and their social feelings gradually broadened into "a zeal for their common country, or even to a more extensive *philanthropy*."[54] It may be recalled from Chapter II that at the ideal academy which Fordyce envisioned, much attention was paid to instilling public spirit into the youths. Chapman, also viewing a school as a society, suggested that such an institution would make a boy "see the necessity of government, in order to cure the ignorance, and to check the disorders, of mankind." Another of its benefits, according to him, was that of training in oratory, so desirable for the servant of the state. "Being accustomed to deliver orations at the public examinations of the school," Chapman said, "and to declaim more frequently in English before his companions," a boy would "be better qualified for a more public appearance, if he aspire after the honour of serving his country at the bar, in the pulpit, or in the senate."[55]

The claim that private tuition, from various causes, left a gentleman rather ignorant was also brought forth as proof that the public schools provided the best preparation for service of the state. In order to fill a public office well, we remember, a gentleman was to have a considerable degree of learning. Defoe's conviction that tutors taught their pupils very little led him to say in his *Compleat English Gentleman* that whereas men educated at schools "have been the glory of their country, the ornament of the court, the supports both of prince and people," those educated in private "have been the meer outsides of gentlemen, useless in their generacion, retreated from the State" (page 8). Acording to Swift, British noblemen no longer took a prominent part in national affairs because private tutelage, which he termed "the frequent, corrupt, and sottish methods of educating those, who are born to wealth or titles," left gentlemen of twenty-eight with "the same understanding, the same compass of knowledge" as they had had at eight.[56]

One of the arguments intended to show the superior intellectual training received at public schools has been reserved for mention here. It was a well-established theory in education that a boy learned more if he studied from a desire to excel his fellows. Emulation acted as an incentive to mastering his lessons. Obviously, this competitive spirit occurred more frequently at the public schools than in the privacy of a home. If a boy was his tutor's sole pupil, it was impossible; if two or three other young gentlemen were under the same tutor, it perhaps existed, but only to a limited degree. Opponents of public education fully recognized that emulation was a merit of the system. "The advantages of schools are great," Burnet admitted; "for since emulation is that which presseth children most effectually to their studies in schools, they have many provocations that way." Although Burnet preferred private training for other reasons, he stipulated that the privately educated boy should be brought up in company with another child, in order to promote a competitive spirit.[57] Locke himself granted that "the emulation of school-fellows often puts life and industry into young lads."[58]

Supporters of public education cried up emulation as a shining advantage of their system. Knox invited his readers to look at the boy relegated to private tuition, "who with languid eye is poring, in solitude, over a lesson which he naturally considers as the bane of his enjoyment; and consequently feels no other wish than to get it over as soon as he can with impunity." Such a youth could profit little from his lessons. On the other hand, emulation spurred students to study diligently at school. Since the boy at the head of his class was regarded as a hero by his classmates, he would "spare no pains to maintain his honourable post; and his competitors, if they have spirit, will be no less assiduous to supplant him."[59] In his *Treatise on Education*, Chapman based his praise of the schools for fostering emulation on his conception of a school as a society in miniature. "There is implanted in the human mind," he believed, "an ardent desire to excel. This desire, operating with greater force in society, proves a strong motive with the generality of boys, and keeps some awake, who would otherwise languish in sloth." With an oblique slur on private upbringing, he announced: "This emulation, this virtuous rivalship for knowledge, ought never to be checked" (pages 43-44). Moore thought just as highly of it: "The active principle of emulation, when allowed full play, as in the chief schools in England, operates in various ways, and always with a good effect."[60]

Some commentators said that the employment of praise and censure, which was generally viewed as a useful method for inducing students to industry, had better results in public than in private training because at the schools it encouraged a competitive spirit. A pupil, Maidwell explained, "reaps an Advantage, by the Shame of this Lads Idleness, and the Praise of the Others Industry. Commendation provokes Æmulation, and he wil think it dishonourable to yield to his Æquals, and glorious to excel his Seniors."[61] Sheridan demonstrated in his *Plan of Education* that a schoolboy, seeing the master reprimand some children and laud others, would strive to be among those praised. "The love of glory will serve him as an incentive to take pains. He will be ashamed to give place to his equals, and will take pains to excel the most forward. A good scholar will use his utmost endeavours to be the first in his form, and carry the prize." By using praise and censure with a single pupil, a tutor could perhaps stir him to some diligence, but before the application of this technique could be really effective a whole class was needed, in which the emulative spirit was strong. In Sheridan's own proposed school, emulation was to be furthered as much as possible. The prospect of rising from class to class on the basis of progress in studies, and the competitive examinations held once a week to determine such progress, were calculated to promote in the boys a desire to excel (pages 75-76, 68-69).

Still another advantage of public education, occasionally mentioned along with its other merits, was the contraction of friendships at school. They had their practical side, for they could be of great service in later life. In illustration of this, Budgell in the *Spectator* No. 313 (February 28, 1712) related the story of two gentlemen who had been friends at Westminster but who found themselves in opposite camps during the Civil Wars, one being a judge under Cromwell, the other a Royalist officer. The latter was taken prisoner and brought before the judge, who, remembering his old school friend, pleaded to Cromwell on his behalf and thus saved him from the fate of the other captives. Similarly, Burgh declared in *The Dignity of Human Nature* that the "useful and valuable friendships a youth might have contracted at school . . . often hold through the whole of it, and prove of the most important advantage" (page 122). Knox was aware that "the formation of connections which may contribute to future advancement . . . has always been a powerful argument in support of the preference of public schools," but he added that connections formed solely with an eye toward personal advantage were not commendable.[62] Although Chapman realized that friendships begun at school were "often the means of advancing a man's fortune in the world," he, like Knox, valued them chiefly for their less tangible merits: "Friendship, by the tender sympathies which it produces, is known to heighten our joys, and to soften our cares. . . . When begun in youth, it has been found to grow up gradually, and to last as long as life itself. Public education furnishes the best means of forming this amiable tie: it accustoms us to live in society; it calls forth the social affections; it gives kindred souls a better opportunity of meeting while they are most susceptible of friendship, and of all the generous passions."[63]

The number of opposing points mentioned in this chapter makes a brief recapitulation advisable. No conclusion is possible as to whether public or private education was more favored for gentlemen in the Restoration and eighteenth century. On the whole, Restoration commentators preferred the private method, whereas in the eighteenth century the balance of approval shifted to public training. Aristocrats themselves found private upbringing more to their taste; yet many were brought up publicly, at least in part. Some theorists, such as Burnet, Gailhard, Locke, and Stockdale, exclusively supported private tutelage; others, such as Maidwell, Swift, Defoe, Costeker, Chapman, and Knox, just as exclusively championed the public schools. Still others, notably Walker, Clarke, and Burgh, recommended a small private boarding school rather than a public school or tuition at home. There was very little willingness to compromise; Budgell and Sheridan, and possibly those who advised a private boarding school, were among the few writers who could see the advantages and defects of both systems.

Adherents of the private method maintained that it led to virtue whereas the public schools promoted vice by exposing the boys to the influence of ill-assorted company and by allowing the master scant opportunity to oversee the conduct of individual pupils. Instruction could not be adapted to particular students at the populous schools, defenders of private education affirmed; all the boys were subjected to the same lessons regardless of individual genius, all were put in the same classes regardless of mental capacity, and all were submitted to the same pedagogical technique regardless of differences in personality. As a result, they learned less than they could have at home. Higher salaries for schoolmasters and an increase in the proportion of masters to pupils were occasionally proposed as remedies for these disadvantages.

The corporal punishment common at schools was condemned for its cruelty, for hardening boys against persuasion to virtue, and for breaking the spirits of young gentlemen. Objections to the emphasis on Latin and to modes of teaching Latin, treated in Chapter III, were often directed specifically at public education. Private training was said to assure good breeding, in contrast to public training, which produced only rowdiness and ill manners. Fashionable parents often disapproved of the public school for this reason, as well as because it obliged their well-born sons to mingle with social inferiors.

Advocates of public education, like advocates of the private system, maintained that virtue was the result of their method. They declared that tutors encouraged vice in their pupils and that association with schoolfellows was virtue-forming. One of the greatest arguments against upbringing at home was that it held the danger of indulgence from doting parents. A tendency on the part of parents to spoil their children was generally decried during the Restoration and eighteenth century, as it made the children vicious by subjugating their reason to their passions and as it disabled them from surmounting the problems they would meet in adulthood. Even champions of private education admitted that the likelihood of parental indulgence was the special defect of their method. Those proposing public education added the further point that since a tutor received his income from his pupil's parents, he was helpless if the parents interfered with his province. According to critics of private education, fond mothers often did so, rendering ineffectual his efforts to give the boy an adequate degree of learning as well as moral discipline. Sometimes, however, the tutors themselves were blamed for imparting little knowledge; they were depicted as negligent or otherwise ill-qualified.

Public education was extolled because it prepared a young gentleman for an active participation in the affairs of the world, teaching him how to deal with others and developing his self-reliance. For this reason and others, it was said to equip him for serving the state in a public capacity much better than tutelage at home could do; the gentleman brought up in his parents' house, where he was shielded from the world and where his intellect was perhaps poorly trained besides, was pictured as incapable of benefiting the nation. The emulation characteristic of schoolboys was also considered an advantage of public education, since it spurred them on to greater progress in their studies. Friendships entered into at school were mentioned as still another merit of the public system.

It may be noted that the controversy as to the superiority of public or private training involved all the principal ideals in gentlemanly education—virtue, ability to serve the nation, book knowledge, a knowledge of the world, and good breeding.

Notes to Chapter VII

1. See Furnivall, *EETSOS,* XXXII, vi-xxvi, lii-lxii.

2. Francis Coventry, *The History of Pompey the Little: Or, The Life and Adventures of a Lap-Dog* (London, 1751), p. 80.

3. *Compleat English Gentleman,* p. 55.

4. *Ibid.,* p. 7. J. W. Adamson, in the *Cambridge History of English Literature,* IX (Cambridge, 1920), affirmed: "The well-known decline in the number of boys at public schools during the greater part of the eighteenth century to some extent confirms Defoe" (p. 398). But this decline in attendance did not have reference entirely to boys of genteel parentage.

5. *Course of Liberal Education,* pp. 6-7.

6. *Plan of Education,* p. 52.

7. See *Of Education, Especially of Young Gentlemen,* pp. 23-24; *Essay upon the Education of Youth in Grammar-Schools,* p. 204; and *Dignity of Human Nature,* pp. 121-125.

8. *Thoughts on Education,* p. 21.

9. *Compleat Gentleman,* 1st Treatise, pp. 17-18.

10. *Some Thoughts Concerning Education,* pp. 50-53.

11. P. 193. For quotations from Locke, see pp. 212-219. See also the anon. *Essay on Modern Education,* p. 22, and Burgh, *Dignity of Human Nature,* p. 125.

12. *Some Thoughts Concerning Education,* pp. 49-50.

13. *An Examination of the Important Question, Whether Education, at a Great School, or By Private Tuition, Is Preferable?* (London, 1782), p. 7.

14. *Plan of Education,* pp. 74, 63, 67, 71.

15. *Treatise on Education,* pp. 50-51, 231, 226.

16. See *Compleat Gentleman,* 1st Treatise, pp. 64-70.

17. *Examination,* p. 2.

18. See *Treatise on Education,* pp. 52-54, 230-232.

19. *Plan of Education,* pp. 79, 51.

20. *Examination,* pp. 15-16. See also the anon. *Essay on Modern Education,* p. 22.

21. *Essay on Modern Education,* in *Prose Works,* XI, 52.

22. See *Uses of Foreign Travel,* p. 44.

23. See *Some Thoughts Concerning Education,* pp. 49 and 52, and *Spectator* No. 313 (Feb. 28, 1712).

24. *Letters,* IV, 1494, 1516.

25. See his *Essay on Modern Education,* ed. cit., p. 52.

26. *Essay Upon the Necessity and Excellency of Education,* pp. 14-15.

27. *Liberal Education: Or, A Practical Treatise on the Methods of Acquiring Useful and Polite Learning* (London, 1781), pp. 33-35. See Stockdale's attack on these remarks in his *Examination,* pp. 34-36.

28. *Compleat English Gentleman,* p. 56.

29. *Essay on Modern Education,* ed. cit., p. 54.

30. *Examination,* pp. 13, n., and 12. See also pp. 22-24, wherein Stockdale laid down strict moral and religious requirements for the tutor, who was to inculcate virtue beyond all else.

31. See *Essay on Modern Education,* ed. cit., pp. 55-56.

32. *View of Society and Manners,* I, 293-294.

33. See *Gentlemans Companion,* pp. 7-8.

34. See *Of Education, Especially of Young Gentlemen,* pp. 13-25. See also Osborne, *Advice to a Son,* p. 35; Ayres, *Vox Clamantis,* pp. 42-43; and Grenville, *Counsel and Directions,* pp. 85-86.

35. See *Compleat Gentleman,* 1st Treatise, p. 14.

36. See *More Fruits of Solitude,* in The Harvard Classics, ed. Charles W. Eliot, I (New York, 1909), 402-403.

37. See, for example, Fordyce, *Dialogues Concerning Education,* II, 289, and Chapman, *Treatise on Education,* p. 25.

38. *Dignity of Human Nature,* pp. 69-70.

39. See *Thoughts on Education,* pp. 23-24.

40. *Examination,* pp. 13-14.

41. *Fine Gentleman,* pp. 10-11.

42. *Treatise on Education,* p. 42.

43. *Compleat Gentleman,* 1st Treatise, p. 17.

44. *Essay on Modern Education,* ed. cit., pp. 53-54.

45. *Dialogues Concerning Education,* I, 160.

46. *Compleat English Gentleman,* p. xvi.

47. *Education of Youth in Grammar-Schools,* pp. 193-195.

48. Costeker, *Fine Gentleman,* p. 12.

49. *View of Society and Manners,* I, 292.

50. *Dignity of Human Nature,* pp. 121-122.

51. *Education of Youth in Grammar-Schools,* pp. 8-10.

52. *Some Thoughts Concerning Education,* pp. 49-51. See Stockdale, *Examination,* pp. 8-11, wherein he also pointed out that a schoolboy's boldness represented an undesirable kind of worldly knowledge and that conversation with a virtuous tutor would teach a virtuous knowledge of the world.

53. *Plan of Education,* pp. 12-14.

54. *Dialogues Concerning Education,* I, 299.

55. *Treatise on Education,* p. 49. See also Knox, *Liberal Education,* pp. 38-39.

56. *Essay on Modern Education,* ed. cit., pp. 51, 54.

57. *Thoughts on Education,* p. 21; see pp. 22-23. See also Gailhard, *Compleat Gentleman,* 1st Treatise, p. 18.

58. *Some Thoughts Concerning Education,* p. 49.

59. *Liberal Education,* pp. 37-38. But see Stockdale, who denied that emulation was encouraged at the public schools (*Examination,* pp. 5-6).

60. *View of Society and Manners,* I, 296.

61. *Essay Upon the Necessity and Excellency of Education,* pp. 15-16.

62. *Liberal Education,* pp. 39-41. Stockdale used this latter point to derogate public education; see his *Examination,* pp. 17-20.

63. *Treatise on Education,* p. 47.

Bibliography

I

Recent Studies

Adamson, J. W. "Education," chap. xv in *Cambridge History of English Literature,* IX. Cambridge: Cambridge University Press, 1920.

————. *Pioneers of Modern Education 1600-1700.* Cambridge: Cambridge University Press, 1905.

Bates, E. S. *Touring in 1600. A Study in the Development of Travel as a Means of Education.* Boston and New York: Houghton Mifflin Co., 1911.

Betz, Siegmund A. E. "Francis Osborn's 'Advice to a Son,'" in *Seventeenth Century Studies,* 2nd Ser., ed. Robert Shafer. Princeton: Princeton University Press for University of Cincinnati, 1937. pp. 3-67.

Coxon, Roger. *Chesterfield and His Critics.* London: G. Routledge & Sons, Ltd., 1925.

Craig, Hardin. *The Enchanted Glass: The Elizabethan Mind in Literature.* New York: Oxford University Press, 1936.

Einstein, Lewis. *The Italian Renaissance in England.* New York: The Columbia University Press; London: Macmillan & Co., Ltd., 1902.

————. *Tudor Ideals.* New York: Harcourt, Brace & Co., 1921.

Furnivall, Frederick J. "Education in Early England," *Early English Text Society,* Orig. Ser., XXXII (1868), iv-xliii.

Godley, A. D. *Oxford in the Eighteenth Century.* New York and London: Methuen & Co., 1908.

Graves, Frank Pierrepont. *A History of Education During the Middle Ages and the Transition to Modern Times.* New York: The Macmillan Co., 1915.

Gulick, Sidney L. *A Chesterfield Bibliography to 1800.* Chicago: University of Chicago Press, 1935.

Heltzel, Virgil B. *A Check List of Courtesy Books in the Newberry Library.* Chicago: Newberry Library, 1942.

————. "Chesterfield and the Anti-Laughter Tradition," *Modern Philology*, XXVI (1928), 73-90.

————. "*The Rules of Civility* (1671) and its French Source," *Modern Language Notes*, XLIII (1928), 17-22.

Holme, James W. "Italian Courtesy Books of the Sixteenth Century," *Modern Language Review*, V (1910), 145-166.

Howard, Clare. *English Travellers of the Renaissance*. New York . . . 1913.

Jones, Richard Foster. "The Background of the Attack on Science in the Age of Pope," in *Pope and his Contemporaries: Essays presented to George Sherburn*, ed. James L. Clifford and Louis A. Landa. Oxford: Clarendon Press, 1949, pp. 96-113.

Kelso, Ruth. "Sixteenth Century Definitions of the Gentleman in England," *Journal of English and Germanic Philology*, XXIV (1925), 370-382.

————. *The Doctrine of the English Gentleman in the Sixteenth Century*. University of Illinois *Stud. in Lang. and Lit.*, XIV (Urbana, Feb.–May, 1929), 1-288.

Landa, Louis A. "Jonathan Swift and Charity," *Journal of English and Germanic Philology*, XLIV (1945), 337-350.

Mallet, (Sir) Charles Edward. *A History of the University of Oxford*. 3 vols., London: Methuen & Co., Ltd., 1924-27. Vol. III.

Mason, John E. *Gentlefolk in the Making: Studies in the History of English Courtesy Literature and Related Topics from 1531 to 1774*. Philadelphia: University of Pennsylvania Press, 1935.

Mead, William Edward. *The Grand Tour in the Eighteenth Century*. Boston and New York: Houghton Mifflin Co., 1914.

Mullinger, J. Bass. *A History of the University of Cambridge*. London: Longmans, Green, & Co., 1888.

Noyes, Gertrude E. *Bibliography of Courtesy and Conduct Books in Seventeenth-Century England*. New Haven: Yale University Press, 1937.

Parks, George B. "Travel as Education," in *The Seventeenth Century: Studies in the History of English Thought and Literature from Bacon to Pope by Richard Foster Jones and Others Writing in His Honor*. Stanford, Calif.: Stanford University Press, 1951, pp. 264-290.

Quintana, Ricardo. "Notes on English Educational Opinion During the Seventeenth Century," *Studies in Philology,* XXVII (1930), 265-292.

Shellabarger, Samuel. *Lord Chesterfield.* London: Macmillan & Co., Ltd., 1935.

—————. *Lord Chesterfield and His World.* Boston: Little, Brown, 1951.

Thompson, Elbert N. S. "Books of Courtesy," in *Literary Bypaths of the Renaissance.* New Haven: Yale University Press, 1924.

Ustick, W. L. "Advice to a Son: A Type of Seventeenth-Century Conduct Book," *Studies in Philology,* XXIX (1932), 409-441.

—————. "Changing Ideals of Aristocratic Character and Conduct in Seventeenth-Century England," *Modern Philology,* XXX (1932), 147-166.

—————. "Seventeenth Century Books of Conduct: Further Light on Antoine de Courtin and *The Rules of Civility,*" *Modern Language Notes,* XLIV (1929), 148-158.

Vogt, George McGill. "Gleanings for the History of a Sentiment: Generositas Virtus, non Sanguis," *Journal of English and Germanic Philology,* XXIV (1925), 102-124.

Watson, Foster. *The Beginings of the Teaching of Modern Subjects in England.* London: Sir I. Pitman & Sons, Ltd., 1909.

—————, ed. *The Encyclopaedia and Dictionary of Education.* 4 vols., London and New York: Sir I. Pitman & Sons, Ltd., 1921-22.

—————. *The English Grammar Schools to 1660: Their Curriculum and Practice.* Cambridge: Cambridge University Press, 1908.

Woodward, William Harrison. *Studies in Education During the Age of the Renaissance 1400-1600.* Cambridge: Cambridge University Press, 1906.

Wordsworth, Christopher. *Scholae Academicae: Some Account of the Studies at the English Universities in the Eighteenth Century.* Cambridge: Cambridge University Press, 1877.

II

Original Sources

This list does not include well-known works, such as *Sir Charles Grandison, She Stoops to Conquer,* and the *Dunciad,* to which I may have referred once or twice. It does include certain prominent courtesy books of the Renaissance and early seventeenth century. For works of which a first edition was not used, the date of the first edition is indicated in parentheses; when pertinent, the date of composition is indicated in parentheses.

Adventurer, The, ed. Alexander Chalmers. In *The British Essayists* (Boston, 1856), XIX-XXI. (1752-54.)

Allestree, Richard, attrib. *The Gentleman's Calling. Written by the Author of The Whole Duty of Man.* London, 1677. (1660.)

Amhurst, Nicholas. *Oculus Britanniae: An Heroic-Panegyrical Poem on the University of Oxford. Illustrated with divers beautiful Similes, and useful Digressions.* London, 1724.

––––––. *Strephon's Revenge: A Satire on the Oxford Toasts.* 4th ed., London, 1724. (1718.)

––––––. *Terrae-Filius: Or, The Secret History of the University of Oxford; in Several Essays. To which are added, Remarks upon a late Book, entitled, University Education, by R. Newton, D. D. Principal of Hart-Hall.* 2nd ed., 2 vols., London, 1726. (Appeared periodically, 1721.)

Ascham, Roger. *The Scholemaster,* ed. Edward Arber. London, 1870. English Reprints No. 23, Vol. X. (1570.)

Ayres, Philip. *Vox Clamantis: Or An Essay for the Honour, Happiness and Prosperity of the English Gentry, And the whole Nation: In the promoting Religion and Vertue, and the Peace both of Church and State.* London, 1684.

Barrow, Isaac. *Sermon XLVII. Of Industry in Our Particular Calling, as Gentlemen and Scholars.* In *Theological Works,* ed. the Rev. Alexander Napier (3 vols., Cambridge, 1859), III, 415-452. (1693.)

Beattie, James. *Remarks on the Utility of Classical Learning.* In *Essays,* Edinburgh, 1778, pp. 487-555. (Written 1769.)

Bentham, Edward. *A Letter to a Fellow of a College. Being the Sequel of a Letter to a Young Gentleman of Oxford.* London, 1749.

————. *A Letter to a Young Gentleman of Oxford.* Oxford, 1748.

————. *Advices to a Young Man of Fortune and Rank, Upon his Coming to the University.* Oxford, n. d.

Blacow, the Rev. Richard. *A Letter to William King, Principal of St. Mary Hall, Concerning a Particular Account of a Treasonable Riot at Oxford, February 1747.* London, 1755.

Boyer, Abel. *The English Theophrastus: Or, The Manners of the Age. Being the Modern Characters of the Court, the Town, and the City.* London, 1702.

Brathwait, Richard. *The English Gentleman.* London, 1630.

Brokesby, Francis. *A Letter of Advice to a Young Gentleman at the University. To which are subjoined, Directions for Young Students.* London, 1751, repr. from 1701.

Brooke, Henry. *The Fool of Quality,* with Biog. Preface by Charles Kingsley and Life by E. A. Baker. London and New York, 1860. (1765-70.)

Brown, the Rev. Dr. John. *An Estimate of the Manners and Principles of the Times.* 2nd ed., London, 1757. (1757.)

————. *Sermons on Various Subjects.* London, 1764.

Burgh, James. *The Dignity of Human Nature; Or, A Brief Account of the Certain and Established Means for Attaining the True End of Our Existence.* 2nd. Amer., from 1st London ed., Hartford, 1802. (1754.)

Burghley (Burleigh), William Cecil, Baron. *Certaine Precepts or Directions, for the Well Ordering and Carriage of a Mans Life.* London, 1617.

Burnet, Bishop Gilbert. *History of His Own Time.* 6 vols., Oxford, 1823. ("Conclusion" written ca. 1708.)

————. *Thoughts on Education,* ed. John Clarke. Aberdeen, 1914. (1761; written ca. 1668.)

Burton, John, pseud. Phileleutherus Londinensis. *Remarks on Dr. King's Speech at the Dedication of Dr. R————'s Library.* London, 1749.

Castiglione, Count Baldassare. *The Book of The Courtier,* trans. Sir Thomas Hoby (1561), ed. (Sir) Walter Raleigh. London, 1900. (1528.)

Chapman, George. *A Treatise on Education, with A Sketch of the Author's Method.* 3rd ed., enl., London, 1784. (1773.)

Chesterfield, Philip Dormer Stanhope, 4th Earl of. *Letters,* ed. Bonamy Dobrée. 6 vols., London, 1932.

Clarke, John. *An Essay upon the Education of Youth in Grammar-Schools. In which the Vulgar Method of Teaching is examined, and a New one proposed, for the more Easy and Speedy Training up of Youth to the Knowledge of the Learned Languages; together with History, Chronology, Geography, &c.* 2nd ed., enl., London, 1730. (1720.)

—————. *An Essay upon Study. Wherein Directions are given for the Due Conduct thereof, and the Collection of a Library, proper for the Purpose, consisting of the Choicest Books in all the several Parts of Learning.* 2nd ed., London, 1737. (1731.)

Cleland, James. *The Institution of a Young Noble Man,* ed. Max Molyneux. New York, 1948. (1607.)

Connoisseur, The, ed. Alexander Chalmers. In *The British Essayists* (Boston, 1856), XXV-XXVI. (1754-56.)

Costeker, John Littleton. *The Fine Gentleman: Or, The Compleat Education of a Young Nobleman.* London, 1732.

Coventry, Francis. *The History of Pompey the Little: Or, The Life and Adventures of a Lap-Dog.* 2nd ed., London, 1751. (1751.)

Croft, G. *General Observations Concerning Education, Applied to the Author's Method in particular.* Hull, 1775.

Dalton, the Rev. John. *Two Epistles. The First, to a Young Nobleman from his Praeceptor. Written in the Year 1735-6.* London, 1745.

Darrell, William, attrib. *The Gentleman Instructed, In the Conduct of a Virtuous and Happy Life. . . . . To which is added, A Word to the Ladies, by way of Supplement to the First Part.* 6th ed., London, 1716. (1704.) •

Davies, Dr. Richard. *The General State of Education in the Universities: With a particular View to the Philosophic and Medical Education.* Bath, 1759.

Defoe, Daniel. *The Compleat English Gentleman,* ed. Karl D. Bülbring. London, 1890. (Written ca. 1728-29.)

Della Casa, Giovanni. *Galateo: Of Manners & Behaviours,* ed. J. E. Spingarn. Boston, 1914. (1558; trans. 1576.)

"Dialogue *between a* Beau *and a* Scholar," *Gentleman's Maga-zine,* XLIX (1779), 464.

Dykes, Oswald. *The Royal Marriage. King Lemuel's Lesson . . . Practically Paraphras'd; With Remarks, Moral and Religious, upon the Virtues and Vices of Wedlock.* London, 1722.

Ellis, Clement. *The Gentile Sinner, Or, England's Brave Gentleman: Characterized In a Letter to a Friend, Both As he is, and as he should be.* Oxford, 1660.

Elyot, Sir Thomas. *The Boke Named The Gouvernour,* ed. H. H. S. Croft, 2 vols., London, 1883. (1531.)

Enquiry into the Plan and Pretensions of Mr. Sheridan, An. Dublin, 1758.

Essay on Modern Education, An. London, 1747.

Essay upon Education; Shewing How Latin, Greek, and Other Languages May Be Learn'd more easily, quickly, and perfectly, than they commonly are, An. London, 1711.

Fielding, Henry. *An Essay on Conversation.* In *Works,* ed. William E. Henley (London, 1903), XIV, 243-277. (1743.)

————. *The Covent-Garden Journal,* ed. Gerard Edward Jensen. 2 vols., New Haven, London, and Oxford, 1915. (1752.)

Fordyce, David. *Dialogues Concerning Education.* 2 vols., Glasgow, 1768, repr. from London, 1745.

Forrester, Colonel James. *The Polite Philosopher: Or, An Essay on That Art, Which Makes a Man happy in Himself, and agreeable to Others.* In *The Magazine of History with Notes and Queries,* XXI, Extra No. 83 (Tarrytown, N. Y,. 1922), 97-131. This is a repr. of 15th ed., 1758. (1734.)

Foxton, Thomas. *Serino: Or, The Character of a Fine Gentleman; With Reference to Rerigion,* [sic] *Learning, and the Conduct of Life. In which are inserted Five Poems . . . Written by Mr. Addison.* 2nd ed., London, 1723. (1721.)

Gailhard, Jean. *The Compleat Gentleman: Or, Directions for the Education of Youth as to their Breeding at Home and Travelling Abroad.* London, 1678.

————. *Two Discourses. The first concerning A Private Settlement at Home after Travel. The Second concerning*

the Statesman, Or Him who is in Publick Employments.
London, 1682.

Gentleman's Library, Containing Rules for Conduct in All Parts of Life, The. London, 1715.

Goldsmith, Oliver. *The Citizen of the World,* ed. Austin Dobson. 2 vols., London, 1891. (1760; 1762.)

Gordon, Thomas. *The Humourist: Being Essays upon Several Subjects.* 2 vols., London, 1720-25.

Grenville, Archdeacon Denis. *Counsel and Directions Divine and Moral: In Plain and Familiar Letters of Advice from A Divine of the Church of England, to A Young Gentleman, his Nephew, Soon after his Admission into a College in Oxford.* London, 1685.

Guardian, The, ed. Alexander Chalmers. In *The British Essayists* (Boston, 1856), XIII-XV. (1713.)

Hale, Sir Matthew. *A Letter of Advice to His Grandchildren.* Boston, 1817. (Written ca. 1673 but not published till this ed.)

Hall, Bishop Joseph. *Quo Vadis? A just censure of Travell, as it is commonly undertaken by the Gentlemen of our Nation.* London, 1617.

Higford, William. *Institutions: Or, Advice to His Grandson.* London, 1818. (1658, of which above ed. is a repr.)

Huartes, Juan de. *Examen de Ingenios,* trans. Richard Carew. London, 1594. (1578.)

Hurd, Bishop Richard. *Dialogues on the Uses of Foreign Travel; Considered as a Part of An English Gentleman's Education: Between Lord Shaftesbury and Mr. Locke.* London, 1764.

Idler, The, ed. Alexander Chalmers. In *The British Essayists* (Boston, 1856), XXVII. (1758-60.)

James I, King of Great Britain and Ireland. *Basilikon Doron.* Edinburgh, 1603.

Jenyns, Soame. *The Modern Fine Gentleman.* In *Works,* ed. Charles Nason Cole (2nd ed., 4 vols., London, 1793), I, 63-69. (Written 1746.)

King, Dr. William. *A Poetical Abridgement, Both in Latin and English, of The Reverend Mr. Tutor Bentham's Letter to*

A Young Gentleman of Oxford. London, 1749.

————. *A Proposal for Publishing a Poetical Translation, Both in Latin and English, of The Reverend Mr. Tutor Bentham's Letter to a Young Gentleman of Oxford.* London, 1748.

————. *Dr. King's Apology: Or, Vindication of Himself from the Several Matters Charged on Him by the Society of Informers.* Oxford, 1755.

————. *Elogium Famae Inservens Jacci Etonensis, sive Gigantes; Or, The Praises of Jack of Eton.* Oxford, 1750.

————. *Oratio in Theatro Sheldoniano habita. Die Dedicationis Bibliothecae Radclivianae.* London, 1749.

————. *Some Remarks on the Letter to a Fellow of a College.* London, 1749.

————. *The Last Blow: Or, An Unanswerable Vindication of the Society of Exeter College.* London, 1755.

Knox, Vicesimus. *Essays Moral and Literary,* ed. James Ferguson. In *The British Essayists* (London, 1819), XLI-XLIII. (1778.)

————. *Liberal Education: Or, A Practical Treatise on the Methods of Acquiring Useful and Polite Learning.* London, 1781.

Lancaster, Nathaniel. *The Plan of an Essay upon Delicacy. With a Specimen of the Work.* London, 1748.

Law, William. *A Serious Call to a Devout & Holy Life.* London and New York, 1906. (1728.)

Leigh, Edward. *Three Diatribes or Discourses. First of Travel, Or a Guide for Travellers into Forein Parts.* London, 1671.

Letter to a Young Gentleman upon his Admission into the University, A. London, 1753. Signed "Corderius."

Letter to Dr. King Occasioned by His Late Apology, and in Particular by Such Parts As Are Meant to Defame Mr. Kennicott, A. London, 1755.

Lingard, the Rev. Dr. Richard, attrib. *A Letter of Advice To a Young Gentleman Leaving the University Concerning His Behaviour and Conversation in the World,* ed. Frank C. Erb. New York, 1907. (1670.)

Locke, John. *Some Thoughts Concerning Education,* in *The Educational Writings of John Locke,* ed. John William Adamson. Cambridge, 1922. (1693.)

"Lord Chesterfield's Creed," *Gentleman's Magazine*, XLV (1775), 131.

Mackenzie, Sir George. *Moral Gallantry. A Discourse, Wherein The Author endeavours to prove, that Point of Honour (abstracting from all other types) obliges Men to be Virtuous. And that there is nothing so mean (or unworthy of a Gentleman) as Vice*. Edinburgh, repr. at London, 1669.

Mandeville, Bernard. *The Fable of the Bees: Or, Private Vices, Publick Benefits*, ed. F. B. Kaye. 2 vols., Oxford, 1924. (1705.)

Maidwell, Lewis. *An Essay Upon the Necessity and Excellency of Education With these Consequences, That the Excellence of Education is best obtain'd by the Application of the Genius to the Dictat of Nature. That al Wise-Governments have praefer'd an Education, necessary to their Constitution, and Interest; and for this Reason England oblig'd to cultivat the Art of Navigation*. London, 1705.

Mar, John Erskine, 11th Earl of. *My Legacie to My Dear Son Thomas, Lord Erskine*, ed. the Hon. Stuart Erskine. In *Scottish History Soc.*, I Ser., XXVI (Edinburgh, 1896), 157-191. (Dated March, 1726.)

Martyn, William. *Youths Instruction*. London, 1612.

Miller, James. *The Humours of Oxford. A Comedy*. London, 1730.

Milton, John. *Of Education*. London, 1644.

Mirror, The, ed. Alexander Chalmers. In *The British Essayists* (Boston, 1856), XXVIII-XXIX. (1779-80.)

Moore, Dr. John. *A View of Society and Manners in France, Switzerland, and Germany*. 2 vols., London, 1779.

Mulcaster, Richard. *Educational Writings*, ed. James Oliphant. Glascow, 1903. *Positions* (1581) and *Elementarie* (1582).

Nelson, Robert. *Instructions for the Conduct of Young Gentlemen in Their Travels thro' Foreign Countries. In a Letter from Robert Nelson, Esq., to His Kinsman Sir George Hanger*. London, 1718.

Observations on the Present State of the English Universities. Occasion'd by Dr. Davies's Account of the General Education in them. London, 1759.

Of Education. London, 1734.

Osborn (e), Francis. *Advice to a Son, Directing him How to demean himself in the Most Important Passages of Life.* 4th ed., London, 1716. (1656-58.)

Oxford Honesty; or, a Case of Conscience . . . . Occasioned by the Oxford Speech and Oxford Behaviour, at the opening of Radcliffe's Library, April 13, 1749. London, (1750?). (1749.)

Panton, Captain Edward. *Speculum Juventutis: or, A True Mirror, where Errors in Breeding Noble and Generous Youth, with the Miseries and Mischiefs that usually attend it, are clearly made manifest; as likewise Remedies for every growing Evil.* London, 1671.

Peacham, Henry. *Compleat Gentleman 1634,* ed. G. S. Gordon. Oxford, 1906. (1622.)

Penn, William. *Fruits of a Father's Love.* London, 1726.

————. *More Fruits of Solitude,* ed. Charles W. Eliot. In The Harvard Classics, I (New York, 1909), 385-416. (1702.)

————. *Some Fruits of Solitude,* ed. Charles W. Eliot. In The Harvard Classics, I (New York, 1909), 329-384. (1693.)

Penton, Stephen. *New Instructions to the Guardian. . . . With a Method of Institution from Three Years of Age, to Twenty One.* London, 1694.

————. *The Guardian's Instruction, Or, The Gentleman's Romance. Written for The Diversion and Service of the Gentry,* with Introd. by Herbert H. Sturmer. London, 1897. (1688.)

Petrie, Adam. *Rules of Good Deportment, or of Good Breeding. For the Use of Youth.* In *Works* (Edinburgh, 1877), I, 1-136. (1720.)

Philpot, Stephen. *An Essay on the Advantage of a Polite Education Joined with a Learned One.* London, 1747.

Postlethwayt, Malachy. *The Merchant's Public Counting-House.* London, 1751. (1750.)

Pretty Gentlemen; or, Softness of Manners Vindicated From the false Ridicule exhibited under the Character of William Fribble, Esq., The. In *Fugitive Pieces, on Various Subjects* (2 vols., London, 1761), 1, 197-221. (1747.)

Priestley, Dr. Joseph. *An Essay on a Course of Liberal Education for Civil and Active Life.* London, 1765.

————. *An Essay on the First Principles of Government, and on the Nature of Political, Civil, and Religious Liberty, Including Remarks on Dr. Brown's Code of Education, and*

on Dr. Balguy's Sermon on Church Authority. 2nd ed.,
corr. and enl., London, 1771. (1768.)

Principles of the University of Oxford, as far as Relates to
Affection to the Government, Stated, The. London, 1755.

Proposals For the Reformation of Schools & Universities, In
order to the Better Education of Youth. Humbly Offer'd
to the Serious Consideration of the High Court of Parliament. N. p., 1704.

Puckle, James. The Club: In a Dialogue Between Father and
Son. London, 1817. (1711.)

Raleigh, Sir Walter. Instructions to his Sonne, and to Posterity.
London, 1632.

Rambler, The, ed. Alexander Chalmers. In The British Essayists (Boston, 1856), XVI-XVIII. (1750-52.)

Ramesey, William. The Gentlemans Companion: Or, A Character of True Nobility, and Gentility. London, 1672.

Ramsay, the Chevalier Andrew Michael. A Plan of Education
for a Young Prince. . . . To which is added, A Thought
relating to Education, Offer'd to the Examination of such
as have Noblemen and Gentlemen (from the Age of Eight
to Twelve, aut circiter) under their Care. London, 1732.

Reynolds, Sir Joshua. Discourses. London, 1924.

Satire upon Physicians, A. . . . To which is added A Curious
Petition to an Hon. House in Favour of Dr. King. London,
1755.

Shaftesbury, Anthony Ashley Cooper, 3rd Earl of, attrib. Several
Letters Written by a Noble Lord to a Young Man at the
University. London, 1716. (Letters dated 1707-10.)

Shaw, Peter. The Reflector: Representing Human Affairs, As
they are; and may be improved. London, 1750.

Sheridan, Thomas. A Plan of Education for the Young Nobility
and Gentry of Great Britain. London, 1769.

————. British Education: Or, The Sources of the Disorders
of Great Britain. London, 1769. (1756.)

Some Doubts Occasioned by the Second Volume of An Estimate
of the Manners and Principles of the Times. London, 1758.

Spectator, The, ed. George A. Aitken. 8 vols., London and
New York, 1898. (1711-14.)

St., C. L. The Real Character of the Age. In a Letter to the

Rev. Dr. Brown, Occasioned by His Estimate of the Manners and Principles of the Times. London, 1757.

Stockdale, Percival. *An Examination of the Important Question, Whether Education, at a Great School, or By Private Tuition, Is Preferable? With Remarks on Mr. Knox's Book, entitled Liberal Education.* London, 1782.

Swift, Jonathan. *Prose Works,* ed. Temple Scott. 12 vols., London, 1897-1908. The following essays:
> *A Complete Collection of Genteel and Ingenious Conversation.* XI, 195-301. (1738.)
> *A Treatise on Good Manners and Good Breeding.* XI, 77-84. (1754.)
> *An Essay on Modern Education.* XI, 47-57. (*Intelligencer* IX, 1729, as *The foolish Methods of Education among the Nobility.*)
> *Hints on Good Manners.* XI, 85-88. (1765.)
> *Hints Towards an Essay on Conversation.* XI, 65-75.

Tatler, The, ed. George A. Aitken. 4 vols., London, 1898-99. (1709-11.)

"Thoughts on Education, by Way of Introduction." Prefixed to *The Pleasing Instructor: Or, Entertaining Moralist.* 6th ed., London, 1768.

Vaumorière, Pierre d'Ortigue de, attrib. *The Art of Pleasing in Conversation,* trans. John Ozell. London, 1736. (1688.)

Walker, Obadiah. *Of Education, Especially of Young Gentlemen.* Oxford, 1673. (1672.)

Waterland, Daniel. *Advice to a Young Student. With a Method of Study for the First Four Years.* 2nd ed., Oxford, 1755. (1755; but appeared in an incorrect and shorter form in *The Republick of Letters,* Dec., 1729.)

West, Gilbert. *Poetical Works.* Edinburgh, 1781. *On the Abuse of Travelling* (1739) and *Education* (1751).

Wilson, Bishop Thomas. *The True Christian Method of Educating Children: A Sermon Preached in the Parish-Church of St. Sepulchre. . . . On May 28, 1724.* 5th ed., London, 1787.

World, The, ed. Alexander Chalmers. In *The British Essayists* (Boston, 1856), XXII-XXIV. (1753-56.)

Index